WHEEL ESTATE

The Rise and Decline of Mobile Homes

Allan D. Wallis

WHEEL ESTATE

New York   Oxford

OXFORD UNIVERSITY PRESS   1991

Oxford University Press

Oxford   New York   Toronto
Delhi   Bombay   Calcutta   Madras   Karachi
Petaling Jaya   Singapore   Hong Kong   Tokyo
Nairobi   Dar es Salaam   Cape Town
Melbourne   Auckland

and associated companies in
Berlin   Ibadan

Copyright © 1991 by Oxford University Press, Inc.

Published by Oxford University Press, Inc.,
200 Madison Avenue, New York, New York 10016

Library of Congress Cataloging-in-Publication Data
Wallis, Allan D.
Wheel estate: the rise and decline of mobile homes / Allan D. Wallis.
p.   cm.   Includes bibliographical references.
ISBN 0–19–506183–7
1. Mobile homes—United States—Psychological aspects.
2. Mobile homes—United States—Sociological aspects.
3. Mobile home industry—United States.
4. Mobile home living—United States.
5. Housing policy—United States.   I. Title.
HD7289.62.u6w35   1991
338.4'7690879'0973—dc20   90–31275

9 8 7 6 5 4 3 2 1

Printed in the United States of America
on acid-free paper

Preface

This is a book about mobile homes—those curious wood-framed, metal-clad boxes that dot the highways and populate communities across America. The mobile home may well be the single most significant and unique housing innovation in twentieth-century America. No other innovation addressing the spectrum of housing activities—from construction, tenure, and community structure to design—has been more widely adopted nor, simultaneously, more broadly villified. The mobile home is the dream of the factory-built house come true, yet few advocates of that dream are proud to acknowledge its manifestation in the present form.[1]

At every phase of its development, the mobile home has been shaped by market demands that conventional alternatives, sanctioned by the housing industry and the institutions which guide it, were unable to meet: from the Depression, when it offered itinerant workers shelter, during the war when it provided temporary housing, then after the war as mobile housing, and finally as an alternative to the ideal of affordable detached housing. Each of these junctures had been marked by a change in market, form, meaning, and name.

Today, mobile homes provide shelter for more than twelve and-a-half million Americans. For the last two decades they have comprised over one-fourth of the new housing produced annually, yet they have been the subject of a sustained and contentious debate for sixty years. In the current era of manufactured housing, the industry appears to be poised at a critical crossroad once again. With sales declining at the same time that affordable housing needs go unanswered, the industry and the institutions of housing should not neglect the opportunity to press this innovation into further service. But despite the mobile homes past success and increased legitimacy, its future is far from clear.

Where the use of mobile homes has not been challenged, they have largely been ignored. While there are several books about design innovations such as the log cabin or the roadside diner, surprisingly little had been written about mobile homes or their aesthetics. Twenty years ago Margaret Drury stated the situation aptly when she subtitled her book about mobile homes *The Unrecognized Revolution in American Housing.*[2] Since then, the silence has barely been broken. The few major mobile-home studies which have appeared since 1969 have focused primarily on public policy issues, specifically standards and regulations for safety, use, and appearance. The Center for Automotive Safety published a muckraking study in 1975 that was the impetus for the National Mobile Home Safety and Constuction Act of 1974.[3] Several years later, under the sponsorship of the Department of Housing and Urban Development, Arthur Bernhardt wrote *Building Tomorrow: The Mobile/Manufactured Housing Industry,*[4] which considered public policy issues as well as industrial policy affecting the industry's present and future organization. More recently, Thomas E. Nutt-Powell's *Manufactured Homes: Making Sense of a Housing Opportunity*[5] offered policy makers a straightforward description of the industry and its products.

The focus of the present book is different. It considers the mobile home as both the object and agent of change: as an addition to our inventory of housing options that must be brought into conformance with our expectations, but also as an option that forces us to reconsider what we understand about the character of American housing. Rather than prescribing ways in which mobile homes could be made more acceptable, I consider how standards of acceptability are devised in a social and cultural context, then manifested in public policy. While I consider the future role of the mobile home industry, particularly in providing affordable housing, I am less concerned with economic factors driving demand than with the perceptions and beliefs of members of the industry, politicians, and consumers.

The basic thesis of this book is that two processes have shaped the use, form, and meaning of the mobile home. The first process is one of invention, or innovation, carried out by mobile home manufacturers, park developers, and the people who live in mobile homes. These people, driven by necessity and entrepreneurship, have created a new form of housing, figured out how to relate it to land and community, and how to finance, insure, and otherwise protect and market it. The innovation that has occurred in the development of the mobile home is characteristic of American vernacular design in general.

The second process affecting the mobile home has been one of regulation or categorization carried out primarily by institutions: zoning and building agencies, mortgage bankers, and insurance companies. In large part, the institutional process of categorization has been conservative. Its motivating force had been the desire to preserve the "order of things." Such conservatism serves an important function; it helps make housing choices predictable. Thus, by limiting the range of acceptable housing, institutions maintain the stability of the market while preserving their own power and authority over it.

These two processes together—one pushing at the boundaries of acceptability by coming up with new alternatives that expand the range of available housing, the other attempting to restrict and preserve the established order—have played off against each other to produce the mobile home as it appears today. This book traces the development of the mobile home over a period of about sixty years, revealing in its course something about the processes of transformation.

Since perceptions of mobile homes are often distorted by misinformation and prejudice, the first chapter of this book attempts to give a sense of the people who live in them and of their communities. It introduces the theme of the countervailing processes of categorization and innovation that have shaped the mobile home over the course of its evolution. The five chapters which follow it are a chronological account of the development and use of mobile homes in the United States. The final chapter returns to the discussion of categorization and innovation, considering their relationship to public and industry policy shaping the built environment.

The term mobile home is used in the subtitle of this work, despite the fact that I have been informed by many people in the industry that the offical name now is manufactured housing. I want to acknowledge at the outset that I am aware of this term and appreciate the desire of the industry to use it. The fact remains that most people still think about the housing discussed here as mobile homes, and many still hold on to the dreaded term trailer. All of these terms appear here, corresponding to the periods of their coinage and reflecting the political context of their use. I also have kept the term mobile home because it conveys better than any other the basic hybrid character of the innovation and the essential basis for the conflicts it has engendered.

Acknowledgments

Having offered my apologies for the title of this book, I would like to acknowledge the help of some of the individuals in the industry who have assisted me in my research. Sid Adler of Sarasota, Florida; Holt Blomgren, former President of the National Manufactured Housing Federation and Dan Gilligan, current President; Lemoyne "Brownie" Brown, Executive Director of the Colorado Manufactured Housing Association; Ricky Bucchino of the Mobile Home Old Timers; Jerry Conners of the Manufactured Housing Institute; Elmer Frey, "Father of the Tenwide"; Danny Ghorbani, Director of the Association for Regulatory Reform; Harold Platt of South Bend, Indiana; Ken Rhoton of the Mobile Home Hall of Fame; and, finally, Paul and Phyllis Yohey and the residents of Freedom Acres Mobile Home Park in Muncie, Indiana. In the course of my research I have interviewed dozens of individuals associated with the industry, ranging from developers, and dealers, to manufacturers. I apologize for not acknowledging all of them by name.

The intellectual orientation of the argument presented here owes much to my teachers and colleagues. Professor Richard Bender, when at The Cooper Union, first introduced me to the idea of mobile homes as a form of industrialized housing. William Ittelson, one of the founders of the environmental psychology program at the City University Graduate School, kindled my interest in the issues of technology and change. Leanne Rivlin and Susan Saegert offered their help and encouragement during the early stages of this research. Langley Keyes and Martin Rein of MIT shared their insights on the nature of categorization. Ludwig Glaeser, whose scholarship in the history of architecture helped displine my own naive ventures into historical research. The work of J. B. Jackson on the nature of the American landscape has been an inspiration to me, and I have benefited from his comments and encouragement regarding the investigation of mobile homes. My colleague Dr. Donna Morganstern offered valuable suggestions on content and style, and Lynn Lickteig provided assistance with photography.

Since books take far longer to write than most authors care to imagine, I wish to acknowledge the patience, love, and encouragement of my wife, Peggy, who was a tireless sounding board for my ideas, and who agreed to live in a mobile home so that I could better understand what I was writing about. To my children, Jennifer and Phillip, thanks for the sunshine and for allowing me to hog the computer; and thanks to my parents and sister for their unqualified love and support.

Boulder, Colorado   A. D. W.
September 1990

Contents

WHEEL ESTATE

Mobile Homes in Middletown

The Byrds Build a Nest

The flat field, which has yet to be filled in with houses, is bounded on one side by the embankments of a new highway overpass and on the other by railroad tracks. The streets and lighting have already been constructed where just two years ago there were neat rows of cornstalks. Near the new north entrance of the park, a single mobile home, still unskirted and with its wheels showing, serves as a sales office. The entry is marked by a low curved brick wall, surmounted by a three-foot-long model of a mobile home. Beneath it, raised letters spell FREEDOM ACRES.

In the early days of October, the trees are still showing their colors. The poison ivy that grows profusely on the barbed-wire fences is now bright red and the sky is more frequently gray. The trains pass more often now, carrying grain to the port in Chicago or multitiered stacks of automobiles on their way to regional distribution points. One train of boxcars has stopped on the tracks at the edge of the park. For a few moments there is a telling juxtaposition of boxes on wheels set against boxes on wheels: some with shutters and front stoops, others with the logo of the Burlington Northern or the Santa Fe. Boxes with shallow rounded roofs and horizontal corrugated metal surfaces. At the instant the train starts to move again, it is difficult to tell what has been thrown into motion, the houses or the railroad cars.

Part of the original Freedom Acres, Muncie, Indiana.

Freedom Acres was started by Phyllis and Paul Yohey in 1947. They hoped to serve returning veterans caught in a tight housing market. Mobile homes weren't called that then; they were unapologetically "trailers." Trailers had become a familiar sight during the war, when they served as temporary housing for tens of thousands of war workers. At Freedom Acres the first lots were a modest 35' x 80'. Trailers were set in close parallel order so that they were easy to back in and out. The simple site plan allowed utility lines to be laid out more quickly and economically. Today the lots are bigger. Some of the new homes are almost as big as the old lots: 24' x 50' double-wides with shingled, saddle roofs and horizontal lap siding. They even have gutters and eaves, and an occasional fireplace.

The original part of Freedom Acres is still in use. It is occupied mostly by widows and widowers living in older, used units: narrow single-wides that still fit comfortably on the small lots. It is a real community, with neighbors looking after one another. This section of the park still looks out on the fast disappearing fields, corn giving way to houses that will share the sound of the train whistles breaking the crisp autumn nights.

Number 36, in the old part of the park, is occupied by Alma and Herbert Byrd. Their front door is framed by a brilliant flowering clematis vine. Within, their homey living room is cluttered with many of the cherished antiques Alma purchased at flea markets and yard sales during her first marriage. Her treasured collection includes a marble-top ice-cream-parlor table with twisted wire legs, and a plaster-cast statuary lamp of a bare-chested black man in bright red turban and loin cloth, who holds up a shaft supporting a fringed shade. There are also several scrollwork knickknack shelves filled with "collectibles," consisting mostly of colored-glass Avon bottles between which delicate ceramic cats peek. One cat holds, in perpetual suspension, a ball of porcelain yarn. The television set, as usual, is on. It is a source of company, and during the day it is usually turned to the soaps.

Alma, by her own description, is a "large" woman, tall and full-bodied. She does not simply occupy, but fills the small space she lives in. Alma often walks around her home until midafternoon with colored plastic curlers in her hair. She constantly unrolls and rerolls the smaller ones over her forehead as she talks to friends on the phone. Often those friends are sisters in the lodge that she and Herbert attend every Wednesday night. The lodge has many members who, like Herbert, are postal workers.

The Byrds' home was built in a factory in northern Indiana, an area where most of the major manufacturers of mobile homes are located. Herbert took a day off from work so that he and Alma could visit the factory while their home was being built. It is a source of pride for them that they know how it was constructed and that, in a sense, it was built for them, under their watchful eyes. "Never buy a mobile home that's been built on a Monday or Friday," Herbert suggests, based on advice learned at the factory. "On Friday the workers are too anxious to finish off the week, and on Monday they're still recovering from the weekend."

Fortunately, the Byrds' home was built on a Wednesday. The factory, a large metal shed surrounded by asphalt-covered yards, was of medium size by industry standards. It produced eight to twelve units a day. In one corner of a yard there were several finished units. Some ready to be transported had WIDE LOAD signs attached to their rears. The two sections of a double-wide unit, standing next to each other, looked as if they had been severed by a giant chain saw. The open wound had been covered by huge sheets of clear plastic that allowed Alma to see the completely finished and furnished interior.

A small brick structure, tacked to the front of the factory, housed management personnel. All the office suites, as if demonstrating an affinity in taste, were paneled and carpeted with the same materials found in the mobile homes. The Byrds were

The idea of homes built like automobiles on a factory assembly line was realized in mobile/manufacturing housing production, but not in a form that most advocates of industrialized housing were willing to recognize.

A completed double-wide mobile home awaiting shipment from the factory.

escorted from the offices to the factory floor, where they were invited to watch as long as they pleased. The first element of a mobile home is its steel chassis, which is usually prefabricated by the steel producer and shipped to the mobile home manufacturer. Stacks of chassis were stored for use in a part of the yard near the doors of the shed. One was hoisted up, its wheels and tires attached, and then it was placed on dollies so that it could be rolled sideways once inside.

At the first station, the wood frame of the floor platform was constructed. Arranged around the work table were stacks of precut wood joists and all the other materials required for the assembly. Nailing-guns and jigs, which position the wood members in their proper place, were used to facilitate fabrication. Blankets of pink batt insulation were placed between the floor joists, and then the duct work and piping were laid on top. Once assembled, the frame was flipped off the work table and on to the chassis, to which it was attached by lag bolts. Plywood flooring was quickly nailed to the frame. At the narrow end of the unit was a rack with rolls of linoleum exactly the width of the floor platform. The pattern that the Byrds had selected was drawn off the roll across the entire length of the platform, which had been spread with glue. This glue, which was used in many aspects of the assembly, contains formaldehyde as a drying agent. The smell of formaldehyde, which gave Alma a headache, is part of the ambiance of the factory, and one of the lingering odors of the new mobile home. Finally, holes were cut through the flooring for the duct work and the pipes that had already been laid beneath. It seems as if the mobile home is not so much built as assembled.

The floor and chassis of the unit were now rolled to the next station, where several workers were fabricating the interior walls on jigs. The wood studs of the wall frame, which had been glued on one side, were laid down on plywood sheets that would form the interior paneling. The other face sheets of paneling would be put on later, after interior wiring and plumbing had been completed. Next, the finished interior walls were hoisted onto the floor of the unit and nailed through the linoleum flooring, followed by the bathroom and kitchen fixtures that were connected to pipes and tubing in the floor. At this point, the Byrds' unit looked something like a stage set, with finished interior walls, plumbing fixtures, and cabinets, but without exterior walls to obstruct the view.

At the next work station, the exterior walls were fabricated; with pink fiberglass batt insulation stuffed between the studs, they were hoisted onto the floor frame and strapped in place. The electrical wiring was then woven around the outside

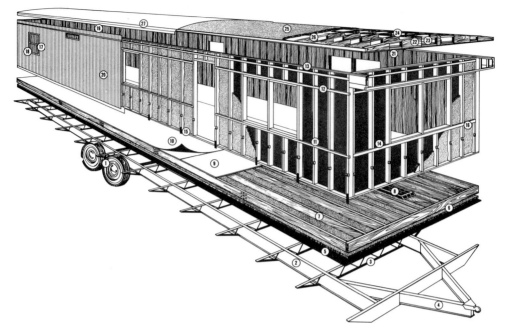

Exploded axonometric view of the construction of a mobile home.

through reinforced notches cut in the studs and pulled through holes to the location of the interior outlets. Activity in the factory was suddenly halted by the lunch whistle. The morning had passed, and the Byrds stood before their half-finished home that looked big, pink, boxy, and roofless, but nevertheless enclosed, and wired and plumbed too.

Alma remembered that the family room her first husband added to their brick house had taken over two months to complete. Even then, it was weeks until the carpeting was delivered and laid, drapes hung, and furniture selected and arranged. The sum total of work hours that had gone into the assembly of her new mobile home up to this point was about forty. Sixty more hours, compressed into the afternoon, would bring it to completion.

After lunch, the workmen returned to lay bow trusses on a large jig next to the unit. The trusses were attached to other framing members that completed the roof structure; then batt insulation was laid between the trusses. The end of the roof, which would eventually sit over the living room, was rounded, giving a kind of brow to its leading edge. A large sheet of galvanized aluminum roofing was pulled off a roll and attached to the roof frame. The completed roof was then hoisted on top of the waiting unit and attached to the walls with straps.

Off to the side of this work station were huge rolls of aluminum sheeting that had been prefinished in a variety of colors. The rolls were held vertically on stands, which allowed the workmen to pull out sheets, like huge pieces of wrapping paper, and apply them to the exterior walls of the unit. As the sheets were pulled out, they passed through deforming rollers that crinkled a pattern into their surface. For the front of the unit, a diamond pattern was used, while the sides were formed into shallow, closely spaced, horizontal corrugations. The aluminum sheets were attached to the exterior wall studs with rivets. Electric shears were used to cut openings for windows and doors. The prefabricated aluminum-frame windows and doors were fitted into place with a thick bead of caulking to ensure a seal. Aluminum shutters, made elsewhere in the factory, were riveted, forever fixed and open, to the sides of the windows. The edges of the metal skin were sealed with trim strips covering beads of caulking. The elevation of the unit, as seen looking down its long side, was remarkably flat. The windows, doors, and shutters hardly provided any relief to the surface. The overhang of the roof consisted of the half-inch thickness of a piece of trim. The thinness of it all gives the surface the appearance of a truck trailer or railroad car, rather than a dwelling. It is a thinness justified by the need to optimize the container: maximizing the interior space within, while observing the restrictions imposed on an object designed to be towed down a highway. It is a thinness which constitutes an aesthetic of its own.

At the next work station, remaining interior finishes, including doors, were attached. Further on, beside a loading dock, the refrigerator and other appliances would be wheeled in to complete the units. Since the Byrds had not ordered a furniture package, furniture, which otherwise would have been delivered here was left out. Aside from checking for leaks in the plumbing and faulty wiring, the job was done. The Byrds' finished home was delivered two days later and set up in the park within three hours. Today, homes built in factories are generally larger than the one made for the Byrds. While there are more inspections now, as mandated by federal regulations, the process is largely the same.[1] After fifteen years of use, the Byrds feel that their home has stood up pretty well. They hope to have it for another fifteen.

In five years, Herbert expects to retire from his job and, at the age of fifty-five, enjoy years of traveling around the country. The Byrds already own an 8' x 35' trailer that will make the trip. It is now parked beside a small pond, a few miles outside of town, where they use it as a summer cottage, a miniaturized country home that is in scale with their home in the city. Although they look forward to traveling during most of the year, they intend to keep their present home. "A person has to have roots," Alma explains. "You need a place to come home to."

Two lots south of the Byrds is the home of Helen Norris. It sits in a trim yard bordered by a white plastic chain. A family of ceramic ducks is arranged around the front. They emerge from under a flowing geranium set within the flanges of the hitch. Helen is a slight, white-haired woman in her mid-eighties. She knew Alma Byrd before moving to Freedom Acres. They were sisters in the same lodge. There are other lodge sisters in the park as well. It was Alma who told Helen that the unit near her was for sale.

Helen Norris is a fastidious housekeeper. She has scrubbed the walls of her living room so often that in less than a year she has begun to erase the printed wood grain from its paneled walls. She has lived alone since her sister, her lifelong companion, died two years ago. A large house near the center of town, which her parents left them, had been her home from childhood until she left it eight months ago. With its high-ceilinged rooms, tall windows with valanced curtains, fireplaces, and yards to take care of, the house had become too much for her. "The windows were so tall that I had to get up on a stepladder to reach the top of them. Well, after nearly falling off the ladder three times I said, this is it, I am selling it. I thought, what would happen if I fell and broke a hip. If I couldn't get around any more and had to go to a rest home. It might take up all my money that way."

At first she moved into a garden apartment. The space was fine and the appliances were new, but she could never quite get used to the noise: people coming and going at all hours, cars starting up, and televisions blaring. One of the things that Helen likes most about her mobile home, is that, despite its size, it has privacy. She can walk around the outside of this home, and the walls are all hers. There is privacy from neighbors, yet they are close enough that if she hasn't come out by midmorning to retrieve her paper, someone will be concerned enough to call on her. Helen also likes owning her own home, as do 80 percent of the householders in the park. Her entire dwelling is less than five hundred square feet, but within that area she has her own bedroom, a full bath, a living room/dining area, and a kitchen—a manageable space, with ceilings low enough for her to mount a small stool and compulsively whisk away any cobwebs in the corners.

Helen Norris purchased her home from Steve and Penny Seramur, who live a few blocks away in another section of the park. Helen's trailer had been their home until they moved into a

Tightly spaced mobile homes in Helen Norris's section of Freedom Acres.

larger one four years ago. Before moving to Freedom Acres, they rented a duplex apartment in an older house downtown. Moving here, at the edge of the city, meant quieter streets for four-year-old Kevin to play in. It also meant owning a home rather than renting one. "Every month you just felt like the rent check was going out the window, and you weren't building anything. This place still wasn't much," observes Penny, "but it was equity."

The Seramurs are in their early thirties. They met and married while attending the state university here, and decided to stay after graduation. Their current home is an "expando," so called because the room that projects out of its side can be slid back into the body of the mobile home for ease of transport. The pull-out room creates a T-shaped plan. It has a roofed porch in the crux of the T that serves as an entry. The Seramurs' home has three bedrooms, so that Kevin and his younger brother can each have a room of his own. Space, however, is still tight, and Steve misses having a garage where he can work on his cars.

When the Seramurs moved to Freedom Acres, Penny was still finishing her training as a dental technician. Steve was beginning his first job in town. Now he is a supervisor at a local manufacturing plant. Both earn good salaries and have additional income from some other units they own in the park and rent to people like Helen Norris. They like their home and community, yet they feel pressured, perhaps by family or friends, to move up to something better, something larger and more permanent. "This town has certain social cliques," Penny explains, "and according to these cliques, there are certain acceptable places to live . . . and this is not one of them. . . . But then it depends on your priorities. I would rather spend money on vacations and clothes than on house payments."

The Byrds, Helen Norris, and the Seramurs, though separated by age, have several things in common. Perhaps the most important is that under each of their dwellings there are axles that can be fitted with wheels so that their homes can be towed away. They, and their neighbors in Freedom Acres, prefer to call their residences mobile homes. Slip the word "trailer" into a conversation, and you will soon be corrected. Yet all, on occasion, refer to their dwellings as "trailers." They described them by their exterior dimensions—not as a "three-bedroom ranch," but as a "12' x 50'." They all think their homes are better maintained by an occasional Simonize.

The people of Freedom Acres feel that it is important to have roots and to honor the ideals of family and community, but they occasionally feel pressed to defend their commitment to these things because of the housing they live in. Steve Seramur recalls that

> acquaintances, not friends of mine, who have had occasion to come here, are just astounded with what they have found. Some of them still think that mobile homes are like travel trailers. Someone who has never experienced being inside of one, or who has only seen one behind some farmer's place where his field hands live, have no idea that this is a modern normal facility. . . . Some people have just not realized yet that you can build the same type of facilities here as in a conventional home. Often the mobile home communities that you see from the highway are not the best looking ones, and this is what people most often see. But slowly people are beginning to realize that this is going to encompass an awful lot of the housing market shortly.

Choosing to Live in a Mobile Home

In Middletown,[2] where Freedom Acres is located, 5 percent of all housing consists of mobile homes, and the concentration is higher in the county. The situation is common nationally. In 1975, over 212,000 mobile homes were shipped, at an average cost of $11,440.[3] By 1985, the number of units shipped had increased to 283,489, at an average cost of $21,800. In the decade between 1975 and 1985, approximately one-fifth of all new houses sold in this country, and well over two-thirds of all low-cost single-family homes were mobile homes. Since 1985 sales have declined. In 1988 only 218,429 units were shipped, the lowest rate in thirteen years. Despite the current decline, mobile home sales have accumulated to the point where in the United States today, one dwelling out of ten is a mobile home, providing housing for over 12.5 million people. The use of mobile homes had been most concentrated in the high-growth Sunbelt states (the Southeast, Texas, Arizona, and California). The top ten states in mobile home occupancy contain almost half of the year-round mobile homes in the country. These are also the states with high percentages of seasonal occupancy.

The reasons for choosing to live in mobile homes are as varied as their occupants. For Steve and Penny Seramur, those reasons include developing equity so they can eventually buy a site-

Contribution of Mobile Homes to Single Family Housing Production

Year	Total completions of single family housing units	Site-built and site-fixed single family housing completions[1]	Mobile home shipments[2]	Percent of total completions in mobile homes
1968	1,176,550	858,600	317,950	27.0
1969	1,220,190	807,500	412,690	33.8
1970	1,202,990	801,800	401,190	33.3
1971	1,510,570	1,014,000	496,570	32.9
1972	1,736,140	1,160,200	575,940	33.2
1973	1,526,500	1,197,200	566,920	37.1
1974	1,269,600	940,300	329,300	25.9
1975	1,087,490	874,800	212,690	19.6
1976	1,280,320	1,034,200	246,120	19.2
1977	1,523,545	1,258,400	265,145	17.4
1978	1,644,871	1,369,000	275,871	16.8
1979	1,578,382	1,301,000	277,382	17.6
1980	1,178,316	956,700	221,616	18.8
1981	1,059,407	818,500	240,907	22.7
1982	870,308	631,500	238,808	27.4
1983	1,218,779	923,700	295,079	24.2
1984	1,320,093	1,025,100	294,993	22.3
1985	1,355,989	1,072,500	283,489	20.8
1986	1,364,860	1,120,200	244,660	17.9
1987	1,355,398	1,122,800	232,598	17.1
1988	1,106,449	1,084,600	218,429	19.7

[1] Department of Commerce reports on housing production, which include factory-built housing permanently affixed to a site but not HUD Code housing. *Source: Construction Reports: Housing Completions, C-22* (U.S. Department of Commerce, annual).

[2] Although mobile home shipments shown here may differ from actual sales, they correspond most closely to housing completions. *Source: Quick Facts About the Manufactured Housing Industry* (Manufactured Housing Institute, annual).

built home. The quiet of the community as a place to raise children is also important. The Manufactured Housing Institute reports that median average monthly housing costs for mobile home owners in 1989 was $251 compared to $364 for home and apartment renters.[4] In a 1988 survey conducted by the Foremost Insurance Company,[5] 30 percent of the mobile home owners questioned were under thirty. Since the late 1950s, mobile home households have generally been younger, less educated, and poorer than site-built home owners. The Foremost survey, however, suggests that a change may be occurring. Twenty-four percent of the households listed themselves, as would Steve Seramur, as white-collar workers. In addition, the survey found that the median household income level for the new mobile home buyer has been rising. In 1988 it was $21,900, still below the median household income for all households in the United States, which was $24,826 that year.

Helen Norris's reasons for choosing mobile home living were slightly different from the Seramurs'. She wanted economy, but ease of maintenance was a central concern. She also wanted a community of caring neighbors, and she felt that she could find it in a park. Nineteen percent of mobile home occupants in the Foremost survey were sixty years of age or older, and over 80 percent were retired. Like Helen Norris many of these people previously lived in a conventional site-built home. They did not feel that they were losing face in retiring to a mobile home, in part because they had already enjoyed the status of home ownership.

The Byrds, by contrast, are part of a traditionally underrepresented group of mobile home households. Households headed by a person between forty and forty-nine years of age are the smallest group of mobile home owners, but one of the largest groups of site-built home owners. Conventional wisdom, promoted by the mobile home industry itself, holds that the young couple starting out in a mobile home saves equity to be able to move eventually into a site-built house, presumably before the age of forty. Yet, as the cost of a conventional home increases, along with interest rates and the size of the down payment, it is becoming increasingly difficult for couples who do not already own a home to save enough to enter the site-built housing market. With the cost of new site-built housing in 1989 averaging $148,700 and existing homes averaging around $118,000, fewer than 20 percent of young households not currently in a site-built home can afford to buy one. Even though nominal interest rates have been declining, real interest rates (adjusted for inflation) remain historically high, and the "affordability gap" shows no signs of narrowing.[6]

Among the reasons that mobile home owners give for choosing their form of housing, one that ranks surprisingly low is the desire for mobility. As the size of mobile homes has increased, the cost of moving them has risen as well. A rough estimate of the cost to relocate a single-wide unit one hundred miles is between $2500 and $3000. Relocating a multisection mobile home the same distance can cost between $10,000 and $12,000.[7] In addition to these costs, used mobile homes sold on a dealer's lot rather than in a park can lose much of their resale value. It is estimated that of the mobile homes being purchased today, only 3 percent will ever be moved once they are set up on their first home site.

At one level it might appear that the choice of a mobile home is no more than an economic consideration: people buy one because it is what they can afford. Affordability, however, is a consideration constrained by acceptability. People do not settle for the cheapest housing, but for housing that gives them the greatest satisfaction for the part of their income they dedicate to housing. When people select housing, it is not simply shelter that they are choosing. Along with the utilitarian aspects of shelter, characteristics symbolic of the stability and propriety of conventional houses and implicit social status are a concern.[8] Location, too, is associated with a certain status, which is a consideration along with convenience and services.

Sociologists Kenneth Tremblay and Don Dillman, in *Beyond the American Housing Dream: Accommodation to the 1980s*,[9] suggest that Americans' housing preferences are based on four basic norms: ownership, detached dwelling, private outdoor space, and conventional construction. All four norms are best satisfied by a single-family detached home. But what happens when this alternative is too expensive?

> If the most preferred housing situation is not attainable, people substitute a housing situation which most closely satisfies a similar number and similar kinds of norms as met by their first preference. When people cannot obtain ownership of a conventional single family detached home, they tend to select owning a mobile home and lot (loss of conventionality) or renting a single family home (loss of ownership) which both satisfy three norms. Therefore, if ownership of a conventional single family detached home becomes problematic in the future, we can expect certain types of alternative housing to be relatively acceptable based on knowledge of our four housing norms.[10]

Although Tremblay and Dillman look at housing choices as the buyer's rational evaluation of alternatives, it is not clear how commonly mobile homes take their place in the list of choices. For many people a barrier of prejudice surrounds the mobile home, and they may fear the stigma of living in one. It is difficult for people to separate their concept of housing needs from the types of housing that society has taught them are acceptable. Even for children who have grown up in apartments, the ideal home is a single-family house. In this regard, it should be recognized that a sense of novelty still surrounds mobile homes and park living—a barrier for some households. It may well be that the mobile home will continue to have its greatest market among people at a stage in their lives when they neither need nor want a traditional single-family house.

Locations: Parks and Private Lots

Today, approximately 46 percent of all mobile home owners live in parks. There are over 24,000 parks in the United States, containing more than 1.8 million home sites. After the Second World War, most parks were of the "Mom and Pop" variety: consisting of 40 to 60 spaces, with the owner/managers living on the premises. Parks now average 150 to 175 spaces and often contain separate sections for families with children. A small but growing trend in the development of new mobile home communities is the creation of subdivisions and condominium parks, which offer the advantages of land, as well as home ownership.

Half a mile down the road from Freedom Acres is the Holiday Mobile Home Park. Like its neighbor, it has about 250 home sites. There are other parks as well in this city of 100,000. Some are older and not so well maintained. White's Trailer Park, which, like Freedom Acres, was started after the war, hasn't changed much. The manager's home is set at the entrance. The roads are unpaved, there is no street lighting, the homes are generally older and smaller than those in newer parks, but lot rents are also significantly lower, and there are fewer lease restrictions. Often the older parks now found in cities were once located beyond the city limits. As urban areas grew, they annexed the parks along with everything else. Zoning ordinances were revised to recognize the parks as a land use, but even then the only land zoned for them was often what they already occupied. Today many of the older parks are disappearing or losing lots as the highways along which they were located are widened or as land values soar, making other uses more profitable to owners. In addition, fewer new parks are being built, especially outside the Sunbelt states. The high cost of developing a park can mean lot rents that would make mobile homes noncompetitive with rental housing.

To understand the mobile home as an innovative housing alternative, it must be considered along with the development of parks. These communities still allow the mobility valued in the early days of mobile homes as well as an affordable and desirable form of housing. Parks provide more than services and utilities, they offer a genuine sense of community. Larger parks often feature such amenities as separate sections for family and recreational facilities such as pools and clubhouses, but even in smaller parks, people are attracted to the informal sense of community. Florida planner Frederick Bair, Jr., suggests that mobile home parks may be the last genuine communities in the United States,[11] an observation that has been supported by several investigations of park life.[12] Ironically, parks are often seen as an undesirable form of land use, incompatible with permanent housing and therefore justifiably relegated to commercial and industrial areas.

While parks are usually associated with mobile home living, fully 54 percent of all mobile homes are on private, individual lots. A recent survey found that approximately two-thirds of these are on property owned by the household, while the others are on friends' or relatives' property.[13] It is not uncommon in rural areas to see a mobile home parked beside an old farmhouse. What is surprising is that it is not always there for the farm hands, but for the farmer who has retired and turned operations over to a son. Likewise, in smaller cities and towns a frequently requested zoning variance is to allow a mobile home to be placed on a lot with an existing site-built house, as a dwelling for an aging parent.

Mobile homes on private lots are found in many parts of Middletown. Like the older parks, most were sited on land still located in the county. Others, however, were located in the city before more restrictive zoning was enacted. Today many major cities allow for the single siting of mobile homes in residential districts, but land costs and minimum lot size requirements are often incompatible with the economy that attracts so many people to mobile home living.

In a working-class area of the city not far from Freedom Acres is the home of Mel and Betty Schlichter. Although it is set on a permanent foundation, it is more a "trailer" than a mobile home. The original unit is an 8' x 51', Gear Trailer built in Phoenix, Arizona. Attached to it is a site-built extension measuring 12' x 34', built in three phases over a period of ten years. There is also a freestanding garage and a walk-in toolshed out back. Beginning in the late 1930s, Mel worked in heavy construction, building bridges, dams, and highways in just about every region of the country. "People who worked construction like us called each other 'tramps.' We lived in our own trailers or

The Schlicter's home with its site-built additions.

company trailers, following the work, usually with the same firm. Trailer life lets a family stay together: brings them closer together. You become a real community with other families. People caring for each other."[14]

Mel's last construction job was in Vernal, Utah. By then he was a foreman. The company supplied him with the trailer he lived in. Betty stayed with her recently widowed sister in Middletown during Mel's last three years in Utah. That's when she decided that they ought to buy land in town, so that when Mel retired they would have a place to settle down. When the job in Vernal was completed, Mel bought his trailer from the company and had it towed back to Middletown.

With the purchase of land, the Schlichters could set up a permanent home for the first time in their thirty years of marriage. "It meant a lot to us to have a place that was roots," Betty recalls. "The years of traveling were great, and not having any children of our own made it a lot easier; but after a while you don't want to think about when the next move is gonna come. I've always liked to have a garden, and that's something that's hard to move with you. Seemed like just when you got one mulched enough to produce you'd have to abandon it."

The site-built family room of the Schlichter's home is a

cheerful, sun-filled space. There is a row of jalousie windows along one side, knotty-pine paneling on the walls, and shag carpet on the floor. Betty's green thumb is evident. The room is full of plants. The television, which forms a focal point, is always on. The one distinguishing element in this otherwise ordinary space is the aluminum siding of the trailer that forms its fourth wall. It stands there, unaltered, looking like part of a truck that has come crashing through the wall. The windows in the trailer part of the house, with their green aluminum shutters riveted in place, now peer out into the family room. To get into the trailer, one must climb two steps up from the level of the family room and open the metal-clad door, with its diamond-shaped window. The same bold contrast is evident from the exterior where there is no embellishment, camouflage, or apology for the collision of forms. The hitch is still evident, as are the running lights on the corners.

The one thing that disturbs the Schlichters about their housing is the response it gets from people in town. "People think because you live in a trailer you're trash. It don't matter if you own, or if you keep your place better than theirs. I look at some houses on either side of me, and I know that this one is in better shape." Even though they own their own land, until a few years ago the Schlicters paid personal rather than real property tax on their house. As such, it did not qualify for the homestead exemption. All of this just seemed another way of telling them that their home was not a house.

The same prejudice that non-mobile home owners have against mobile homes, especially those sited on private property, is shared by some of the people living in house-like mobile homes located on their own property. From the outside, as well as within, these homes look just like site-built houses. They have pitched shingled roofs, overhanging eaves with gutters, and permanent foundations. Usually they are multisectioned units whose length and width fit the conventional house footprint. They are often sited parallel to the street, like conventional homes, rather than in the perpendicular arrangement characteristic of the mobile home park. They may even come with a single deed and mortgage for house and property. To the occupants of such units, the way in which their houses were made, or the historical origins of this type of dwelling, may be of as little concern as knowing that one's breakfast rolls were made in a factory. Nevertheless, they may find their homes lumped with the likes of the Schlichters' because technically all mobile homes are alike.

Since the way an object is categorized affects the way it is seen, the way mobile homes have been defined has affected the ability of people in the community to locate or choose their housing. Middletown now permits the single-lot siting of mobile homes by right; they can be located in zones designated for single-unit siting. In most cities, however, to place a mobile home in a residential district requires a special variance, which often provokes highly contentious public hearings. Indeed, a particular sense of rage seems to be reserved for zoning hearings at which the issue of mobile home siting is raised. It is an occasion for prejudice to be vented about both the housing type and its occupants.

A year after the Schlichters located their home, and before the new ordinances were passed in Middletown, Katherine Armstrong requested a variance to place a mobile home on property that she owned in the north end of the city. Though still a relatively undeveloped area, it had been zoned R-1, for single-family residences. Many of the surrounding property owners objected to Katherine's request. "People who live in mobile homes just don't take care of their property. You see trashed out cars, propped up on milk crates, sitting in the front yard for years at a time. What's that kind of thing going to do to our property values?" After two hearings, the requested variance was denied. Four months later, Elmer and Marguerite Herbert asked for a variance to allow a mobile home to be placed in the rear yard of their half-acre home site, so that Mrs. Herbert's ailing parents could live with them. Because of the close ties that the Herberts had established with their neighbors, no public complaints were aired at the hearing. The commissioners approved the use, but for only a two-year period.

Attempting to place a mobile home on a lot through the granting of a variance is a time-consuming and often traumatic process for the applicant. Nevertheless, in many municipalities this is the only way that the single siting of a mobile home can be approved. By the late-1980s, the legislatures or high courts in twenty-two states had moved to eliminate zoning practices that discriminated against mobile home use; but municipalities, especially in strong home-rule states, continue to resist these efforts. Ironically, many of those same cities are deeply committed to providing affordable housing for their citizens.

Can't Live with 'Em, Can't Live without 'Em

In many respects, the mobile home must be regarded as a genuine innovation, meeting needs which conventional housing has left unsatisfied. The mobile home has become the predominant unsubsidized type of affordable housing in the United States, and its significance should continue to grow. In addition, mobile homes and mobile home communities have developed to serve many of the newer housing submarkets, especially elderly retired people. Finally, the way mobile homes are built, sold, and transported is unique among American housing types.

Despite its many obvious and often innovative contributions, the mobile home frequently generates social criticism. Users are often looked down upon and feel compelled to justify their choice of housing, as is obvious in the defensiveness of people like Steve and Penny Seramur. And neighborhoods frequently resist the intrusion of individuals or park developers seeking land for mobile homes, fearing the effects on house values and social stability. The irony of the mobile home is that it successfully satisfies so many needs, yet many people, and particularly housing institutions, would rather ignore its existence.

There are several frequently offered explanations for the mobile home's contradictory status, ranging from obvious complaints about its appearance to more subtle explanations of its relationship to American housing ideals and values. One explanation suggests that the mobile home is ugly and unsafe and, hence, a threat to nearby property. Since housing represents a family's single largest investment, protecting that investment inevitably raises a hostile response from the owners of conventional housing. Besides its appearance and safety, the potential, if not the actual, mobility of the mobile home is perceived as a threat. How can people who live in houses on wheels honor a commitment to community?

Concerns over appearance, safety, and mobility often are surrogates for concern about conventionality. In this sense, the mobile home is not a threat because it is ugly, but because it is identifiably different. Yet Americans are supposed to value differences and object to excessive conformity. What standard is being applied here? As for safety, current building standards require mobile homes to meet safety standards that are equivalent to the uniform codes adopted by most municipalities. Nevertheless, building officials balk at the idea of "equivalent performance," because mobile homes are constructed differently and built away from the site. Finally, the concern over mobility is essentially moot given the current pattern of immobility that characterizes most mobile homes today.

It is also said that mobile home owners do not pay for the public services they use. This argument has been around since the mid-1930s, yet several states at that time charged fees to cover services provided for mobile home households. Today mobile homes are subject to a property or a real estate tax. The endurance of this notion despite the facts may be the result of ignorance, but it often betrays prejudice.

That prejudice commonly influences the response to mobile homes is the basis for yet another argument, which states that complaints about mobile homes express class bias. Since mobile homes are widely associated with lower income groups, resistance to their use is really a way of excluding working-class families from middle-class neighborhoods. The argument of class bias is illustrated in the landmark *Mount Laurel II* decision, in which the New Jersey Supreme Court declared as unconstitutional the use of zoning to exclude mobile homes.[15] The court ruled that such exclusion was effectively a form of class discrimination.

The class-bias explanation offers important insights into not only the response to mobile homes but public housing policies in general. Yet elements of the paradox remain. Why is it that even in communities where affordable housing is mandated, the mobile home is rarely considered an alternative? If mobile homes are low-income housing, why are minority groups with a high percentage of low-income households so significantly underrepresented among owners? Likewise, if class bias is so strong a part of the response to mobile homes, why doesn't it preclude the use of mobile homes in fairly luxurious retirement communities? Regional differences are clearly involved here,[16] but something more is at work; something inherent in the most fundamental attitudes of Americans toward their housing.

Margaret Drury has made the following provocative observation, providing the foundation for a different explanation:

> The basic conflict that mobility causes in housing is related to the American concept of "home." This conflict is the product of the image of "home" or any architectural form as having time-honored roots; thus, the image of "home" is one of stability and rootedness. This "home" is so sacred an American ideal that "stability" has come to be looked upon as a virtue. Conversely, lack of stability has been looked down upon as less than virtuous.
>
> But America has always been a mobile nation. In the pioneer days, Americans going west moved from one piece of land to another. Now we move from one place to another but we still have to put down our roots, so we buy land.
>
> Because of the nation's mobility, and, at the same time, its need for this feeling of "permanence," we have had a conflict in our ideology. This conflict is reflected nowhere better than in the housing situation as seen in the mobile home. It is in this situation that the conflict of the conventional, the stable, the home-rooted environment versus the temporary, the mobile, the transient environment comes into the open.[17]

If Drury is correct, the paradoxical place of the mobile home in American housing—as both necessity and pariah—may be found in conflicts within our most fundamental beliefs about

The mythic image of housing sustains our perception of the ideal. Here mobile homes flank a log cabin in Debeque, Colorado. Both are in fact forms of temporary housing: expedient and affordable.

home and community, conflicts between conformity and individuality, between the place-bound community and the expectation that individual freedom means freedom to move. It is also the conflict between the factory-built and the site-built: between the ideal of a mass production/mass consumption society and belief in the values of individuality and authenticity. In light of these conflicting beliefs, the mobile home may be shunned not because it fails to satisfy American housing ideals, but because it makes these contradictions between ideals apparent.

All of the explanations of the mobile home's paradoxical status share one theme in common; they consider some aspect of the process of categorization. Questions about whether the appearance or structural integrity of the mobile home is acceptable; questions about whether it conforms to or violates ideals of housing, are different aspects of the process of deciding whether it is housing and, if so, what kind. These are questions which obviously concern people who live in mobile homes, but they are also at the core of the response of institutions whose actions can restrict or facilitate the use of mobile homes.

A Moving Categorization System

The gradual and grudging institutional acceptance of the mobile home reveals the boundaries around that set of objects recognized as housing.[18] Within those boundaries a wide range of style is permitted: Cape Cod saltboxes, Los Angeles Deco bungalows, southeastern board houses, southwestern adobe, A-frame chalets, and miniaturized Southern plantations, not to mention penthouses, tenements, and brownstones. The housing domain also contains different types of tenure, and different forms of community. Despite this diversity, there are limits, and they have often been tested by the mobile home. "It's not housing," some have argued, "because it has wheels." "It's not housing because it wasn't built at the site," or more simply, "It's not housing, because housing doesn't *look* like that."

While most people would assert that they know what housing is, they would be hard pressed to define its primary characteristics. Nevertheless, it seems easy to recognize and agree on what is not housing. Thus, while the mobile home has often been declared "not housing," that is, outside the boundaries of acceptability, little clear advice has been offered on how to make it acceptable. Would different windows do the trick, hiding the wheels, raising the roof, lowering the floor? Even when such recommendations are made people find that it still isn't enough.

The role of public and private institutions is crucial in determining acceptability: mortgage banks, zoning and building authorities, state and federal housing agencies, all have a vested interest in maintaining the definition of housing they are empowered to support. Mortgage bankers, for example, want to be assured that the houses on which they make loans will have a resale market, and that they will retain their value over the life of the mortgage. Institutions are generally conservative: they are effectively "gatekeepers" of the housing domain. Try to slip an alternative in and you may find that you can't get a mortgage or you can't find land where you are permitted to build. By limiting alternatives, these gatekeeping institutions serve an important function: they help assure the predictability of the housing market.

If the power of gatekeeping institutions lies in assuring a predictable environment for investment, their authority is threatened when large numbers of people cannot find the kind of housing they have been taught to strive for and which they believe should be available and affordable. When this happens, buyers either have to adjust their aspirations or explore alternatives. This is a situation ripe for innovation, and one in which institutions may be forced to open boundaries and admit new types of housing.

Significant advances in the use and design of mobile homes have occurred primarily in periods of unmet housing demand. Even in those times, mobile homes were frequently categorized in such a way as to limit their use; for example, by classifying them as emergency housing, not as permanent housing; or as a kind of multifamily housing to be restricted to parks, not as the equivalent of single-family homes. These different categorizations depend, just as the mobile home's admission to the housing domain did in the first place, on the features or aspects that gatekeeping institutions select as significant. This selectivity is illustrated by a 1982 decision, *Comeau v. Brookside Village*, handed down by the Texas Supreme Court. Henry Comeau had petitioned the City of Brookside Village to place a mobile home on his own property. City ordinances restricted mobile homes to parks. Comeau argued that this restriction was an unconstitutional infringement on his right to use his property. The Court, finding for Brookside Village, noted:

the inherent structural difference in such manufactured housing can make them vulnerable to windstorms and fire damage; and their mobile nature may lead to transience and detrimentally impact property values if scattered through the municipality. [The Court concluded that] mobile homes are different and thus may be classified separately from other residential structures for purposes of regulation. . . . We find such classification reasonable, as bearing a substantial relationship to the preservation of public health safety, morals or general welfare.[19]

In this decision, the court chose to focus on mobility, disregarding that a mobile home permanently attached to a foundation is actually immobile. The court could then distinguish mobile homes from other forms of housing, effectively placing them in a category of their own.

The *Brookside Village* ruling illustrates the process used by regulatory institutions confronted with an innovation. If the use of an innovation is at the center of a legal case, the courts must find a way of dealing with its novel elements in terms of established precedent. Legal scholar Edward H. Levi describes this process as reasoning by analogy or example:

The basic pattern of legal reasoning is reasoning by example. It is reasoning from case to case. It is a three step process described by the doctrine of precedent in which a proposition descriptive of the first case is made into a rule of law and then applied to a next or similar situation. The steps are these: similarity is seen

The hybrid character of mobile homes is heightened with the use of site-built additions. At times an ensemble of house and additions looks like the product of a collision. This home is near New Castle, Colorado.

between cases; next the rule of law inherent in the first case is announced; then the rule of law is made applicable to the second case.[20]

Legal reasoning is based on analogies: seeing a new object or practice in terms of an established situation. The analogy is developed and guided by the perception of similarities and differences. A mobile home, for example, is said to be like a vehicle because it has a chassis and wheels. As the analogy is elaborated and applied to making judgments, discriminations are refined and the analogy itself is adjusted. Thus, even though the mobile home is vehicle-like, it is used as a dwelling and should therefore be required to have the features and performance characteristics of a dwelling.

Levi goes on to describe legal reasoning as a "moving classification system." The classifications are set up by case law, legislation, or the Constitution, but they are subject to modification, which allows for the inclusion of new cases and the exclusion of cases previously covered. Through this process a legal category is "stretched" to accommodate the new situation.

The process of accommodating new situations may also change the structure of the system of categories itself. Separate categories may merge, as the boundaries between them are made less distinct, or new categories may be differentiated, as distinctions previously regarded as insignificant gain new importance. Again, Levi:

> Therefore it appears that the kind of reasoning involved in the legal process is one in which the classification changes as the classification is made. The rule changes as the rule is applied. More important, the rules arise out of the process which, while comparing fact situations, creates the rules and them applies them.[21]

The process is not confined to legal institutions. It is evident in the actions of all regulatory agencies. When a federal mortgage agency, for example, considers whether a mobile home qualifies for a particular program, it often uses analogical reasoning to determine what kind of housing the mobile home is like and whether the category fitting such housing can be made to include the mobile home as well.

The "moving classification system" results from the need to accommodate new or innovative situations while maintaining continuity with established practices and the authority of existing institutions. The use of analogies allows institutions to see and then act on new situations in familiar and established terms. At the same time, the new situation has the potential of altering the analogy and, in turn, transforming the institutions which use it.

The mobile home poses special problems for classification and hence institutional regulation, by virtue of being a hybrid. Some of the elements which make up the mobile home are physical features, like wheels and chassis, and others are behaviors, like camping or homemaking. Depending on the aspect of the innovation that is focused on, it may be perceived or categorized in different ways. In *Brookside Village,* the court accepted the mobile home as a dwelling but wanted to restrict its placement. It was saying that the similarity or analogy extends only so far, and that its limits justify confining the mobile home to parks. In a contemporary Michigan case, *Robinson Township v. Knoll,* the State Supreme Court ruled that a zoning ordinance restricting mobile homes to licensed mobile home parks "had no reasonable basis in police power.[22] The court went on to observe,

> The mobile home today can compare favorably with site-built housing in size, safety and attractiveness. To be sure, mobile homes inferior in many respects to site-built homes continue to be manufactured. But the assumptions that all mobile homes

are different from all site-built homes with respect to criteria cognizable under the police power can no longer be accepted.

To say [as the town ordinance does] that a dwelling was "constructed to be towed on its own chassis" or "designed without permanent foundation" speaks only to its origins and not to its present character.

The Michigan court focused on different features than the Texas Court had, concluding that mobile homes belong in the category of permanent housing, rather than segregated in a category of their own.

Underlying questions of acceptability are those of comparability and compatibility: is the new thing like other things in this category; is it similar to things the regulatory institution knows how to deal with? A hybrid like the mobile home invites multiple categorizations, resulting in conflicting responses between users and regulators and problems in coordinating actions between institutions. Over time there is pressure to isolate the acceptable elements, and to alter the object to unambiguously fit the categorical scheme. Gradually, a complex process of fitting and sorting takes place, both revealing what the gatekeeping institutions think housing is, and suggesting contradictions in our beliefs about what makes a type of housing acceptable.

In the case of the mobile home, the process of fitting is apparent; the object itself changes over time, becoming less vehicular and more house-like. Its physical transformation corresponds to changes in its use and meaning. The travel trailer becomes a house trailer, a mobile home, and finally manufactured housing, with each name change revealing a different categorization and equilibrium between the institutions involved.

While the role of institutions is important in the process of categorization, and especially in fitting, they do not control it. The makers and users of the innovation are also active participants. The mobile home industry is not centrally organized or dominated by a few large manufacturers; there are hundreds of firms building models, as well as park developers and dealers, participating in the design, all of whom must work with a variety of regulatory institutions. The occupants of the mobile homes themselves, not only constitute the market, determining what models are acceptable, they also modify their homes over time and decide how they will be sited and related to the ground.

The evolution of the mobile home is a play between these two sets of actors: institutions on the one side, makers and users on the other, both struggling to create a common framework that permits them to coordinate their actions while satisfying their specific needs. For institutions, the problem is to maintain a predictable categorical order. For individual households and mobile home manufacturers, it is to satisfy housing needs. This book traces this process over time. Chapters are ordered chronologically, corresponding to major periods of development. Chapter 2 focuses on the travel trailer period beginning in the mid-1920s and ending around 1939. It was a period dominated by designer/manufacturers who were exploring alternative forms and meaning as they attempted to anchor the innovation in terms of familiar categories drawn from the past, as well as popular images of the future. By its end, the actions of regulatory authorities had narrowed the meaning and uses of the trailer, designating it an autocamping accessory. Chapter 3 covers the period from 1940 to 1953, when travel trailers become house trailers. The central issue considered here is the trailer as industrialized housing. Its performance is compared with other contemporary attempts to realize a house built-like-a-car.

The era of the mobile home proper begins in the mid-1950s, spanning to the mid-1970s. Chapter 4 analyzes the design of mobile homes and the tensions between attempts to make it more house-like rather than vehicular. Chapter 5 considers how mobile homes were related to their individual sites and organized into communities. The latest period of development, beginning in the mid-1970s, in which the mobile home officially became manufactured housing, is reviewed in Chapter 6. This transformation was the result of federal recognition of the role of mobile homes in satisfying the demand for affordable housing. This chapter considers how the sale and use of manufactured housing has benefited and suffered from its new-won status. The last chapter returns to themes introduced in the first, considering again the processes of categorization and invention as they play against each other through the development of housing innovations.

Image and Invention

Back to Nature on Springs of Steel

A special kind of fellowship comes with camping: the pressure of urban life is dispelled and the pattern of daily activities is reduced to essentials. Then the senses are reawakened to the fragrance of the air, the changing color of light, and the quiet rustling of leaves. Rank and station conferred by society lose importance: association is based on propinquity and freedom of movement. In this vein, American naturalist John Burroughs observed: "We grow weary of our luxuries and conveniences. We react against our complex civilization, and long to get back for a time to first principles. We cheerfully endure wet, cold, smoke, mosquitos, black flies, and sleepless nights, just to touch naked reality once more."[1]

One weekend in 1921, the smoke from a cooking fire curled gently toward a clear sky, as people talked and laughed, above the echoes of wood being chopped. The man cutting wood, in striped shirt and bow tie, was Henry Ford. Thomas Alva Edison recorded the event on his motion picture camera, as Harvey Firestone looked on, offering directorial suggestions. Nearby, an open cooking fire sparked while, next to it, a chuckwagon cleverly fitted out from the back of a truck, served as a kitchen. Lunch would soon be served under a white dining fly erected in the center of the campsite. Its interior could barely contain a huge round table, at the center of which a Lazy Susan turned to deliver bowls of salad and condiments. The host of this fresh-air gathering was Warren G. Harding, President of the United States.

The event of an American president and distinguished men of industry camping out together was not altogether novel. Teddy Roosevelt, who advocated a return to the strenuous life as an antidote to the decadence of urban civilization, had hosted many such trips. What distinguished Harding's outing, and excited the public, was its equipment and style. In the few years between the Roosevelt and Harding administrations, the return to "first principles" had become conflated with the invention of the car and the beginning of autocamping. Burroughs himself was an autocamping companion of Firestone, Ford, and Edison. Ironically, the sojourn into nature about which Burroughs wrote was, for these men, apparently not compromised by the use of modern technology.

Among the early celebrated autocampers were other captains of industry, who relished the possibility of enjoying nature without having to endure the traditional hardships. They could be as romantic about technology as Burroughs was about black flies and mosquitos. The president of Packard Motor, for example, went camping in a custom-built motorized van that slept six. Its interior had many of the transformable furnishings associated with Pullman cars: berths that swung out of the wall, folding tables, built-in cupboards, and more.

In 1919, aviation pioneer Glenn Curtiss designed and built his own custom trailer. The Aerocar featured rounded edges and a goosenecked section fitting over the trunk of the tow car. The first issue of *Automobile and Trailer Travel* magazine (later, *Travel Trailer*), described it as "neat as a yacht and beautifully streamlined. Inside were four Pullman type berths, a spotless galley and an airplane type observatory cockpit forward with a glass roof. There were wardrobes and running water and a telephone to the car ahead."[2]

Curtiss referred to his Aerocar as a "motorized Gypsy van" or "motor bungalow" and licensed it for commercial production in the late 1920s. At the top of the Aerocar production line was the 161-BPC model, featuring a cockpit with a row of clerestory windows near the front, which provided a panoramic view from the lounge-type chairs inside. This model was also equipped with air conditioning. Despite its advanced design, the Aerocar achieved only modest sales and went out of production by the late 1930s. Yet it embodied a new synthesis between the ideal of camping as a rustic, natural activity, and the romantic vision of technology winging mankind into a comfortable but adventuresome future.

Glenn Curtiss in 1922 standing outside his Aerocar.

The outings of presidents and captains of industry were worthy of press coverage, because they reflected the public's own enthusiasm for autocamping and its belief in the idea that once outside the structured society of cities and in the open countryside, people could enjoy each other as equals. Ford himself identified this aspect of the automobile as a reason for the Model T's popularity.

> I will build a motor car for the great multitude.
> It will be large enough for the family, but small enough for the individual to run and care for. It will be constructed of the best materials, by the best men to be hired, after the simplest designs that modern engineering can devise. But it will be so low in price that no man making a good salary will be unable to own one— and enjoy with his family the blessings of hours of pleasure in God's great open space.[3]

In 1921, an estimated 20,000 people drove across the country; no mean feat considering the unpaved and rutted roads at that time. The *New York Times* estimated that, out of 10.8 million cars on the road in 1922, approximately 5 million would be used for camping.[4] Other estimates made within the next few years ranged up to 20 million autocampers annually. The growth in car ownership—a clear prerequisite—fueled the popularity of

The Warner Autotrailer "Prairie Schooner" is an example of a commercially manufactured folding trailer popular in the mid-1920s.

autocamping. In 1910 fewer than half a million cars were registered in the United States; by 1920 there were over eight million; by 1925, 17.5 million; and by 1935, over 22 million.[5]

The automobile of the 1920s camping trip was not simply the means of getting to a campsite, but the focus of, and often an excuse for, the trip. The pastime—and obligation—of socializing with neighbors was greatly reduced by the freedom automotive travel offered. Church would sometimes be skipped, and potluck suppers avoided, to get an early start on the road. The automobile greatly expanded a freedom that had been introduced by the bicycle. Perfected in the mid-1880s, the easy-to-ride modern two-wheeler gave family members, especially young singles, the chance to escape a restrictive home orbit. Bicycles became the foundation for social clubs as well as informal and unchaperoned socializing. In the late 1930s, John Steinbeck expressed the magnitude of the new freedom the automobile brought when he suggested that half of the American population was conceived in the back seat of a Ford.

Just as the automobile gave a measure of freedom to individual family members, it could also bring families together for outings and vacations. During the last half of the nineteenth century, it was common for women and children to spend summers in the country or by the shore, while the male head of the household remained at work in the city. By the 1920s, work schedules had been sufficiently reduced and annual vacations had become generally established, so that families could take weekend and vacation trips together. During this same period, the preferred setting for a vacation shifted from formal resort hotels to rural areas, where family members could engage in all types of rigorous outdoor activities. The exposure to different people and places travel provided came to be considered valuable in itself, particularly for the development of children, and camping's popularity rose. It was an era when the ideal of the Christian household, in which children were taught moral virtues around the hearth, was being replaced by the image of the leisure-oriented family.

Do-It-Yourself Campers

The typical camping outfit of the 1920s consisted of an "autotent," whose design ranged from simple lean-to flies, which used the side of the car for support, to elaborate affairs, with windows, hanging bunks, and chuckwagon cook kits. Of the autocampers' outfits, Warren Belasco, in *Americans on the Road*, observed:

> Like hotel guests, only more so, autocampers loved gadgets. Collapsible equipment that minimized work and space could be purchased or designed at home. Bolted to the running board, an autotent unfolded almost automatically into a full scale shelter, complete with cot, springs and headrest—the running board itself. An ABC Sleeper converted the car into a Pullman-like berth. An auto kitchenette carried everything from pots and pans to eggs and stove in a compact box. Most elaborate were the two- and four-wheel trailers: trim wagons that miraculously mushroomed into bungalows with beds, stove, table and screened windows. The more ascetic camper might reduce his outfit to a frying pan, bed roll, and a few cans. Either way, self reliance was the aim and the result.[6]

What is striking about the autocamping ensemble is the intimacy between people and their cars. "Autocampers slept in their cars," Belasco recalls, "cooked on the radiators, and used running boards as headrests in the autotents."[7] The automobile, in some contemporary photographs, looks like an elephant crawling into its trainer's tent to take shelter for the night, asserting itself as a member of the family. One design which captured this intimacy, to a parody, was the 1926 "Honeymoon Special." A converted coupe featuring front and rear seats that could be rearranged to sleep two, came equipped with a radio, camping paraphernalia, and a shower that hooked onto the back of the car.

The advantage of the autotent was that it could be bought, or made, for a small investment. The family unsure of the merits of camping could still afford to give it a try. A major disadvantage was the space the autotent and camping accessories occupied in the car. The soft roof of the Model-T might be rolled back so that tent poles could extend outside, but passengers were still likely to be uncomfortably wedged between canvas and boxes during long and bumpy trips to the campsite. As the hard-topped car became dominant in the late 1920s (the Model-T went out of production in 1927), people were increasingly hesitant to jam equipment inside the more refined and dust-proof interior. The roof, however, was now available to receive the overflow.

A major inconvenience, if the family wanted to stop by the roadside for lunch when autotenting, was that part of the car would have to be unpacked to get chairs, table, utensils, and food, taking away from the precious time that might be used to increase the day's mileage. By the end of the 1920s, the use of autotents started to decline as they went out of fashion. To be seen so equipped, especially at popular private campgrounds, identified the owner as behind the times, cheap, or poor. Vestiges of the autotent, however, remain today in the form of special flies and lean-tos that attach to the side of a car, or in specially fitted vans.

More elaborate than the autotent was the tent trailer that was towed behind the car. Among the advantages of towing was that it left the interior free for passengers. A 1923 brochure for the "Auto-Kamp" trailer emphasized its convenience:

> The "Auto-Kamp" Trailer enables the motorist to take even the longest of tours with independence and comfort. It is a completely equipped home, affording absolute protection from the elements. . . . There is room for everything in the "Auto-Kamp" Trailer, as the car is entirely free for the comfort of the passengers.[8]

Among the earliest commercially produced tent trailers was the 1926 Chenango Camp Trailer, manufactured on an assembly line in Norwich, New York. The Chenango had a buckboard-type bottom, sides and roof of canvas, and a rear door. More elaborate than the Chenango were trailers with wood sides that folded up for travel. In some designs of this type, the trailer looked like a wagon, a few feet high, its base densely packed with equipment, clothing, and food, all covered by the folded canvas and wood sides. When camping, the wooden sides folded out into sleeping platforms and formed the base for a tent-like canvas enclosure.

Another commercially manufactured trailer of the late 1920s was the "Covered Wagon." Designed with a fixed canvas roof, it

The interior of this trailer by Covered Wagon featured details like glass-door cabinets and café window curtains, suggesting the comforts of home.

resembled a small Conestoga wagon mounted on rubber tires. Some contemporary journalists saw a direct connection between the Conestoga and the autotrailer camping fad, an association celebrated in the lines of a poem published in the *Denver Post:*

> Time has not dulled that urge.
>   The wanderlust lives forever in the hearts of men.
> Trails have grown smooth and comfort goes along
>   As covered wagons travel West again.[9]

If the covered wagon provided the mythic, if not literal, precedent for the tent trailer, then one of the prototypes for the solid-bodied trailer was the Gypsy wagon. Even before auto-camping, people were taking to the countryside in campers towed by horses. The Gypsy-style camping wagon had its origins in Europe and was especially popular in England.[10] Of the Gypsy wagons exhibited in the World's Columbian Exposition in Chicago in 1893, the first prize winner was a wagon built for King James Stanley of the Stanley Tribe of English Gypsies. Its exterior was lavishly ornamented with painted and carved decorations. The inside was fitted with a four-poster bed suitably modified to the restricted space. Folding doors, storage space under seats, and a portable stove were inventions designed to cope with the confined interior of the wagons. Access to the

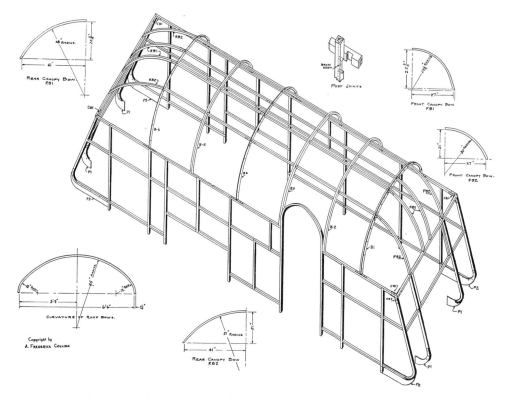

Construction diagram for the wood frame of a do-it-yourself trailer.

inside was typically over the driver's seat, which might fold away, leaving the back wall free for a single or double-decker bunk. Charles Lindberg has a custom-made trailer that incorporated many Gypsy wagon features. Nevertheless, for most Americans the Gypsy wagon and the Gypsy way of life evoked far fewer cultural associations than the covered wagon.

Although custom-made and commercially manufactured trailers were the glory of motoring magazines, the typical trailer from the 1920s through the 1930s was homemade. Curtiss's Aerocar notwithstanding, the early travel trailer was clearly a form of soft or low technology: accessible, understandable, easy to manipulate and alter. The distinction between homemade trailers and those manufactured for sale was often slight. Indeed, several major trailer manufacturers started out building units for their own use, then discovered that there was a market for their creations.

The technology of the tent trailer was sufficiently simple that the backyard do-it-yourselfer could easily copy its design. In fact, many instruction books came with construction drawings.

Chassis parts could be salvaged from the auto junkyard, and the body, made of wood, pressboard, and cloth, could be constructed with familiar, available tools. Throughout the 1930s about three out of four trailers—both the solid-sided variety and the tent types—were homemade.

The do-it-yourself builder was aided by parts suppliers who also served commercial manufacturers. Companies like Coleman began manufacturing gasoline-fueled camp stoves and lanterns in the 1920s. Others, like Hammer Blow Tool, produced axles and running gears. Watson Automatic Machine, a supplier of couplers and hitches, advertised for retail as well as wholesale customers. Some suppliers even offered plans showing how different trailers could be constructed. Parts suppliers also helped make the fledgling trailer industry viable by offering components on credit so that manufacturers could sell their units before their bills came due.[11]

The simplicity of constructing trailers was no small factor in their popularity. With a modest investment, and a little technical knowledge, an adequate trailer could be built. Until the mid-1930s, there were few regulatory restrictions to observe.

Campsites and Mobile Communities

Like the development of the trailers' design, the evolution of the organization of trailer communities was largely ad hoc. In the early days of autocamping, following the end of the First World War, the most common practice was for campers to stop by the side of the road or in a farmer's yard for the night. As the number of autocampers grew, such informal arrangements became unsuitable; farmers grew hostile to the frequent, uninvited guests, who trampled the sites and left their trash by the roadside.

Soon, the growing number of trailers became an incentive for developing specially designed campgrounds. The average small town on a main road might expect to see fifty to sixty cars seeking sites each night. The first auto campgrounds, constructed in the early 1920s, were municipal facilities. Their development was encouraged by local businesses who saw autocampers as potential customers. Ten to fifteen acre sites, usually near the center of town, were made available free to the public. They were supplied with potable water, toilets, electric lights, showers, laundry, and even a central kitchen with stoves and eating areas. Between 1920 and 1924, an estimated three to six thousand municipal autocamps were established. The campgrounds were a source of community pride and an object of rivalry between neighboring towns. To be known as "a nice place to stay" reflected favorably on the whole community.

A typical trailer camp in the mid-1930s with ad hoc awning carports.

By 1924, however, municipal campgrounds were beginning to suffer from their own generosity. A less desirable class of camper was moving in, encouraged by the free facilities, but not likely to spend money in local businesses, except perhaps the gas station. Unlike the vacationing camper, the "hobo tourist" often had no permanent home and was likely to stay on in a campground for as long as possible. As quickly as they had appeared, free municipal camps began to disappear. They were either replaced by private pay camps, or a fee was imposed for the use of the municipal facility. Towns also began to set a limit on the length of stay, often of one to two weeks.

At this same time, autocamping was being challenged by a competitor for the auto vacationing public—the motel. Although the early motel cabin offered little more space than a trailer did, it was more acceptable as a commercial establishment in the community. As the number of motels increased, many motel owners sought to eliminate trailer competition by supporting restrictive zoning; others, however, sought a compromise by renting space between their cottages to autocampers.

By the mid-1930s there were enough travel trailers to justify excluding tents from the campsites. By the late 1930s, the term "park" came into use to distinguish trailer facilities from other types of campgrounds. Since a campground required little capital investment, anyone with a parcel of land supplied with utilities could add some dirt roads and bath and wash facilities and set up business. Some parks started as extensions of gas

The distribution of trailer camps in the U.S. in 1938.

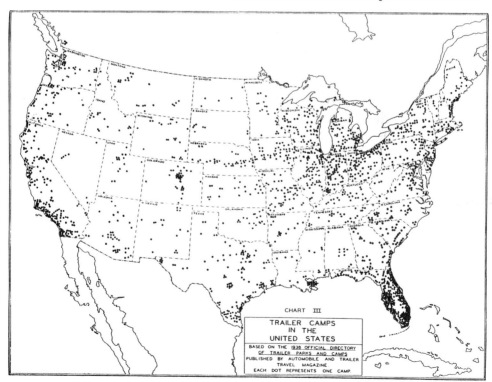

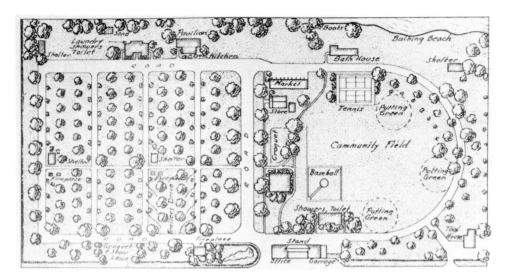

Proposed layout for a trailer park features shade trees, a buffer from the road, and extensive recreation facilities. Despite the generous use of space, the trailers themselves are closely packed, indicating an acceptance of this arrangement even in an idealized plan.

stations or roadside grocery stores: places where trailerites could get supplies and find parking. A home owner in town with an extra large lot might also consider entering the park business. These small "Mom and Pop" parks, so called because the owners often lived in a house on the property, had the advantage of being run by a resident owner. Many, however, lacked rudimentary sanitary and safety features: toilets were often privies, grey water was disposed of in seep holes, and electricity was conveyed to individual units through a web of extension cords. Sanitary codes in many states were soon amended to impose some order, but enforcement, especially in small towns, was nevertheless spotty or nonexistent. It often required an antagonistic party, such as a competing motel owner, to bring authorities in to enforce a code.

In contrast to the casual entry of many people into the park business, developers were planning luxury parks by the mid-1930s, which offered paved parking pads, individual service lines, and toilet facilities. There were also attempts to create national chains of quality parks. Kar-A-Van Trailer Company, for example, developed model site plans which it hoped to develop as a franchise system. No record exists of any parks actually being built by the company. Another firm, Glider Trailers, established uniform standards for the construction, design, and operation of their parks, named "Glider Villes."[12] The first of these developments opened near Bettendorf, Iowa; others were established elsewhere in Iowa, Illinois, and Florida. The war years brought a halt to further development of such chains. The type of system they envisioned, however, would later be the model for such national chains as Kampgrounds of America (KOA), where a uniform, standardized facility was created to accommodate the autocamper.

Since the quality of the Mom and Pop parks, as well as of other trailer campgrounds, varied widely, guidebooks and magazines began to appear in the early 1930s attempting to identify some of the better ones. *Brown's Trailer Park Directory* was the first, followed by *Woodall's Park Directory* in 1937. The first magazine for trailerites, *Trailer Travel*, made its debut in 1936. It included a limited listing of campgrounds, as well as recommending travel itineraries.

Although most vacationing trailer families preferred to follow their own schedules and routes, others chose to move as a group or to rally at a common site. The earliest of these groups was the Tin Can Tourists Association, founded in Tampa, Florida in 1919, whose objective was to promote fraternity among autocampers and to promote a redeeming image of their form of leisure. The association had four announced goals:

A rendering of a KAR-A-VAN Kamp shows the close relationship between the early motel and progressive thinking about what trailer camps might be like.

A rally of the Tin Can Tourists where homemade and manufactured trailers stand cheek and jowl with folding campers. What united them was the fraternity of autocamping.

- to unite fraternally all auto campers;
- to establish a feeling of friendship between them and a friendly basis with local residents;
- to provide clean and wholesome entertainment in camps and meetings
- to spread the gospel of cleanliness to all camps, as well as enforce the rules governing all public campgrounds.[13]

The name "Tin Can Tourists" referred to the canned food autocampers ate. The tin can became a sign of pride, even though it begged association with the hobo's can of beans. The Tin Can Tourists held rallies twice a year. Two thousand participants, housed in six hundred trailers, attended a summer convention in Sandusky, Ohio, in 1936.

Other organizations for trailerites were formed in the 1930s. The Automobile Tourist Association, organized in 1935, held a summer rally in Manistee, Michigan, that attracted 2,728 participants in 685 trailers. The Eastern Campers Association, the New England Tourists, and the National Travel Trailer Association, also started at this time. In the late 1930s, the Airstream Company began to promote gatherings exclusively for owners of its trailers. These organizations created the need for instant campsites. A favorite campsite layout for smaller gatherings was the roundup, in which trailers formed a circle, wagon-train fashion. Like the covered wagon style trailer, the roundup evoked images of the Wild West and the open frontier.

The Ideals of Autocamping

A new medium, Marshall McLuhan observed, takes the old medium for its message. The automotive age emerged just as the American frontier was disappearing. Frederick Jackson Turner, who did so much to solidify the idea of the frontier, published his essay *The Frontier in American History* in 1896. Turner's conception of frontier includes the "wild country," without which the idea of pioneering would be meaningless. "Out of his wilderness experience," Turner wrote, "out of the freedom of his opportunities, [the pioneer] fashioned a formula for social regeneration—the freedom of the individual to seek his own."[14] In Turner's formulation, mobility was equated with individuality. Wilderness provided the challenge, but it was Americans' willingness to move to meet the challenge that allowed the wilderness to have its regenerative effect.

Although the newly mobile public could not easily get to genuine wilderness, it had increasing access to its pastoral counterpart. Weekend auto trips and summer vacations created a demand for the development of national and state park systems, as well as forest recreation areas. The great natural wonders of the country could be seen firsthand, and education was added as justification for travel.

The mass-produced car, which made autocamping popular, was the ultimate mass consumer product. By allowing every household with a decent wage access to the countryside, the car offered an escape from the geographic bounds and the limited social opportunities of a neighborhood or town. By extension, autocamping represented a rejection of the constraints of a fixed community, promoting the free camaraderie of the road.

A return to nature and the ideal of individuality, expressed as physical mobility in a classless society, were the central but not the only themes which gave meaning and justification to the surge of automobile use and autocamping. The evocation of such ideals and images helped to link a cherished recent past and the possibilities offered by an emergent technology, while, in turn, influencing the design and patterns of use of the automobile and trailer.

In announcing the ideals with which its legitimacy was to be historically and culturally associated, advocates of autocamp-

Breakfast of pancakes and coffee

The return to nature was a theme frequently portrayed in trailer ads and magazine articles. The trailer interior here occupied by two hunters suggests a bunkhouse with its "Breakfast of Pancakes and Coffee."

ing also presented the basic arguments against it. Freedom from fixed communities could mean a lack of responsibility to community. Similarly, the droves of autocampers who carelessly trashed the roadside were proof that preserving the wilderness was best achieved by limiting its use. These conflicts would become increasingly apparent as autocamping's popularity increased, creating pressure for restrictions on the activity and its equipment, especially travel trailers.

Commercial Trailers: Images and Inventions

Early issues of *Trailer Travel* magazine tried to identify "The First Trailer," running pictures of traveling salesmen, itinerant workers, and evangelists who had developed either a motorized van or a car-towed trailer in which to live while on the road. It was difficult to locate the first trailer because, in effect, it had not been invented. As an object it was essentially already part of society's inventory. What was innovative was its use in a new activity—autocamping, itself a hybrid of automobiling and camping.

Throughout the 1920s, the vast majority of trailers had been homemade; and even by the late thirties, three out of four were do-it-yourself projects. The question of whether such a product could be the basis of an industry was open to speculation. In 1937, the editors of *Fortune* magazine observed:

> If you study it from a long way off . . . it seems to promise all kinds of wonderful opportunities . . . but when you step closer for a sharper look, you find something else. No matter what the prophets say, the trailer, at least at this stage of its technology, is still only a gadget. . . . Nobody close to the business knows how it will change or where it will go.[15]

By this time, the trailer industry had developed a sufficient sales level and growth rate to be worthy of notice by the general business community. In 1937, sales reached an estimated $55 million; more than double that of the previous year. Though born in the Depression, trailer manufacturing was an industry in which a relatively small investment could return an enormous profit. About four hundred companies were already manufacturing an estimated 85,000 to 100,000 trailers annually.

Just as the 1920s had been a fertile period for the ad hoc invention of homemade and custom-made trailers, the 1930s was fertile for invention and speculation within the emerging trailer industry. Indeed, no other period in the industry's development was more broadly or openly innovative: the manufacturers borrowed freely from many other spheres of activity for cultural associations and images of what the trailer and trailer life could be. Some of the cultural ideals and images associated with the design and use of the trailer had already been evoked in the 1920s, especially that of a return to nature or wilderness. Another was the ideal of individuality as expressd through physical mobility.Trailer advocates stressed the idea of being free from rent and from the necessity of socializing with neighbors not of one's choosing. Trailer manufacturers drew on these

JANUARY-FEBRUARY 1936
$1—12 issues . . . 10c a copy

*Special New 1936 Models and
First National Trailer Exposition Issue*

MAY 27 36

Trailer Travel

ONLY NATIONAL MAGAZINE IN THE TRAILER FIELD

*for all Trailerites . . . owners [present and future], operators
dealers and manufacturers of pleasure and business trailers*

[The Road Chief in the Desert—Courtesy Bowlus-Teller]

N THIS
SSUE

ROGER W. BABSON predicts: "Half
the U. S. will soon be living in trailers."

America's First National Tourist Trailer Show ❦ Official Announcements and
News of T. C. T. and A. T. A. and Industry ❦ Touring Information ❦ Business
Trailer Development ❦ Trailer Designs and Features ❦ Home Builder's Guide

The cover of the first issue of *Trailer Travel* featured the sleek, silver-sided
"Road Chief" crossing the desert: a machine-age vehicle in which to return to
the wilderness.

associations but they also emphasized a romantic fascination
with technology. The image evoked by Glenn Curtiss's Aerocar
was a return to wilderness, but in a high-tech container—an
image that received further expression with the commercial
development of models by Airstream and Silver Dome.

The broad range of cultural ideals associated with trailering in
this period parallels the development of different potential uses.

The attitude of experimentation is most obvious in physical design. If a trailer was designed to evoke an association with advanced technology, details borrowed from yachts and airplanes became appropriate to its form. If a romantic, nomadic lifestyle was the theme, Gypsy wagon details could be incorporated. In many cases, multiple associations were evoked, producing a wild and undisciplined collage. Eventually, external pressures from institutions responsible for maintaining the use and character of permanent and vacation housing narrowed the range of explorations, but for a brief and glorious period the field was wide open.

"Good night, sweet dreams, sonny," read the caption of this trailer ad. The industry at the time wanted to promote the idea that trailer living could support family values, educating children by exposing them to the diversity of American culture and landscape through travel.

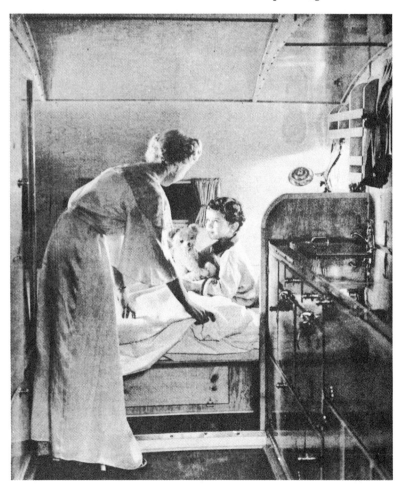

Fortune's assessment that the industry lacked clear direction at this point proved to be prophetic. Many possibilities seemed viable. One obvious direction was for nascent industry to offer travel trailers exclusively for vacationing. Taking advantage of the economy of mass production, the industry would provide an alternative to the homemade trailer. Another direction was to stress the use of trailers as mobile housing. The market would be itinerant workers, traveling salesmen, and others whose occupations or avocations required a good deal of travel. A third, and final direction was to develop the idea of the trailer as an alternative form of permanent housing. In this case, mobility would be played down and the economy of factory production emphasized. During the late 1930s, as manufacturers of trailers begin to form into a recognized industry, all three possibilities—travel trailer, house trailer, and mobile/manufactured housing—were being explored. While production activity at this time centered on vacation travel trailers, the other two products would re-emerge to dominate the industry in later periods.

Travel Trailers

The distinction between homemade and manufactured trailer was often fuzzy. A number of major firms founded in the 1930s began with a camping trip in which the homemade trailer's successful design suggested the possibility of commercial production. The largest firm of the period, Covered Wagon, was founded by Arthur Sherman, a bacteriologist and president of a pharmaceutical firm. An article in *Fortune* reported that his interest in trailers began with a camping trip.

> Knowing from experience the grief of making and breaking camp, he looked around for something ready-made that he could tow behind the family car. All he could find was a wheeled box containing a tent, which the manufacturer claimed you could pitch in five minutes, but which Mr Sherman could not master after an hour of wrestling. Remembering that he had read somewhere about houses on wheels, Mr Sherman decided to build one himself. . . . With that, the Sherman family went a-touring.[16]

The curiosity which his trailer aroused convinced Sherman there was a market for his design. With an initial investment of ten thousand dollars, and working out of a rented garage, he set up commercial production of the Covered Wagon in 1929. In 1931, he sold 117 trailers; by 1936, his assembly line turned out 35 units per day. That year, Covered Wagon was the largest company in the industry, grossing three million dollars in annual sales and manufacturing one out of six commercially produced trailers.

The Covered Wagon model incorporated the main features that had been evolving in solid-bodied trailer design. Its door was on the side rather than the rear, so that people could enter and exit more safely, and less dust would be kicked up into the interior during travel. Placing the door on the side also affected the organization of the interior, which now could be readily divided fore and aft into sleeping/dressing and kitchen/sitting areas. The compartmentalization of the interior marked a shift in design from one that emphasized a total transformation of space and furnishings, to an organization where spaces had fixed functions. Given the small area of the early travel trailer, such changes would seem to be impractical; yet they reflected the American preference for separating dwelling spaces by function.

To some contemporaries, the Covered Wagon's interior suggested a yacht.

> Many persons have commented on the resemblance of yacht interiors to travel trailer interiors, citing kitchen galleys, the compact bunks, the marine type water pumps, the mahogany paneling. They draw comparisons between staterooms on a boat and on a trailer. They even design some trailers with portholes for windows. The fact of the matter is that such design developments Mr Sherman based directly on his cruising experience.[17]

More impressive than the design of the Covered Wagon was its method of production, patterned after Ford's assembly line. Units moved down the line, end-to-end, on their own wheels. Subassemblies, like cabinets and completed body frames, came in from the sides or above the line, where wood, metal, and other shops were organized. Some components, like the chassis, cabinets, and icebox, were purchased from supply firms. Most of the larger trailer manufacturers engaged primarily in assembly, though others produced all of their own components.

The large-scale and efficient organization of the Covered Wagon factory suggested that trailer manufacture would soon take its place alongside other major forms of industrialized production. But this level of organization soon proved a liability. In 1938, the company contracted with Motor Wheels Corporation for delivery of wheels, springs, and chassis for a hundred units per day. Later that year, a general business recession hit and sales fell to five to ten units per day. At the same time, Covered Wagon found itself faced with a change in consumer preferences. Its models were 6½ feet wide, while other manufacturers had turned to 8-foot-wide designs. As the narrower models declined in popularity, the company decided to modify its design with an 8-foot-wide unit. Surplus chassis had to be modified to fit a wider body, adding to the model's cost and reducing its competitiveness.[18]

Covered Wagon's financial problems raised questions about the analogy of the automobile industry to trailer production. Even though the sixteen largest manufacturers accounted for sixty percent of the 17–21-foot commercial units built in 1939, the small marginal producers were important to the vitality of the industry. The modest capital investment required to start a plant, and the suppliers' practice of extending credit until units were sold, encouraged the development of small producers. Automobile production, by contrast, required large capitalization, and model changes involved enormous tooling-up costs. Indeed, the major automobile manufacturers, Ford and General Motors, had investigated the feasibility of entering the trailer market but decided it was too small to justify their production and marketing methods.

Sherman's meteoric success was repeated by others. Schult Trailers was founded in 1934 by Wilbur J. Schult, a former Covered Wagon dealer, and Walter O. Wells. The first Schult trailer was a simple design with two flat, semicircular sides and a rounded roof that met the chassis at both ends. By 1936, Schult was the third largest manufacturer in the industry, with annual sales of fourteen hundred units. The design of the Schult trailer also grew in sophistication. By 1940, its top-of-the-line model was a 17-foot-long unit, with curves confined to the roof line and a slightly swept-back tail section. The efficiently designed plywood interior featured many of the built-in yacht-like features of the Covered Wagon models.

Another major company of the period, Silver Dome, was founded by Norman C. Wolfe. His firm, Wolfe Bodies, Inc., of Detroit, built truck bodies for Ford and Chevrolet until the auto manufacturers took over production of components for themselves. In 1932, Wolfe turned to manufacturing travel trailers. Four years later, he was the second largest producer in the industry. Other automobile body manufacturers also became briefly active in trailer production: Pierce-Arrow, Federal Motor Truck, and the Hayes Body.

The Silver Dome trailer came in deluxe and standard models. Measuring 15'6" long, 92" wide, and 74" high, it could be fitted for camping or commercial use. The organization of the Silver Dome's interior was influenced by the placement of the door in the rear. Shower and toilet closets flanked either side, followed by a kitchenette. The forward section contained two lower berths that served as couches during the day, and two Pullman-type upper berths. The body, a steel chassis surmounted by a

Exterior and interior views of a 17-foot trailer manufactured by Schult Trailer Co. in 1940. Its design is not significantly different from trailers manufactured today.

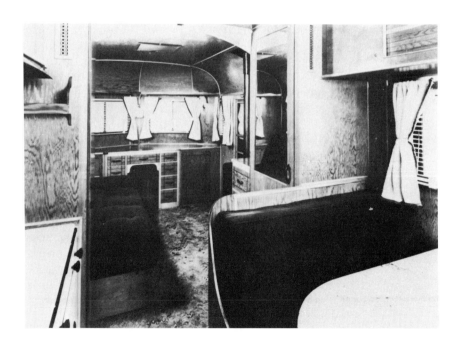

The "Trailer of Tomorrow," designed by Carl X. Meyer, features an aerodynamic shell that is visually exciting but less than efficient in its creation and use of the interior space.

wood and plywood frame, was sheathed with masonite sides and an aluminum roof. With six screened metal, awning-type windows wrapped around the front, the Silver Dome offered a modern appearance. "Perfect 'Silver Dome' streamlining," a company advertisement proclaimed, "as reflected in the V-front and graceful roof contour, makes wind resistance negligible and insures ease of operation. Travel at high speeds is possible with safety. This factor need only be governed by the desire of the driver or the limitations of motive power."[19]

The classic streamlined trailer of the period, the Airstream, was developed by another industry pioneer, Wally Byam. First introduced in 1935, the shape and structural design of the Airstream has changed little to this day. Its shell of aluminum sheets and ribs featured rounded edges forming a giant teardrop. Byam explained the principle of its design based on aerodynamic considerations: "the front was rounded to present an easy edge into the wind, vertically and horizontally. The tail was tapered off to eliminate suction in the rear. It was streamlined underneath as well as on top . . . and planned to give an extremely low center of gravity."[20]

The first issue of *Automobile and Trailer Travel* in 1936 featured an Airstream trailer being towed along a desert highway behind a two-door coupe. Its gleaming sides and round-edged windows made it appear far more advanced in design than the tow car. Yet aesthetically, as well as aerodynamically, the Airstream was conceived as part of a car/trailer complex. The idea of car and trailer as a single ensemble was also expressed in a design by Royal Barry Wills that appeared in the January 1937 issue of *Pencil Points* (later called *Progressive Architecture*). The streamlined aesthetic also proclaimed its association with other products of advanced industrialization: the smooth and integrated features of the body indicated something made by machine.

Although the streamlined aesthetic was justified by the dictates of aerodynamics, many adopted it with little or no appreciation of its principles. One critic observed: "The strangest monstrosities being committed in the name of streamlined designs are bad enough today and will probably grow worse."[21] Indeed, for many manufacturers, streamlining appears to have meant little more than rounding edges and adding motion-line appliqués to the unit's exterior. Nevertheless, the smooth and integrated body of the streamline design was in distinct contrast to most homemade solid-sided trailers.

Another important influence on trailer design was the railroad Pullman car. George Pullman patented his first car, in which seating converted into berths, in 1856. His design used furniture and equipment which could be collapsed or converted to make maximum use of limited space. Pullman-type devices were used in solid-body trailers, cross-country motor-buses, and motorized homes. Although the association with railroads and their technology was welcomed by early trailer designers and users, such details fell out of favor by the 1940s, as the market's preference shifted to more conventional, house-like interiors.

The concept of transforming the interior by using folding and collapsible furniture was taken a step further in attempts to make the trailer shell itself transformable. It was an approach that had already been taken with the tent trailer, whose rigid sides and canvas tops unfolded to produce larger stationary units. The problem was how to achieve similar transformations with the solid-body trailer. Perhaps the earliest attempt was the 1930 Split Coach tourist trailer. Its travel dimensions were 5' x 6' x 10'6". When set up, the coach split in half lengthwise and the roof was raised, opening up a space that was 7^1/$_2$ feet high, 12 feet wide, and 10^1/$_2$ feet long and accommodated four sleeping berths. *Motor Vehicle Monthly* reported,

The ingenious Patrick Collapsible House offered a hybrid between tent and trailer. Attached to the top of the car for travel, it could be lowered to the ground and unfolded into a one-room cabin. The idea was revived thirty years later in the Odyssey Collapsible Trailer.

At night complete privacy is afforded the four occupants by a curtain which is suspended from the roof and divides the vehicle into two equal halves. It is unnecessary to split the vehicle in order to use its equipment. The night curtain can further shut off the rear of the Split Coach whereupon this area becomes a combined dressing room and bathroom, where conveniences are at hand, including three seats, running water for drinking and washing, drawer and cupboard space, toilet arrangements, and hooks for wearing apparel.[22]

Another variation on the pop-up, fold-out method of expansion was the 1938 Klesa "Tourhome," whose travel dimensions were 12'6" x 5'8" x 5'6". At the touch of a switch, the roof of the trailer could be raised to 8'10", and sides unfolded to a width of 12'6". As the trailer opened, a retractable step descended, along with four parking legs that stabilized it on the ground. The fold-out side wings functioned like similar sections of a tent trailer, providing a foundation for sleeping berths. The Nicraluminum skin of the Tourhome, a material used in dirigibles, gave it the appearance of an armored folding tent trailer.

Manufacturers of the 1930s borrowed from several different sources to create the modern trailer. On the one hand, hoping to establish a positive association with advanced technology, particularly in transportation, they borrowed from railroad cars, yachts, and airplanes. Such details as Pullman berths were not only functional, but also helped identify the trailer as a technological object, rather than a homemade, scrap-heap assemblage. On the other hand, they appropriated physical features and alluded to images such as the covered wagon that associated the trailer with a romantic American past. That yacht details were used in an object called a covered wagon was riotously inconsistent, but this was hardly an issue. The composition of the whole was a collage, the power of which came from the juxtaposition of ready-made elements. The process itself was largely intuitive, collective, and uninformed by contemporary aesthetic theory and, therefore, all the more attuned to popular tastes.

The "Tourhome" was another experiment in expandability. It had a telescoping top and sides that folded out.

Designs by respected engineers like Glenn Curtiss and Wally Byam demonstrated that the trailer could legitimately emerge from the domain of ramshackle do-it-yourself projects and join the ranks of advanced industrial products: boats, planes, trains, and, of course, automobiles. Its use, however, confined it to being an automobile vacation accessory. By contrast other industry pioneers saw more radical possibilities for the trailer, as a form of year-round mobile housing.

The idea of a house trailer was already part of autocamping folklore. The Gypsy wagon was in effect year-round housing, and its imagery of roaming freely had been positively associated with autocamping. A no less exotic, but more utilitarian example of a traveling home was the trailers used by evangelists. One of the earliest recorded automobile travel trailers was built by an evangelist minister from Kansas. Built for a cross-country trip in 1915, it consisted of a wooden framed box covered with canvas and mounted on buggy wheels and axles.[23] In addition to evangelists, traveling salesmen and itinerant workers used early automobile trailers.

An estimated 10 to 25 percent of the trailer population were year-round users, with most occupying homemade models. Some industry visionaries projected that a vast segment of the population would take up a trailering way of life, thereby freeing themselves from rent and fixed communities. Undoubtedly the most immodest estimate of the future of year-round trailer use was made by economist Roger W. Babson, who had gained fame by predicting the stock market crash of 1929. "I am going to make an astonishing prediction," he wrote in the pages of *Trailer Travel*, "Within twenty years, more than half of the population of the United States will be living in automobile trailers."[24] Babson identified several "contributing causes" to support his prediction.

> In the first place, as I see it, this movement on the part of our families is a natural expression, a revolt of our people against what they apparently feel to be a condition of oppression. Here are the salient features of it:
> - When a man moves with his family into a home he has the feeling that he is anchored; that he is in the grip of his employer, to begin with.
> - He further feels that he is in the clutches of politicians.
> - He is marked by the tax assessor and collector, and must submit to any levies made on him.
> - He cannot be certain that the landscape surrounding his residence will remain the same from one day to another, and he has no control over the creation of unsightly neighboring structures.

- He must put up with objectionable neighbors, should they move close to him, and cannot alter conditions detrimental to his children in this respect.
- Increases in tax rates have done much to bring about the present state of affairs. The grip of union labor on the building industry has played a part, as well.

Those of our people who have turned to rolling homes have been influenced by a characteristic feeling of Americans—resentment against oppressive taxation and a desire for independence and freedom of movement.[25]

After reviewing the costs of trailer living, and reporting on his own inspection of a Curtiss Aerocar, Babson concluded that "the American urge to be on the move will be indulged. The covered wagon era is living again."[26]

Arguing along similar lines was another advocate of the house trailer, Corwin Willson, an "integrating" engineer and industrial designer. In a series of articles in *Trailer Travel*, Willson tried to promote the idea of the "mobile house" by illustrating its advantages over fixed housing. His fictional spokesman was a "thin, grey little man," who the people around the trailer park called "the Professor."

In the veins of most of us is the blood of pioneers. And what is a pioneer? He is usually a restless fellow who thinks his life was given him by his creator for some purpose more lively than squatting down in one place under a thirty year mortgage and meeting his interest payments promptly . . . to support a leisure class.[27]

The answer the Professor offered to this dilemma was the trailer.

You don't mean that the trailer is going to turn into a house [asks a skeptical bystander]?
What is it now, if not a house? Of course it's not a feudal castle, a huge fort built from stone, a Spanish or Italian villa. . . . It's honestly what it looks like, no more nor less. . . . It is rapidly growing better in every way for the simple reason that it promises to tap the greatest need of the past twenty centuries: a good home that the average income [family] can own or rent new and the less than average income can secure at second or fifth hand cheaply just as it now secures a used car, without mortgaging the future of its children's children.[28]

If the trailer/mobile home was to serve as year-round housing, more space was essential. Consequently, proposals stressed experiments in transforming or expanding space. Designers were highly innovative in searching for this space, again borrowing freely from a number of sources. There was explicit acceptance of a machine aesthetic, evident in details such as

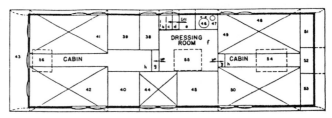

second floor plan

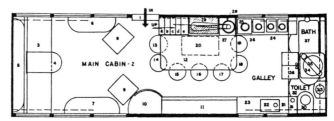

first floor plan

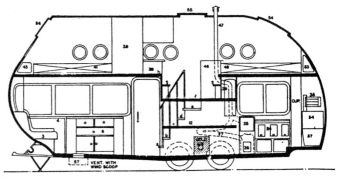

longitudinal section

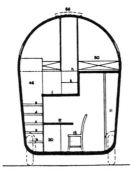

transverse section

Plans and sections of Corwin Willson's "Mobile House." The main cabin, on the first floor, is 8' x 17'6". Willson proposed that the unit be made out of lightweight molded plastic sections.

streamlined edges, porthole windows, and metal skin exteriors. The finished object was to be an industrial age object comparable to ships, trains, and planes. Its designers operated under the modernist belief that the imagery of the conventional house could be dispensed with in a mobile dwelling, and that users would prefer a form resulting from the objective analysis of functional requirements.

Willson's solution to the scarcity of space was presented in *Architectural Record* in July 1936.[29] His "mobile house" has a first floor with bath, kitchen, and dining spaces, and a sitting area which could be made up for sleeping. The upper level, with porthole windows, contained four fixed berths and wardrobes. Because highway regulations in most states limited trailer height to $12^1/_2$ feet, the upper level of the "mobile house" was too low to stand up in. As a sleeping area, however, such arrangements were acceptable and are still used in many modern recreation vehicles. While Willson apparently never built a full-scale version of his mobile house, several manufacturers began marketing double-decker trailers in the late 1950s. They realized limited success until double-wide units—two trailers joined longitudinally—made them a virtually obsolete solution to the problem of finding space.

In one article, Willson illustrated the idea of the mobile house with a design by William Stout, an automotive and industrial engineer whose design accomplishments included the Ford trimotor plane, the Scarab car (shaped like an Egyptian scarab), and the streamlined exterior of the Union Pacific's M-1000 train. Stout took a different tack than Willson, pursuing an approach that had been successful in the folding tent trailer. In many of those designs, fold-out platforms and canvas roof and wall sections expanded a small towable trailer into a more spacious stationary dwelling. Soft, uninsulated walls, however, made these trailers unsuitable for extended use, especially in colder climates. Stout took the idea of expansion, and adapted it to rigid panel construction.

On the road, Stout's house trailer measured 18' x 6'6" x 8'. Its front and rear edges were rounded to reduce wind resistance. The core contained kitchen and bath facilities, and provided storage for furniture to be used in the stationary unit. Once on location, the trailer could be set up in twenty minutes. First the roof sections, which formed the long sides of the folded trailer, hinged up; then the side walls were folded out, and finally the floor section was folded down. Thus expanded, the trailer was almost three times its travel size. Sleeping space for up to six materialized, as well as a living room measuring 13' x 16'.

Stout's design was meant for extended use. Like Willson, he

viewed the house trailer as an alternative to apartment living and as a way for itinerant workers to migrate together with their families. He took the idea further, however, by proposing a national chain of standardized parks, for his mass-produced trailers. The trailers and parks would have an orderly appearance, which, he expected, would help win local approval for their construction and operation. At the same time, the accommodations would meet uniformly high standards.

As a recognized member of the emerging field of industrial design, Stout seems to have been conversant with the work of contemporary innovative designers, including R. Buckminster Fuller. In many respects Stout's proposal recalls Fuller's ideas, first expressed in *4-D Time Lock* (1927) and later expanded in *Nine Chains to the Moon* (1938). In those works, and through his own housing proposals, notably the Dymaxion 4-D House, Fuller suggested that housing be considered a service in which people purchased or leased a standardized unit that could be replaced or traded in as more technologically advanced models were introduced. While these units were to be demountable and transportable, Fuller did not propose using trailers, nor a site development system that would allow units to be plugged into different communities.

In 1938, Stout toured the country towing his folding house trailer. In an article for *Trailer Caravan*, he described his experiences and argued for the widespread use of trailers as an alternative form of primary housing. In the closing paragraph of the article he observed:

> the trailer business is an indication of a new house being forced upon us by outside conditions, by the great accumulation of rubbish houses in our cities, which are no longer fit to live in; by an accumulation of real estate tradition and permanent home laws which prevent the laboring man and others from the luxury of owning property.[30]

This statement appears to paraphrase the conclusion of Le Corbusier's famous essay "Mass-Production Houses," first published in English in 1927.

> There reigns a great disagreement between the modern state of mind, which is an admonition to us, and the stifling accumulation of age long detritus. The problem is one of adaptation, in which the realities of our lives are in question.[31]

While Stout appears to have agreed with Le Corbusier's assumptions about the requirements for industrialized housing, he gave his declaration a uniquely American conclusion:

> but it [the trailer fad] is coming just as much from the new feeling on the part of the American public that the ownership of things

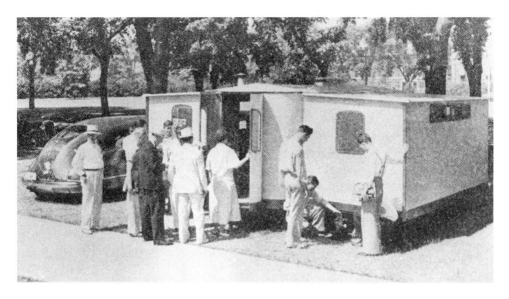

Exterior view of the folding house designed by William Stout exhibited at Purdue University. Seen beside the house is Stout's Scarab car.

Entry hall of the Stout folding house. The tubular steel chair was an icon of modern industrial design and demonstrates stout's acquaintance with that movement.

is not so important as experiences and living, so when all is said and done perhaps it is not the accumulation of unnecessary things but just the "Gypsy in us."[32]

People like Willson and Stout bridged the gap between two traditions: populist and high design. The populist, or modern venacular, tradition consists of the untutored efforts of anonymous designers working in industry or independently to solve immediate, practical problems. These problems are often "vulgar," like the design of a fast-food stand or a tractor seat. The high design tradition, by contrast, consists of the work and writings of individuals regarded as leading professional designers, who, through their connection with the corporate world, help define what is acceptable. They have the authority to elevate the ordinary and vulgar to the status of visibility—worthy of consideration. Through their writing, design demonstrations, and personal contacts, Willson and Stout brought these two traditions into contact and opened, if only briefly, an important avenue for legitimating the idea of the house trailer.

As well developed and visionary as Stout's ideas were, they probably would have remained experimental had it not been for the sudden and tremendous demand for temporary portable housing created by World War II. His design, through the efforts of the trailer industry, would play an important role in meeting that demand. After the war, Stout's folding house continued to be produced in various revised forms, until the double-wide mobile home replaced it.

Just as advocates of the travel trailer drew positive associations between trailering and historically valued ideals of American life, advocates of the house trailer associated their proposals with ideals—physical mobility, the ability to socialize with whom one chooses, and freedom from the burdens of fixed property—that they suggested had made the settlement of the frontier possible. Many of the characteristics of mobile home living which they sought to idealize, however, were precisely those that detractors found offensive and threatening. Freedom from fixed property, for example, could also be seen as a form of tax evasion, just as the freedom to choose one's neighbors might be interpreted as an abdication of community responsibility.

Mobile/Manufactured Housing

A less pronounced, but no less significant development in the design of the trailer was the idea of a mobile/manufactured home. Like the house trailer, it was to be factory-built and used for year-round living, but it was to remain permanently at one location. By the mid-1930s, trailers had already spontaneously

End view of the double unit, showing the manner of fitting the plans together in the center.

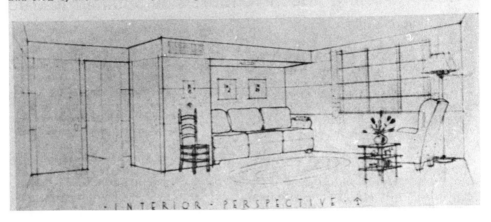

· I N T E R I O R · P E R S P E C T I V E · ↑

Renderings of the Durham Portable House, whose interior and exterior design foreshadowed the development of the double-wide mobile home of the mid-1960s.

begun to be used as fixed residences. People would set up trailers in summer vacation areas, occupy them in season, then close them up for the rest of the year. These trailers, however, were designed for vacation travel, unlike the mobile/manufactured housing proposed as a source of affordable permanent housing.

The idea of mobile/manufactured housing was most clearly presented in a proposal developed by two professors of architecture, M. R. Dobberman and John W. Davis, at the University of Illinois. The Durham House, named after the president of U.S. Club-Car Company who had agreed to build the portable shelters, was, as described in a 1938 issue of *Trailer Travel*,

> not intended to be towed across the country generally. Instead, they are constructed as regular homes with their patented framing

design to enable them to move without damage or loosening by means of large truck trailers. The designers correctly assume that persons who will buy their houses will contemplate remaining at one site for a considerable period of time, but that circumstances may at some future date require their removal. In such an event, the house may be lifted from its cinder block foundation and deposited on the truck trailer and delivered to its new location for about the same cost that ordinarily would be required to move the normal household's furniture.[33]

In concept, the Durham House was essentially like today's modular home. It did not have permanently affixed chassis and axles but was transported on flatbed trucks. The Durham House was proposed for commercial uses, such as motels, as well as the residential market for affordable housing. The estimated price, depending on size, was $1500 to $3000, including appliances, beds, window and floor coverings, but not land or site preparation.

Three basic plans were to be offered. The smallest, 25' x 8', had built-in bunks, appliances, and storage closets all lined up along one side. A rendering suggests that curtains could be drawn at night for privacy between the two sleeping areas. The rendering also suggests a very house-like interior. Details derived from transformable furniture, yachts, and railroad sleeping cars were replaced by hooked rugs, chintz curtains, and crossbuck house-type doors.

A more elaborate plan was the "double unit" consisting of two 8' x 25' sections joined longitudinally. It featured a living/dining area measuring 10'6" x 15'6", and 7'6" x 9' bedroom, and a 5'4" x 7' kitchen. Each section had a pitched shingled roof, so that when the two halves were connected they formed a complete saddle. The roof included a false brick chimney enclosing the furnace flue. There was clapboard siding, a large corner picture window, and an optional detachable porch. Renderings showed the unit close to the ground, as if set on a foundation. The Durham House, in short, looked like a scaled-down version of the kind of double-wide mobile home that would become popular in the mid-1960s.

The significance of the Durham House rests not in its conventional house-like appearance, which it shared with other commercial models, such as the clapboard sided Batavia Trailer, but rather in the idea that the trailer could be fixed to a site, and made large enough for permanent living by being transported in sections. By contrast, the house trailers Willson and Stout proposed emphasized transportability. A family might live in a trailer as its primary housing, but only because the head of the household was engaged in some type of transient work, such as construction. In the Durham House, transportability is important for bringing the house from the factory to the site, but, in the double-wide unit at least, it is not desirable to move it around very often. It would take two vehicles to transport such a house, raising the expense and inconvenience of any move considerably.[34]

The economics of transporting the Durham House suggested that its success would depend on serving an urban market, for which it could provide an affordable housing alternative. Whether the unit would qualify for mortgage money was another important aspect of its affordability. *Trailer Travel* announced that the manufacturers of the Durham House had secured FHA approval for mortgage insurance. Under that program a double-wide unit attached to land on which the purchaser held title would qualify for a twenty-five year mortgage at 5 percent.[35] Given the local resistance which similar siting meets today, it seems doubtful that FHA approval was actually received. In any event, there is no evidence that the Durham House went into production. The concept, however, was clearly a prototype for the modular and manufactured housing that exists today.

The Durham House's potential as affordable housing for an urban market was explored in a 1939 report to the Massachusetts State Planning Board. Karl M. Tomfohrde, author of the report, observed:

> Although the trailer was originally designed chiefly as a more convenient and cheaper mode of vacation shelter, many people are now using trailers as a permanent home. Statistics indicate that the city is faced with a housing shortage, that there has been extreme under building in the depression years and that a large population is living in substandard housing. Neither government subsidized nor stimulated private housing will meet the actual needs. The trailer may have effective potentialities in the field of housing since it may be the basis for the design of a new type of low-cost home on a mass production basis. In fact such an occurrence has taken place in the development of the "Durham Portable House."[36]

> The trailer may offer inspiration to builders and architects in meeting the demands of the low-cost housing market, a market which has been almost completely ignored in the past. It seems but a step, no doubt a long one, from the mass production of trailer homes to the mass production of stationary homes.[37]

The report acknowledged the need for trailers as both temporary and permanent housing. Stringent zoning and sanitary regulations would be necessary, however, if "trailerite slums" were to be avoided. The report nevertheless suggested that provision should be made for this type of housing, and it particularly encouraged the use of trailers as permanent housing.

The Durham House proposal illustrates how attempts to apply trailer technology to the problem of supplying permanent housing carried with them the desire to employ conventional housing forms. Its proponents seemed to understand that institutional, as well as public, acceptance would be conditional on the product's appearance. By contrast, more radical contemporary proposals for industrialized housing, such as Buckminster Fuller's Dymaxion 4-D House, made polemical the ideal that an object produced by advanced factory technology should reject the site-built aesthetic of the traditional house. That aesthetic, however, holds such strong associations with the ideals and values of home that to reject it, while asserting the identity of the resulting object as a home, required an ideological commitment far beyond the capacity of most people simply in search of affordable housing.[38]

Consolidation of Identity

The travel trailer, which emerged in a period of national prosperity, evolved into an industry during the depths of the Great Depression. It developed from a curiosity into a fad, and finally into a national movement which could no longer be ignored or dismissed. The broad-ranging experimentation with the form and use of trailers that had characterized the first decade of development drew to a close as state and local agencies turned their attention to regulating this new form of housing on wheels. By the latter half of the 1930s, an established identity was being formed. On one hand, institutions empowered to regulate land use, and to protect the health and safety of the public, saw the trailer as a potential threat. On the other hand, trailer users and members of the emerging trailer industry found it necessary to form their own associations to defend the trailer and to work toward consolidating an identity that would assure continued, if more restricted, use.

By the mid-1930s, trailers could be seen along the highways of every state, particularly in the Sunbelt, and in droves at national recreation areas like Yellowstone Park. For the 1939 World's Fair alone, a trailer park with 1200 spaces was set up on Hunt's Point in the Bronx. Contemporary estimates of the exact extent of use varied widely. *Fortune* magazine stated that 55,000 trailers were produced in 1936, of which 35,000 were factory made,[39] and estimated that production in 1937 would reach 100,000. The American Automobile Assiciation, in 1936, estimated 300,000 trailers, with one million people using them for vacation or year-round living.[40] *American Cities* magazine, in

IN NOMAD'S LAND

When Half the Nation Lives in Trailers.

The cartoon "In Nomad's Land" originally appeared in the Chicago *Tribune,* probably in response to Roger Babson's prediction that soon half the population of the United States would be living in trailers.

March of 1937, offered the figure of 400,000 trailers and a user population of 1.25 million people. Sociologists Clark and Wilcox, in their 1938 analysis of the house trailer movement, suggested that there were 250,000 trailers with one million users.

If estimates of the total number of trailers and trailerites were difficult to fix, then the percentage of users who lived in their trailers year-round was even more speculative. An industry survey in 1939 estimated that 10 percent of new commercially manufactured trailers were being bought as full-time housing.[41] The principal buyers were skilled itinerant workers, most of whom were in the construction industry, and retired professionals. These trailerites had a higher level of income and education than the general population. The cost of larger manufactured trailers used for full-time housing would, perforce, exclude unskilled and migrant laborers, who used homemade trailers or tents. Following these assumptions, the percentage of year-round trailer users might have been as high as 25 percent of all trailerites. If so, most of the trailers being used for housing were probably inferior to the manufactured trailers. It is little wonder that the industry, as it began to consolidate and develop an official position, wanted to distance itself from the idea of trailers as permanent housing. An industry spokesman went so far as to suggest that, given the small size of units, a family forced to live in a trailer would soon be at each other's throats.[42]

Federal reaction to the use of trailers by migrant workers was to try to reinforce the ideal of fixed housing, rather than encourage the use of alternatives. In 1936, author Ernestine Evans took the Resettlement Administration to task for its attempts to supply a handful of people with decent, conventionally built rental housing, when many more could have been helped with the same dollars if trailers were recognized as an acceptable alternative.

> Why the government in general, and the Resettlement Administration in particular, has been so slow to experiment with trailer-houses I do not know. There are 150,000 migratory workers on the west coast, the stoop-labor that bends over the lettuce and peas, and reaches for the oranges. They live wretchedly. True, Resettlement has built two camps for them with community utilities. But when so many of the workers were desperately trying to house themselves in makeshift trailers, got together from materials found in the Marysville dump, badly constructed and often too heavy for their ancient tin lizzies to haul, it seems a pity that neither Rural Resettlement nor the special skills division of RA have actually put on the payroll an instructor to help these people use new materials, or master the tricks of coupling, water-proofing, and so on.[43]

Just as the Depression encouraged year-round trailer use, it also fueled resistance to the trend. Communities were concerned that trailerites, especially migrant worker families, would descend upon them *en masse*, draining local services. Given the rate of housing foreclosures, the concomitant loss of taxes, and the rising use of trailers, this concern is not difficult to understand.[44]

Community Resistance

Communities responded to the trailer threat by enacting restrictive zoning, requiring parking permits that limited the duration of stay, and imposing new taxes and fees. Detroit, for example, passed an ordinance limiting trailers to a ninety-day stay, to ensure their transience. Before the ordinance was passed neither the Building Department nor the Health Department could determine who had jurisdiction over trailer housing.[45] Similarly, Toledo, Ohio enacted an ordinance limiting visits to three months a year. For its part, the industry, represented by the Trailer Coach Manufacturers Association, endorsed Toledo's ordinance as "both reasonable and equitable."[46] Thus, with industry support, municipalities moved to block the use of trailers as fixed housing.[47]

The courts were soon embroiled in battles over an emergent house form and land use which did not fit neatly into established categories. The situation is illustrated by a widely reported court case of the time, *People v. Gumarsol*.[48] In the summer of 1936, Mr. Hildred Gumarsol placed his travel trailer on a rented lot in Orchard Lake, Michigan. Rather than remove his trailer at the end of the season, he set it on blocks, added a porch, and left it there over the winter, expecting to return the following summer. The suit was brought by nearby landowners who were concerned that others would follow Gumarsol's example, and that Orchard Lake might soon become a shantytown of trailers, lowering their own propery values. In fact, there were already other trailers around Gumarsol's. "These people," Police Chief Clarence Carson stated, "roll in their trailers and proceed to enjoy all of the privileges of the lake without paying taxes . . . and they aren't discreet in getting into bathing suits either."[49]

Gumarsol and five other trailerites were arrested for violating a town ordinance requiring that a dwelling have an area of at least 400 square feet. In his defense, Gumarsol argued that his trailer was not a dwelling but an automobile accessory. Justice Green, to the contrary, ruled:

> It is the opinion of this court that a house trailer of the type occupied by the defendant and having a great many appointments of

Ad hoc trailer park, such as this one, on a Detroit lot, created concern among
municipal officials who responded by imposing limits on the length of stay
of trailers and by enacting restrictive zoning ordinances.

a modern home would come under the scope of a human dwelling
whether it stands upon blocks or the wheels attached thereto
or whether it be coupled to or detached from an automobile.[50]

Justice Green added that "trailer shantytowns will no longer
be allowed at Orchard Lake." In ruling that a permanently sited
trailer should be categorized as a dwelling, the court implicitly
legitimated it for that use while making it virtually impossible
to meet the code requirements. A trailer that was 7$^1/_2$ feet wide
would have had to be 54 feet long to meet the minimum area
requirement of the dwelling code. A trailer of this length, if it
could be towed, would have violated most vehicular regulations.[51]

While Justice Green's position in *Gumarsol* was clear, it was
not characteristic of all court decisions at the time. In the case of
Boxer v. Town of Harrison (1940), for example, the court struck
down an ordinance requiring a nonrenewable permit of occupancy that would be valid for only two weeks. In its ruling, the
court stated that "as the ordinance reads, the plaintiff could
have neither the use of his real property for the storage of his
trailer, nor the right to full enjoyment of his personal property."[52]

Yet, despite contrary rulings, the *Gumarsol* case typifies the common objections to trailers: that occupants did not pay their fair share of taxes for public services; that the unrestricted placement of trailers and trailer camps threatened real estate values; and that people who lived in trailers tended to behave immorally, threatening the standards of the community. The issue of taxation would be answered in this period by imposing registration fees and personal property taxes. The threat to real estate would be met using permits to limit the stay of trailers and frontage consents and other zoning devices to ban the use of trailers in a jurisdiction. Finally, the question of morality would be raised in the courts in an attempt to have trailers and camps declared a nuisance per se.

In the attempt to impose restrictions on the travel trailer, its categorization as a vehicle or dwelling was a constant source of difficulty. If it was a vehicle, could it be regulated through land use controls? If it was not a vehicle, was it a building? How could it be considered a building if it was on wheels? Is the nature of an object determined by its use, the intention of the user, the perceptions of others, or its objective physical features? What analogies apply in categorizing the innovation?

In the case of *Spitler v. Town of Munster* (1938),[53] the town ordinance limited the length of residence in a hotel to thirty days. The town argued that trailerites in tourist camps were like occupants of hotels and that their stay should be similarly limited. The court found for the town, citing that the plumbing code set requirements for places of permanent residences, and that these requirements were not ordinarily met by temporary residences such as trailers in tourist camps. The court further acknowledged that the purpose of the code was to ensure the transient character of such camps.[54]

The ruling in *Spitler v. Town of Munster* affirmed the power of municipalities to define what constitutes a "temporary residence," but it did not overtly express the idea that the very transitory nature of trailer homes posed a threat to the stability of the community. In another case, *Cady v. City of Detroit* (1939), concerning a municipality's right to limit the stay of a trailer to ninety days, the court took that more extreme position.

Ordinances having for their sole purpose regulated municipal development, the security of home life, the preservation of a favorable environment in which to rear children, the protection of the morals and health, the safeguarding of the economic structure upon which the public good depends, the stabilization of the use and value of property, the attraction of a desirable citizenship and the fostering of its permanency, are within the proper orbit of the public power.[55]

In general, the court rulings of this period had the effect of defining the trailer as a temporary and mobile residence. Someone moving from place to place in a trailer was treated as a transient, not unlike a person staying in a hotel. Like a hotel, the trailer park could be classified as a permanant land use, but not the trailers in it. The ambiguity of these rulings reflects legal traditions that assume that proper dwellings are *attached* to land, whether or not that land is owned by the occupant. They also suggest that, although the mobility of families is not a threat to community stability, the actual or potential mobility of dwellings is.

The freedom from taxation that many trailer advocates saw as a major advantage of full-time trailer living was a dilemma for municipal authorities concerned with the demand for additional services that the trailer population would generate. A 1937 bulletin from the American Municipal League concluded that the first and foremost problem was the question of how trailer use should be taxed: as a dwelling or a vehicle?[56] When classified as a vehicle, the most appropriate means of taxation was to impose a registration fee, to which a special user's fee might be added. In Florida, for example, a $12 fee, was assessed on trailer households with children. Twenty states extended their personal property tax to include travel trailers.

Taxation was both a way to secure the costs of providing trailer-related services and to exclude the trailer, particularly when used on a permanent basis. Contemporary sociologists Clark and Wilcox observed:

> Trailerites and manufacturers are figuratively holding their breath as they wait for taxes to strike in full force. Thus far the vehicle license had been the usual direct assessment. However, a tax war is impending. Real estate interests, small hotels, tourist camps, and other businesses have in some localities launched a movement to tax the trailer out of existence, believing that it represents a serious threat to their welfare. Their forces will be joined by many municipalities confronted by troublesome problems of regulation, and reluctant to provide essential services. The least that trailerites may hope for ultimately is that the added costs of governmental agencies, of police and fire protection, health and sanitation, safety and other services be made the measure of taxes.[57]

While taxes, together with exclusionary zoning and restrictive permitting, limited or eliminated the presence of trailers in a community, they simultaneously encouraged the development of trailer parks and the placement of individual trailers on property outside municipal boundaries. As cities grew and extended their boundaries, the parks and private trailers were

Freedom from landlords, portrayed in a cartoon in *Trailer Travel*, 1937.

The travel trailer in the crossfire between regulatory agencies.

Well, maybe someone can tell us just what it is all about. Any way sooner or later trailerites will know.

simply incorporated, and their use grandfathered (allowed because they were existing uses) into municipal regulation. A more effective strategy would have been to regulate trailer land use at the state level, but many strong home rule states were, and remain, opposed to such an approach.

In 1939, Michigan became the first state with legislation that superseded local laws and ordinances affecting trailers and trailer parks. Under the Michigan Trailer Coach Park Act, the stationary trailer was considered a building and regulated as such, while the transient trailer fell under vehicular regulations. The Michigan Act was formulated with the support of the trailer industry, which hoped that it would serve as a model for other states.

The various efforts to regulate the trailer at state and local levels can be seen as attempts to define it as an object, identify its use, and ultimately categorize it to determine how it should be treated. The process of categorization often fixes on clusters of significant features and extrapolates from them to the object as a whole.[58] Thus, if wheels and a hitch are important bases for categorization, then the fact that the object doesn't move may be ignored. At times this is done intentionally, for instance to exclude trailers from a community. If they were defined as permanent housing, for example, such exclusion might be easier to achieve. But categorization is also influenced by hidden, unarticulated, yet deeply felt, assumptions about what is and is not appropriate. The process of categorization makes these assumptions explicit, forcing participants in the process to identify and explain what they find objectionable.

The Industry Attempts to Define Itself

While regulations posed a potential threat to the development of the infant trailer industry, they also offered certain advantages to commercial manufacturers. Standards imposed on unit design, for example, could discriminate more effectively against homemade trailers, whose builders might be unaware of the requirements to which they were expected to conform. Restrictions against the use of trailers as year-round housing could help to assure a nervous public that trailers were not a threat to real-estate values but, rather, a legitimate automobile accessory used for vacationing. An organized industry could thus work for higher standards and support restrictions while improving its image and eliminating some of its competition. A telling cartoon in an early issue of *Trailer Travel* depicted a dilapidated trailer, clearly thrown together from odd parts, entitled "The Lousy Lounge Deluxe." This disparaging image notwithstanding, the distinction between the commercially manufactured units and those made in the backyard was not always as clearcut as the industry might have liked.

One possibility for the early organization of the industry was that manufacturers, dealers, park owners, and trailerites would join together to enhance their effectiveness in fighting restrictive regulation. In 1938, *Trailer Travel* magazine tried to form an industrywide association that would include all of these parties. Though it succeeded in establishing the American Travel Trailer Association, the association received little support and was soon eclipsed by the growth of the manufacturers' associations and the development of a separate association for dealers.

In 1936, a group of companies formed the Trailer Coach Manufacturers Association (TCMA) to represent manufacturers east of the Rockies. In the same year, the Trailer Coach Association of California (later the TCA) was formed to represent West Coast firms. One TCMA member observed:

> When the manufacturers got together for this [1937] annual meeting and election of officers it was the first time they ever actually felt the need for such an organization, but the problems of a legislative and public relations character as well as those within the industry itself during the past season brought them up . . . solidly behind the association which they had only half formed the year before.[59]

In 1937, the TCMA drafted a twelve-point legislative program, proposing, among other things, that states establish a licensing fee based on unit weight; vehicles be required to have lights; their wiring meet building codes; and adequate couplers be required between car and trailer. The Association hoped that all states would adopt the model standards to assure reciprocity of regulation. TCMA was also concerned that trailers be defined as automobile accessories rather than classified as dwelling structures, a categorization that could readily encourage greater restrictions. In 1939, J. L. Brown, speaking for TCMA, suggested:

> In view of the fact that trailers are conceded by most authorities to be vehicles, we doubt seriously the ability of anyone to place them under the housing code. . . .
>
> The experience of those in the trailer industry parallels to some extent that of the pioneers of the automotive industry. We all can well remember the attempts that were made by municipalities to ban the use of the automobile within corporate limits, and of course you know what happened. It is also a known fact that the percentages of people living in trailers who have been or are on relief is almost negligible.[60]

TCMA, which had worked with the state of Michigan in developing its Trailer Park Act, also worked with Toledo to establish a zoning ordinance it hoped would serve as a model for other cities. In addition to this type of effort, the industry began to work with various private national laboratories to establish voluntary standards and codes. In 1937, for example, the National Fire Protection Association established a Committee on Trailers and Trailer Camps; their first standards, which appeared in 1939, included sanitary requirements, site layout standards, and enforcement procedures.

Initially formed to encourage favorable regulation, manufacturers' associations also conducted annual trade shows where their members could display models to dealers and trailerites. Some of the early trade shows were held as part of new car shows, others were incorporated into rallies organized by automobile camper associations. A rally sponsored by the Trailer Coach Association of California in 1937 attracted over 375 trailers and 1000 participants to Palm Springs. Even though such trade shows were intended to promote sales, dealers also began to organize to support their own objectives. In 1940, the Trailercoach Dealers National Association was founded "to dignify the dealer's place in the industry" and with the following objectives:

- to counteract unduly restrictive regulations for trailer parks and occupancy of trailers;
- to provide better trailer parking and service facilities;
- to obtain cleaner and closer competition among dealers and their source of supply.[61]

Their concern with providing better parks and service facilities suggests that dealers were more sensitive than manufacturers to the need for attractive parks. A dealer in the Sunbelt who could assure a customer of space in a good park for a long vacation would be in a better position to close a sale. In fact, many dealers soon became park owners and vice versa. Both businesses were bound up with local communities, whereas the larger manufacturers saw themselves as addressing a national market.

In general, restrictive legislation spurred the formation of associations within different segments of the trailer industry and among trailer users. Just as proponents of such legislation were interested in categorizing the trailer to narrow its range of uses, trailer advocates wanted it defined in a way that would promote its use, while appeasing resistance. The main advocates were the larger manufacturers and the more affluent trailerites, who preferred a definition of trailers as recreational

Dealers played an important role in the industry; they not only sold trailers, but serviced them, and often were involved in the development of parks.

vehicles and tried to play down the use of trailers as year-round housing. Both supporters and detractors tried to influence the categorization of trailers and their use, each calling on fundamental American values to bolster the validity of their claims.

Mickey's Trailer

The travel trailer era, the beginnings of which were illustrated by the camping trip of President Warren G. Harding, can be summarized by another camping trip celebrated in the mass media. In 1938, Walt Disney Studios released "Mickey's Trailer." In the opening, Mickey is shown living in a pleasant, hill-top country cottage, surrounded by a picket fence. When Mickey pulls a large lever set in the floor, immediately, everything begins to change. The house's saddle roof, shutters, door stoop, and porch all fold up into compartments. The picket fence is reeled in through a side door, followed by the lawn. Finally, the entire sky folds up like an oriental fan and is sucked down the chimney. What is left, after the startling transformation, is a trailer sitting in the middle of a city dump, ready to head out on the open road.

Once on the road, the trailer continues to exhibit ingenious transformations. Under the dining room table is a bathtub; a sudden bump on the road can transform it from a table to tub complete with soaking occupant. Well-timed bumps add comic

"EVOLUTION"

The limbs of a tree, and a few dried hides,
　And the Indian had a home.
Some blocks of ice, and some snow cement,
　Made the igloo up near Nome.
The pioneer used the big tree trunks,
　That he piled with mud between.
He built it well, his cabin home,
　A shelter and a screen.
Then came his home of brick or stone,
　A mansion high and wide.
The show place of the village,
　Pride of the countryside.
And each house stood on a plot of ground,
　A door yard or an acre.
And each man proud of the land he owned,
　A private "empire maker."
And houses grew and land grew dear,
　Men bought and fought to gain it.
They staked their claims and staked their lives,
　Their souls, just to obtain it.
A man who roamed, without a home,
　Without a hearth or haven,
A gypsy or a hobo
　Alike,—a man depraven.
Then taxes hit the homestead.
　The mortgage reared its head.
Apartment houses grew apace,
　With kitchenette and bed.
A penthouse or a duplex,
　Man still was anchored fast.
Each night the same path homeward,
　The scene the same as last.
And then he found the gypsy,
　Asleep through all the years,
Awakened in his own staid self,
　The nomad call he hears.
The trailer is the answer,
　A home behind his car.
In every man the longing
　To travel fast and far.
No longer pride of empire,
　No wish for house and land.
There's every living comfort
　When he joins the trailer band.
He comes and goes at pleasure,
　Without roots to hold him fast.
After twenty restless centuries,
　Man's freedom comes at last.

—By Edith C. Gregware

Edith C. Gregware's 1937 poem in *Trailer Caravan* illustrates one of many attempts to draw a positive association between trailer life and America's nomadic and pioneering heritage.

moments to the preparation of breakfast. Predictably, at some point the trailer becomes unhitched, and careens down the mountain, the car in vain pursuit. "Mickey's Trailer" was a curious celebrity endorsement of a product and way of life, acknowledging that the trailer had arrived as a wholesome object of popular culture. In 1943, the publishers Houghton & Mifflin released an elementary school reader in which Mickey and Minnie journeyed across the United States in their trailer. As a book from the war years, it was meant to celebrate the vast greatness of this country.

By the end of the 1930s the trailer's identity had been established as a vacation vehicle. The industry and government officials alike seemed most comfortable with the trailer as a temporary mobile dwelling, yet its possible use as portable year-round housing or permanent factory-built housing had nevertheless been explored and had gained currency, if not acceptability. Their time would come later, when social circumstances favored what they had to offer.

From Travel Trailer
to House Trailer

Willow Run

Between 1941 and 1942, the population of Ypsilanti, Michigan doubled. People took in boarders until their houses were filled. Garages were converted into apartments. Men who came for work held off from sending for their families until they could find housing. Families who had used their small travel trailers for camping trips now paid to park them in somebody's backyard or front lawn. Extension cords and lawn hoses went from house to trailer like artificial umbilical cords. In 1941 the War Department had opened its Willow Run Bomber Plant and Ypsilanti became a boom town.[1]

At its peak, in 1943, the Willow Run plant employed more than forty-two thousand. Tens of thousands more, dependents and support workers, were added to the population. Over half of the newcomers lived in trailers. A small percentage found space in a government trailer camp; the majority lived in sixteen private trailer camps, or on private lots in Ypsilanti and surrounding Washtenaw County. Most were new to trailers as a form of year-round living. Many had left their own homes to take advantage of the employment opportunities. Since the severity of the housing shortage was obvious, they felt no stigma living in their trailer dwellings. Rather, it was regarded as evidence of their sacrifice to help win the war. One of Ypsilanti's trailerites noted in her diary:

War workers' housing in Wichita, Kansas. The trailer provided some privacy and personal control. The alternative for many was a crude shack.

I have wondered many times how many less employees would Willow Run Bomber Plant have if it were not for the men and women living in trailers—men and women who, like us, are praying and hoping for the day when they can go back home again, back to normal living![2]

Life in the private camps was an ordeal: trailers were cramped, with children underfoot, communal facilities for bathing and laundry were inadequate, and mud was abundant after every rain. Moisture would condense on the ceiling, and in the winter the hair of sleeping occupants sometimes froze to the walls. Over two-thirds of the trailers had only one room.

If the cramped space inside the trailers was a source of friction, the inability to keep any distance from neighbors was at times even more annoying. Two contemporary sociologists, Lowell Carr and James Steiner, in their study of Willow Run, observed of the trailer parks:

> Outside of the individual trailer it was impossible to maintain social distances. As one trailerite observed, it was "impossible to select one's associates on a money basis any longer." Or on any other basis, for that matter. Selection was out for the duration. The bomber plant had done the selecting. Ex-bartenders waited for Tennessee drys to vacate the shower baths and middle-class wives from Midwestern Elm Streets took turns at the camp washing machines with eastern foreign-born "creatures" from across the tracks. In the welter of overcrowded utility houses individual discriminations were rubbed out. The easy going shrugged it off. The stiff-necked suffered. But everybody took it, for there was nothing else to do, no place to go.[3]

Most were new to trailer life, and even those who had taken vacations in trailers had difficulty adjusting to year-round trailer living. As soon as they could find the time and materials, people began to modify their new homes: adding an all-important mudroom or utility porch, hanging shelves, building fences, and planting yards. The duration of the war was uncertain, and people wanted to make things as tolerable as possible. The haste with which the camps had been built, however, meant that shallow water and sewer lines froze. Crowding overtaxed utility rooms, which were always running out of hot water, and community trash cans often overflowed with garbage.

Conditions in the one camp built and managed by the government were, by contrast, more orderly and sanitary. The camp was located near the bomber plant, its layout something of a hybrid between a military base and a suburban subdivision. Its streets were boardwalks: an important amenity considering the mud of the rainy season. Lots were 25 to 30 feet wide and 50 feet deep. There was an outdoor recreation area for children. A laundry room with machine washers and drying lines was provided for every fifty trailers, and toilet and shower facilities with adequate hot water for every twenty-five.

The government camp followed an established plan for similar facilities supporting new war materials plants. In a bulletin issued in 1943, the Federal Public Housing Authority defined design standards and camp management. Some camps were

The "Committee trailer" set up in a government camp.

designed exclusively for government-owned rental trailers; others permitted a mixture of government and privately owned trailers. Parking was to be on the street, and sidewalks were provided with neck downs at crossing points. The perimeter of the park was buffered, either by a planted strip approximately 60 feet wide or by an internal road. A generous playground area, with a community building, was a focal point. The use of buffers, as well as the placement of the playground and community buildings along the public street, rather than at the center of the park, suggest that the government planners realized the need to carefully integrate the park into the surrounding community, and to demonstrate that its tenants could be good neighbors.

Though the management and facilities of the government camp in Ypsilanti were superior to its private parks, many preferred the latter because they had fewer regulations. Owners could add mudrooms, sheds, and other site-built structures to their units. Some regarded this privilege as a worthwhile trade-off for the greater order, cleanliness, and space available at the government camp. Regardless of where they parked their trailers, however, life in these cramped quarters was difficult. Carr and Steiner concluded:

> For most bomber workers, and especially families with children, trailer living under the crowded conditions of 1942–1943 was inefficient living. What simplification of housework the trailer itself might have afforded, especially in summertime, was more than counterbalanced by the overcrowding of individual trailers throughout the four seasons, by the overloading of camp facilities, and by the inadequacies of water supplies and sewage disposal. The trailer for vacationing couples is one thing. For harassed families in wintertime it was something else.[4]

The Trailer Market During and After the War

Between the late 1930s and the early 1940s the use of manufactured trailers for year-round housing shifted from 10 percent of annual production to 90 percent. The recently formed industry associations, which in the late 1930s had argued that the trailer should not be regarded as housing, were forced to proclaim only a few years later that it was indeed housing, and therefore appropriate to receive rationed materials. Simultaneously, the idea of the travel trailer was replaced by the house trailer. That this shift in identity was brought on by the industry's struggle to survive is not difficult to appreciate; less predictable and, ultimately, more significant was the fact that this new identity would be retained beyond the war.

As the country began a massive build-up of its war production capacity in 1940, the need for war worker housing soon became evident. Three types of housing were envisioned: permanent housing that would remain fixed and usable after the war; demountable or prefabricated housing that would be used during the war, then removed and disposed of at its end; and mobile housing that could be rushed to areas were there was a sudden increase in population. In November of 1940 the Trailer Coach Manufacturers Association sent a delegation, headed by its former president James L. Brown, to represent its interests

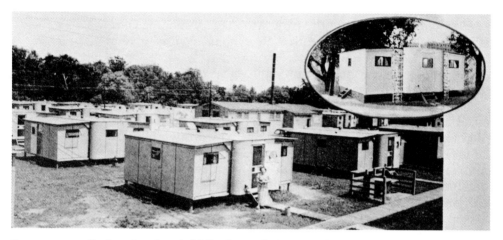

Government trailer based on Stout's folding house design, manufactured by the Palace Corporation. Folding units were also outfitted as laundryrooms and shower houses.

before the Council of National Defense. The group argued the merits of trailers as temporary housing that could be removed at the end of the war, rather than leaving ghost towns. Their low cost meant that trailers could be amortized through rental payments within two years, and scrapped at the end of the war.[5] Since trailers could be made in factories using semi-skilled and even elderly laborers, further demands need not be placed on local work forces to build housing while also serving war plant needs.[6] The recognition of trailers as temporary housing would qualify the industry for the use of critical materials and make workers eligible for deferments. Without that recognition the survival of the industry, which had suffered two years of significantly declining sales in the late 1930s, would have been jeopardized.[7]

In 1940, the government purchased 1500 trailers to house construction workers in defense production centers. This demand came on top of a backlog of orders from private dealers, who were also finding a new market for trailers as temporary housing for war workers. Nearly 9800 trailers were manufactured that year, more than twice the number produced in the industry's dog days of 1938.

To meet its particular needs, and to assure that the bare minimum of critical materials would be used, the Council of National Defense asked the industry to produce a special trailer for wartime housing. The design, presented in January 1941, was developed by William Stout based on his folding house concept. Its travel width was 8 feet, but when unfolded it expanded to 19½ feet. The trailer came in two models, 18 and 22 feet long. The floor plan followed Stout's earlier design with a few modifications, notably the replacement of the metal frame with wood. One wing on the unit contained the living-dining area, the other housed the sleeping area, and the trailer core contained the kitchen and bathroom. The front door was in the living wing, but a side door which opened into the kitchen faced the street and was probably the most frequently used. The kitchen had a double sink, refrigerator, and a propane gas stove. In the bathroom were a toilet, sink, and stall shower. A wall-mounted gas furnace provided heat. The folding trailer was manufactured by the Palace Corporation for $1600 per unit, a price at which it could be offered for a weekly rent of $7.50, including all the electricity a family could draw from a single 10 amp fuse. During 1941, the government bought over six thousand.

In February 1941, the Federal Works Adminstration asked Congress for a $6.75 million appropriation to buy "a flying squadron of trailers."[8] By July 1941, the Defense Department had contracted for delivery of 4935 trailers to areas with housing shortages. It also ordered dormitory room trailers to accommo-

Cutaway view of the folding house trailer.

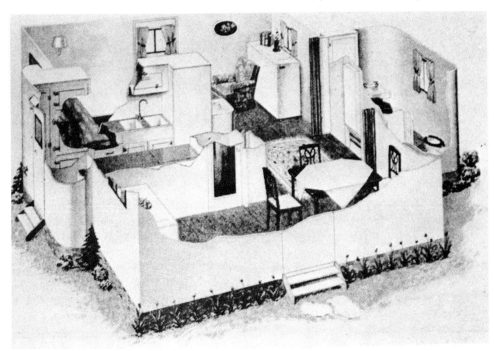

Views of the folding house trailer being erected.

date 2900 men. By the end of the year the industry had manufactured 20,728 units, doubling the previous year's production.

After the bombing of Pearl Harbor in December 1941, the population of shipyard cities boomed. In Richmond, California the government set up 2500 trailer sites to accommodate the influx of workers. In Orange, Texas, the population swelled from 7400 to 50,000. At many sites, the workers arrived before housing could be provided. Again, the trailer industry was called upon to alleviate the demand. Thousands of units were delivered within a month's time. These were not the folding models, but more conventional solid body trailers that could be stacked up on railroad cars for mass delivery. By September 1942 the industry had produced another 16,000 trailers for use at eighty-five sites developed by the Farm Security Administration, the major customer for folding trailers. Their largest project, in Wichita, Kansas, required 600 trailers, while a concentration of five projects in Middle River, Maryland called for 1200 trailer homes. By the end of the year, it was estimated that the trailer industry would produce 50,000 units, all of them for the government or war workers.

The speed with which trailers were being built, and the shortage of construction materials that normally would have been used, meant that the quality suffered. For shipyard areas emergency trailers were ordered with only one door, which workers refused to occupy until a second door was installed.[9] Wood was substituted for steel wherever possible, roofs were covered with painted canvas, electrical wiring was reduced and, in some cases, chassis were made detachable so that they could be returned to manufacturers. The hurried construction and makeshift design of wartime trailers only strengthened many goverment agencies' reservations about the use of trailers, even as temporary housing, and did little to alter the public's prewar impressions of the trailers' suitability for year-round living. Unlike trailer users before the war, of course, many wartime users had little choice but to learn to live in these novel cramped quarters. Again, the industry was called upon to come up with a better design for standardized production.

Early in 1942, the TCMA appointed a War Activities Committee to represent the industry's interests to various federal agencies and to respond to governmental concerns, particularly those regarding construction quality. At the request of the Federal Housing Authority and the War Production Board, three members of the committee developed a new standardized model dubbed the "committee trailer."[10] It was a solid-body nonexpandable unit which, at $750, could be produced for less than half the cost of the folding trailer. The committee trailer measured 8' x 22', and was designed to accommodate up to three people for a monthly rent of $6.50. It was constructed of plywood and pressboard and had a painted canvas roof. Once it arrived at a site, it was set up on wooden sawhorses and its wheels and tires were removed to be re-used.

During the first years of the defense build-up, government control over the public and private sale of trailers had issued from sixteen different civilian agencies, in addition to several different military commands. In February 1942, President Roosevelt established the National Housing Agency (NHA), which consolidated the functions of the civilian agencies involved in the supply of housing. In January 1943, the agency released a bulletin summarizing its policy on trailer housing. The bulletin acknowledged the suitability of trailers for "stop-gap" housing, providing homes for a sudden influx of workers. It also recognized the need to provide trailer camps for workers who owned their own units. The agency soon developed guidelines for the design and management of these parks.

Six months later, over 26,000 trailers were being managed by the NHA, and an additional 8550 trailer sites had been built or were under preparation. Since the NHA had inherited most of its trailers from agencies whose operations it now coordinated, its initial endorsement of trailers could be construed as justifying the use of housing it had in hand. Later that summer, however, a statement issued by NHA Commissioner Herbert Emmerich concluded, that

> While trailers are being used successfully as stop-gap war housing, they do not meet the standards of the National Housing Agency for duration housing for war workers. These wartime standards, moreover, have been cut to a minimum commensurate with providing adequate shelter for war workers and the NHA has no intention of going below them.[11]

The trailer industry was faced with the immediate cessation of government orders and possible further restrictions of authorized private sales. An article in *Business Week* questioned the wisdom of the NHA's decision:

> It takes about 1,000 man-hours to build a house, but only 112 man-hours to make a trailer. It takes husky young men to climb scaffolds and erect a house, but the 4,800 men making trailers are older men working indoors and away from critical labor areas, who can't stand the gaff of the shipyard or plane plant. A man could buy a trailer for $1,000 and move his home, family and chattel away when peace ends his job in an alien city, but with the furniture he'll have to buy to outfit an NHA house he's stuck until he can find a new job and a moving van.
>
> NHA says trailers aren't houses because they are factory built. NHA wants nothing more to do with them. It has told the industry it won't buy any more. WPB [the War Production Board] says trailers are houses because people live in them but won't release critical materials for them if NHA forbids private sales and refuses to buy them itself.[12]

Harold Platt, secretary of the manufacturers' association, argued to the NHA that at least private sales should continue to be authorized:

> It seems that this industry should have a right to exist since it is filling an essential place in the housing field. There is no doubt

but that the time will come when the government will not and should not any longer be a purchaser. But, we know the housing situation is still very critical and more housing is going to be purchased. We know too that there is a market for trailers from private individuals who want to purchase them for housing and at no expense to the Federal Government. We all know too well the fact that in trailer housing we provide a unit with less critical materials, less man-hours and of course much cheaper than any other type of housing.[13]

Although the NHA did not want to purchase more trailers, because it felt that the need for stop-gap housing had largely passed, it was no more enamored of "demountable" prefabricated housing.

In all, 35,000 specially designed trailers were purchased by the government and ultimately managed by the NHA. After the agency's 1943 announcement, however, direct purchases declined and eventually ceased. The trailer industry continued to operate during the remaining years of the war by supplying trailers to certified workers in defense-related industries.[14] Manufacturers also sought alternative uses for their production lines. In some cases, they turned to producing large crates for shipping specialized equipment. Whereas in 1936 there were an estimated three hundred to two thousand trailer manufacturers, by the end of the war the number was down to fifty.

During the course of the war, about four million people moved to defense employment areas. An estimated 200,000 trailers were in use, with some 60 percent in defense areas. Given the level of wartime trailer production, at least half of these trailers would have been prewar models, and over 80 percent of them would have been privately owned. If these estimates are accurate, trailers were used, at one point or another, to house about one in eight migrant war workers. As a result, zoning restrictions enacted in the late 1930s to eliminate year-round trailer housing were temporarily relaxed. The war had forced recognition of the trailer as housing and, in the process, it had significantly reshaped the identity of the industry.

Wartime use of trailers notwithstanding, with the return of peace and the end of gas rationing, the industry again aimed at vacationers traveling by automobile. Palace Corporation ran full-page colored ads in *Trailer Travel* featuring metal-bodied trailers whose streamlined designs were reminiscent of the Curtiss Aerocar. The molds for some of their body designs were, in fact, bought from Buick. Articles on auto vacation itineraries appeared among features on how to be a trailer wife and on army family life in a trailer. The industry, however, was to be shaped again by larger, albeit temporary, social forces.

Following World War II the house trailer market consisted primarily of military and construction workers. Trailer living had been identified with making a patriotic sacrifice to help win the war. This photo, from the cover of *Trailer Travel*, shows a G.I. returning to his family in their trailer.

Trailer manufacturers, who had been languishing during the last half of the war, set a production record of 60,000 units in 1947. That same year, the prefabricated housing industry manufactured 37,400 units. The following year trailer production increased by 70 percent, while the production of prefabricated housing, aided by government support, remained constant. By 1948, an estimated 7 percent of the population of the United States was living in house trailers. That year, a survey of trailerites in Southern California found that most were young families, for whom the trailer was a first home. Almost 70 percent were veterans, and over 95 percent were employed and had an income slightly above the national average for this group.[15] In addition to purchasing new trailers for temporary housing, the government made about 13,000 of its wartime trailers available to colleges and universities to be used as housing for married students on campuses swollen by returning veterans. Thirty years later some of these units were still providing "temporary" shelter.[16]

After the war, the government got out of the business of constructing trailer camps for the private sector but remained an important customer, using trailers to aid disaster victims. After a 1948 flood in Portland, Oregon, 722 trailers were sent to provide temporary housing; and in 1951, 1000 trailers were purchased for the victims of a major flood in Kansas. The military also continued to use trailers as housing for married personnel, even increasing its demand. It purchased almost 4000 units for bases where there were housing shortages and constructed parks for privately owned trailers. In 1954, one fifth of all trailers were owned by military households.

Many of the government's postwar projects, conceived in part to stimulate a recessionary economy, were an important source of growth for the industry. The interstate highway system was a major undertaking, requiring large crews of construction workers, who moved from job to job with their families in trailer housing. Similar mobility was required of the families of workers laying transcontinental pipelines and constructing dams in remote areas. In some cases, the construction companies bought the trailers, but usually they were owned by the workers, who formed tightly knit communities that would move from one job to the next.

The postwar projects that created the biggest demand for house trailers, were the nuclear facilities being built for the Atomic Energy Commission (AEC). In Paducah, Kentucky 5500 workers were hired to construct a uranium refining plant, and federal construction projects in nearby towns employed an additional 2300. At the peak of construction, 2500 house trailers were temporarily housing workers in the area.

The largest of the AEC projects was in Savannah River, where 45,000 construction workers were employed. Many of them came with their families, significantly adding to the population

Trailer park at a university serving returning veterans and their families.

boom. The four parks built in the area, with a total of 4000 rental trailers, were quickly occupied, and approximately 5500 privately owned trailers were scattered among 130 parks in the area. Also under construction nearby were an expansion of the Army's Camp Gordon and the $78 million Clark Hill Dam. Since, once completed, facilities like Savannah River required a relatively small operations work force (in this case only 5400 workers), the housing provided for the construction workers had to be cheap and easy to remove.

The 1950 census revealed that 500,000 trailers were in use. Given postwar production levels, this suggests that over half the occupied trailers were built during or before the war. Four years later, the census found an estimated 700,000 trailer dwellings, a figure again suggesting that the rate at which older units were being retired was low. During this period, almost two-thirds of the trailer houses purchased were for migratory workers; another 20 percent were for military personnel; while only 17 percent were being used by retired people or other occupational classes. The number of trailers purchased exclusively for vacationing was minimal, while their use as housing continued to dominate the market.

Paths to Industrialized Housing

There is no small irony in the fact that, by the mid-1950s, the mobile home had emerged as the preeminent form of factory-built housing in the United States. From a purely technological point of view, it could hardly be regarded as the best of the available alternatives. For its part, the trailer industry had yet to fully recognize and accept that its product was industrialized housing, a circumstance that makes an understanding of the mobile home's development as industrialized housing all the more valuable. To adequately appreciate this development, it is necessary to briefly consider the concurrent development of other forms of industrialized housing from the 1930s through the postwar period.

Comparative Performance During the 1930s

The practice of prefabricating dwellings and shipping them to a site was not a recent development in American housing. Prefabricated shelters were brought to this continent by British colonists, and pre-cut homes were used in the early phases of Western expansion. In the late nineteenth century, prefabricated houses of metal and concrete were developed, and stores like Sears and Roebuck sold prefabricated dwellings through their catalogs. The twentieth century's contribution to the development of prefabricated housing was its industrialization. The Model-T assembly line demonstrated that mass production techniques could be used to manufacture a large object of high quality, in a factory, at greatly reduced cost, thereby providing an important example for industrialized housing.

The general principles of mass production, as enunciated by Henry Ford, seem perfectly applicable to the problem of providing affordable houses:

> The term mass-production is used to describe the modern method by which great quantities of a single standardized commodity are manufactured. Mass-production is not merely quantity production . . . nor is it merely machine production. Mass-production is the focusing upon a manufacturing project of the principles of power, accuracy, economy, system, continuity, and speed. The interpretation of these principles, through studies of operation and machine development and their coordination, is the conspicuous task of management. And the normal result is a productive organization that delivers in quantities a useful commodity of standard material, workmanship, and design at a minimum cost[17]

The concept of mass-produced industrialized housing, as distinct from earlier prefabrication practices, belongs to the period following World War I, and to the new spirit of industrial production Ford exemplified. This spirit was best expressed in Le Corbusier's 1919 essay, "Mass-Production Houses."

> Industry on the grand scale must occupy itself with building and establish the elements of the house on a mass-production basis.
> We must create the mass-production spirit.
> The spirit of constructing mass-production houses.
> The spirit of living in mass-production houses.
> The spirit of conceiving mass-production houses.[18]

The American counterpart to the pamphleteering efforts of Le Corbusier could be found in the writings of people like R. Buckminster Fuller, Albert Bemis, and John Burchard. While differing in details, all of these advocates saw the need to rationalize the production process along the lines of Ford's principles of "power, accuracy, economy, system, continuity, and speed." They were concerned not only with the initial production of houses, but with their life cycle, arguing that housing should be scrapped or recycled as it became technologically obsolete. For this purpose individual housing units would ideally be demountable and designed to fit into some kind of infrastructure at the site, providing utilities and other services. Mobility and demountability were considered integral elements of industrialized housing, along with standardization and assembly-line production.

Translating this bold rhetoric into practice would require the organization and financial resources to manufacture and distribute industrialized housing on a huge scale. Where these would come from was not clear. In Europe, the massive destruction of housing during World War I, coupled with the loss of skilled labor, was an impetus for the application of mass-production techniques. Prefabricated systems of concrete and steel were developed in Britain, France, and Germany, and wood systems in Sweden. While these efforts demonstrated the importance of standardization and modular design in the industrialization of building, their contribution to the total building effort in these countries was small.

In the United States, it took the Depression to generate significant interest in industrialized housing, and then it was primarily as a means of stimulating the economy. In 1937, the *Technological Forecast*, published by the National Committee on Public Policy, identified housing as one of the "lagging" industries in the American economy. The report argued that the advanced production techniques that had resulted in lower prices, improved quality, and wider distribution of other consumer goods, needed to be applied to the field of home building so that more Americans could realize the dream of home ownership.[19] Attempts toward this end were in fact already underway.

In 1932, several large manufacturers, including General Electric, Inland Steel, and Pittsburgh Plate Glass, proposed establishing a new company, General Houses Corporation. The idea behind General Houses, like that of the automobile industry, was to act as an assembler of parts it would order to its own specifications from building component suppliers. Its sponsors predicted that General Houses would become the "General Motors of the housing industry." Its four-bedroom, steel-frame home of 1939 sold for $4500, but its sectional wood-frame house cost only $2980. In 1933, another firm, American Homes, developed a project near Baltimore which included a four-room, steel-frame house priced at $2750 with lot. In 1935, Gunnison Magic Homes began producing prestressed plywood houses. Its 24' x 32' "Miracle House" sold for $2950 assembled, exclusive of lot.

Even greater economies were achieved in some government-sponsored experiments. The Farm Security Administration (FSA), established in 1937 to promote rural self-sufficiency and to resettle migrants in rural areas, conducted several low-cost housing demonstrations. In 1938, it built 1000 homes for sharecroppers in Missouri, using prefabricated walls and roof sections. Each five-room house, measuring 24' x 32', cost $1105. The following year the FSA built fifty steel framed dwellings at a cost of approximately $1650 each.[20] Federal agencies such as the U.S. Forest Service also conducted important work in the development of wood construction technology. New plywood veneering techniques and glues were developed in its Wood Products Laboratory and were used in a stressed-skin plywood panel construction system that formed the basis of many industrialized housing designs.[21]

The performance of the early trailer industry must be seen in light of these efforts. One basis of comparison is the 1938 Durham House, which was least trailer-like and came closest to the appearance and size of a conventional house. The 360-square-foot Durham model cost $1500, while a six-room double-wide model was $3000, both exclusive of land. In comparison with what many prefabricators offered, the price of the Durham House was not spectacular, and its technology, both in the use of materials and assemblies, was less advanced than General, American, or Gunnison production.

Between 1935 and 1940, prefabricators had produced about 10,000 homes, exclusive of pre-cut units, or less than 1 percent of the nation's total production for the period.[22] In 1940, there were only about thirty firms prefabricating houses. By contrast, the most conservative estimate of the number of trailer manufacturers during this period was 200, with a total production of over 75,000 units. Assuming that only 10 percent of these commercially made trailers were used for year-round housing, 7500 households were so sheltered.

Despite this success, advocates of industrialized housing virtually ignored the trailer industry. For their own part, trailer manufacturers eschewed the categorization of house builder. *Architectural Forum* and *Architectural Record,* which featured articles on prefabricated housing in the mid-1930s, did not include trailers in their surveys until the war years.[23] A comprehensive survey published in 1944, *A History of Prefabrication*, featured Willson's "mobile house," along with Buckminster Fuller's first Dymaxion House, as progenitors of the emerging movement in industrialized housing, but ignored the Durham House and Stout's folding trailer.[24] Others viewing the trailer's role in the development of industrialized housing were more skeptical. MIT professor Burnham Kelly, evaluating the experiments of the 1930s from a postwar perspective, observed:

> If a house suspended from a mast [e.g. Fuller's Dymaxion House] was no longer a sensation, then perhaps a mobile house was. The influence of the trailer craze that hit America about 1937 spread into housing circles, and it was not long before someone had figured out how to cure all social ills with mobile dwelling units. . . . Probably all this publicity did more harm than good.

It led people to believe that some miracle would solve the problem, and at the same time it confused them about the nature of
that miracle, what the prefabricated house looked like, and where
it could be bought and for how much.[25]

Despite Kelly's skepticism, the only form of factory-built
housing which met all of the theoretical characteristics of industrialized housing—standardization, assembly-line production, demountability (allowing for the replacement of obsolete
units), interchangeability of units (within a site-fixed infrastructure), and the mobility of individual dwelling units—was
the ensemble of house trailer and trailer court. It was not until
the late 1950s that anyone in the architectural establishment
would seriously note the parallels between what trailer life
actually offered and what industrialized housing advocates had
theorized.

Comparative Performance During the War Years

When the war production build-up commenced in 1940, manufacturers began supplying prefabricated housing for war workers. As part of the Navy's housing program that year, the
Homosote Company completed 100 housing units in New
London, Connecticut, in 42 days, at $2770 per unit, including
site preparation. In 1941, American Houses delivered 251
homes to Portsmouth, Virginia and prefabricated 164 units for
delivery to Charleston, South Carolina. Stran-Steel manufactured house parts for 3862 units at Quantico, Norfolk, and
Newport News, Virginia. A project in Vallejo, California, used
1000 Homosote homes and 700 prefabricated plywood houses.
By the end of 1941, some 18,000 prefabricated houses had been
built.

Despite the impressive record of prefabricated projects
around the country, the Public Building Administration
(PBA), which had principal responsibility over government contracts for civilian war worker housing, remained skeptical.
Presumably to alleviate this skepticism, the agency arranged a
demonstration, in 1941, at Indian Head, Maryland, inviting
eleven companies to erect a total of 650 prefabricated houses.
Although the project was intended to show the value of prefabrication, the PBA insisted that all the units be erected by general
contractors, most of whom had no experience with them; they
were required to erect several different kinds of houses, demonstrating the speed and quality of on-site assembly. The results
hardly showed prefabricators at their best. Outraged by the
whole process, *Architectural Forum* took the PBA to task:

The sectional houses developed by the TVA were an early application of trailer production techniques to the construction of semipermanent housing.

With very few exceptions every PBA official was skeptical of or dead against prefabrication, and the industry therefore went to bat with two strikes against it. . . .

PBA is one of the oldest of all government agencies and it is steeped in tradition. For years it had built up a close relationship with general contractors the country over, most of whom are equally conventional. PBA does not want to jeopardize its position with these general contractors by financing projects which would either leave them out of the picture completely or require them to use construction systems which they and their labor cannot stomach. In most cases, prefabricated projects would do just that.[26]

In conclusion, *Architectural Forum* recommended that the prefabricators band together to form a trade association to more effectively promote government recognition of their product.[27]

Although there were parallel developments in the trailer and prefabricated housing industries from the mid-1930s through the war years, minimal exchanges took place between the two. One exception was the development of a transportable house for the Tennessee Valley Authority (TVA). The idea of a house that could be transported in two sections was proposed in 1937 by Louis Grangent, then chief of the architectural section of the agency, and subsequently developed by Carroll A. Towne.[28] The house, as first built in 1940, featured clean modern lines, with a squared-off bay window in the living room area and a shallow sloping roof. It measured 25'8" x 13'6" and had only one bedroom. The structure was comprised of stressed-skin plywood panels, in which interior partitions provided stiffness and distributed loads. In 1941, the TVA design was adopted by the Federal Works Administration for wartime housing. A pitch roof was added to make it more conventional and, presumably, more acceptable. Units were transported as far as 600 miles.[29]

Burnham Kelly, in *The Prefabrication of Houses*, reported on this development, observing that: "In 1942 the TVA began experimenting with designs that frankly recognized the house section as a trailer and used certain aspects of trailer construction."[30] He concluded that an important asset was that it could be assembled with very little site labor, requiring only four hours to bolt the sections together. Apparently he was unaware that the first TVA units were constructed by Schult Trailers Inc., one of the nation's oldest and largest trailer manufacturers; nor did he acknowledge the debt which the final design may have owed the Durham House, whose dimensions were almost identical to the final TVA house, and whose design was public at the time that the TVA house was first developed.

Another crossover from the trailer industry into prefabricated housing was the "suitcase house" developed by the Palace Corporation. It was similar to the folding house that Palace was producing for defense workers under government contract. Instead of a trailer core, it had a narrow central section, without utilities, that simply held the panels and folding mechanism. Laid on its side, the folded house package stood only 3 feet high and could be stacked on a flatbed truck or railroad car for transport. The unit was designed to serve as emergency shelter.

During the war years, various federal agencies had contracted for, or built, approximately 1.6 million housing units, over 12 percent of which had been prefabricated; of those, over 17 percent had been house trailers.[31] In the government's total housing effort, the role of the house trailer was small, but, in comparison to other forms of prefabricated housing, significant. Whether the trailer should be considered prefabricated housing or a category of dwelling unto itself, however, was still an open question. In 1940, the Defense Council had identified the trailer as "temporary housing," in contrast to prefabricated dwellings, which were initially intended as "duration" housing. This was a distinction that the trailer industry promoted, emphasizing mobility as opposed to demountability. Yet, when the NHA terminated federal trailer orders, the agency's explanation was that trailers were not houses because they were factory-built, the same condemnation it had made of prefabricated housing.

The prejudice of federal agencies such as PBA and the NHA against prefabricated housing and trailers largely confined their use to more remote rural sites where labor was scarce, and demountability and transportability were important considerations. Whenever possible, the agencies preferred to support site-built housing. Tradition-bound as this preference might have been, the way in which it was pursued was innovative in its sheer magnitude.

Before the war, developers would typically subdivide a site into housing tracts and sell them to builders, who would erect anywhere from a few to several dozen houses. During the war, site builders were called upon to develop large projects within a very short time. Levitt and Sons, for example, whose largest development before the war had been a 200-unit subdivision, received a government contract to construct 2350 war workers' homes in Norfolk, Virginia.

The rapid construction of huge housing developments necessitated by the war effort required an unprecedented organization of labor and materials in this country. The different building tasks were laid out in a precise sequence. Crews of specialized workers would first lay foundation slabs, then the framing lumber would be delivered. Small on-site fabrication shops were set up so that trusses and other major structural components could be sent preassembled to the lots. Crews of electricians, plumbers, and roofers would move around the site in an exact sequence. The site was, in effect, organized like a factory, but with the workmen moving to the buidings rather than the dwellings coming to the workers.[32] By rationalizing the construction process by bringing the order of an assembly line to the building site, economies were achieved that could rival prefabricated construction, but at the cost of increased site labor and on-site construction time.

In summary, the war years provided the necessary incentive to translate the housing experiments of the 1930s into practice on a scale which would allow them to be more accurately, if not always unprejudicially, evaluated. Both the prefabricated housing and trailer industries were motivated to organize themselves to represent their interests to government agencies. At the same time, the site-built housing industry changed and, for a brief time, localities relaxed their restrictions.

Industrialized Housing in the Postwar Era

Throughout the war years, Americans had been fed images of the postwar suburban house as a promised fruit of victory. The reality was quite different. In 1947, an estimated six million families were living with friends or relatives, and another half million were occupying Quonset huts or other temporary quarters. Rather than getting "homes for heroes," returning veterans were faced with a housing shortage brought on by fifteen years of depressed production.

One way out of the housing shortage was to revive the dream of the industrialized house, the Depression era image of houses rolling off an assembly line like cars: inexpensive, modern, and beautifully built. In January 1946, President Truman appointed Wilson Wyatt as "Housing Expediter," with responsibility for stimulating the production of housing for returning veterans.[33] Five weeks after his appointment, Wyatt submitted a proposal to the President for a program of 2.7 million housing starts by the end of 1947. The supporting legislation was enacted by Congress in May of 1946, as the Veterans' Emergency Housing Act. An important part of Wyatt's plan was prefabricated housing. He hoped to have 250,000 prefabricated units started in 1946, and 600,000 in 1947. To help encourage production, loans were to be made available through the Reconstruction Finance Corporation (RFC).

The promise of federal support and guarantees to prefabricated builders stimulated growth in that industry. The RFC made available over $50 million in loans. Prefabricators were offered surplus war production plants and were given priority in the allocation of scarce building materials. The number of prefabricators in 1946 was 280, up from fewer than 100 the previous year. Despite this growth and support, only 37,400 prefabricated units were produced in 1946, less than 15 percent of the projected goal. The Democrats' defeat in the 1946 election, coupled with press criticism of the extension of government controls during peacetime, rapidly turned the political environment against Wyatt's ideas. In December 1946 he resigned. As his plans died, so did the fortunes of many prefabricators. By the end of 1947, the number of companies in the industry was again down to around 100.

More effective than Wyatt's program in stimulating housing production were the provisions of the 1944 Servicemen's Readjustment Act, which created the Veterans Administration mortgage program. With the incentives of government-guaranteed mortgages, housing starts in 1946 jumped to 937,000, then to 1,183,000 in 1948, and 1,692,000 in 1950. Merchant builders like Levitt, Eichler, and the Byrne Organization were able to mount huge housing projects, with an effectively guaranteed source of mortgages. Prefabricators, however, had difficulty qualifying for these benefits, and house trailer buyers were simply excluded.[34]

In the years immediately after the war, there were three distinct, if not always acknowledged, forms of industrialized housing. The first, represented by Wyatt's program, was essentially a new kind of house built by a new industry in a factory. The second was the tract house developed by the merchant builders, and the third was the trailer industry's year-round mobile housing. Of the three, only the first was regarded as genuine industrialized housing, yet, it was the least successful. A brief account of the housing developed by each approach—the prefabricated Lustron House, Levittown, and Spartan Trailers—may illustrate their relative advantages.

The Lustron House

The most daring, and ultimately ill-fated, project connected with Wyatt's program for postwar prefabrication was the Lustron-House.[35] Lustron was founded by Carl Strandlund, vice president of Chicago Vitreous Enamel Company, which held important patents on a process for enameling cold-rolled sheet steel. This material, which never needed painting and could be hosed clean, had been used successfully for storefronts and gas stations. Early in 1946, Strandlund decided to apply this technology to house construction, believing that a metal house, manufactured with modern production techniques, well engineered, and made of materials that would never look old, would have great consumer appeal. He requested financial support from the Reconstruction Finance Corporation and received a $15.5 million loan in June 1946. By 1949 Lustron had received over $37 million in RFC loans. The company also was given use of the 1-million-square-foot Curtiss-Wright fighter plane factory near Columbus, Ohio, and obtained priority allocation for rolled sheet steel and other critical materials for its production process.

The basic Lustron House was 1025 square feet in area and weighed 12.5 tons. Its interior and exterior walls, ceiling, and roof were metal. The ititial design specified 3000 separate parts that were to be mounted on a concrete slab poured at the site. As the production process evolved, more prefabrication was tranferred to the factory, and site assembly was reduced to joining 37 subassemblies. These subassemblies, however, had to be carefully packaged in a specially built trailer so that they could be joined in the proper order, which proved to be a time-consuming and costly process.

Lustron house parts were fabricated in a factory, organized around a conveyor belt. A huge press, several stories tall, formed the exterior wall panels, and long tunnel ovens baked the

Exterior view of the two-bedroom model of the Lustron Home.

A special trailer was needed to transport components of the Lustron Home. Loading the trailer in the right order was an additional labor expense that had to be factored into the total cost of the unit.

enamel finish on the panels, which slowly moved through them. Projected production for the factory was 100 houses per day, or 30,000 to 40,000 per year. Factory labor amounted to 280 hours of labor per house. Packing and unpacking the delivery truck took an additional 60 hours, and another 350 hours were required at the site for an experienced crew to finish the home.

Lustron's technology involved significant capitalization costs that would ultimately have to be recouped in the price of the units. The company invested $15 million in tools and equipment and would have spent more if the factory space had not been donated. The break-even point, just to meet expenses, was production of 30 to 50 units per day. By contrast, prefabricators using wood-based technologies, such as stressed skin panels, achieved a break-even point at 4 to 5 units per day. The use of exotic materials and technologies meant that many bugs had to be worked out and special training given to the workmen. Consequently, the start of production was repeatedly delayed.

The price originally projected for the basic house model was $7000 with land. By the time the first units were ready to ship, in early 1949, unanticipated production expenses and variable site preparation and land costs had inflated the price into the $10,000–12,000 range. By contrast, the most successful prefabricators at the time were selling houses in the $5500–8500 range, exclusive of land.

In addition to higher than projected production costs, Lustron faced various institutional problems. In many jurisdictions, local building codes had to be modified to allow the home to be erected and occupied. The legal work necessary to accomplish this was so costly and time consuming that it was only worthwhile in large metropolitan markets. Even in these, the company made little progress in obtaining modifications. Banks also had difficulty adapting their construction loan practices to the prefabricated house. Usually they release funds prorated to the completion of a house. With a prefabricated house, a dealer was expected to put up the money for the whole house before it left the factory and to carry its cost until the house was set up on a site and could be mortgaged.

While marketing the Lustron House was not regarded by the manufacturer as a major concern, other forms of prefabricated housing made of unconventional materials and with exposed joints had met with strong consumer resistance. It is difficult to believe that a metal house, in which pictures were hung with magnets, panels joined by floor-to-ceiling rubber gaskets every two feet, and simple home repairs greatly complicated by unfamiliar assemblies and materials, would be accepted uncritically by consumers.

By the time Lustron was fully ready for production, the conventional housing industry had revived. In 1947, there were 776,000 housing starts, of which less than one half of one percent were prefabricated. By 1948, housing starts had jumped to 1,183,000 units, but even fewer prefabricated dwellings had been produced than in the previous year. To remain competitive, prefabricators were turning out lower-cost models. Lustron was also considering an "economy" version of its house, but the scale and character of its operation made such modifications difficult. In 1950, when there was a record-breaking 1,692,000 housing starts, the RFC foreclosed on its loans to Lustron. Shortly thereafter, President Truman had Lustron's factory reconverted for aircraft production.

Merchant Builders: Levitt and Sons

If Lustron's performance had been disappointing compared to other prefabricators', it was truly dismal compared to that of the merchant builders. After the war, developers applied the lessons they had learned in producing massive war worker housing projects to the creation of large suburban subdivisions. To the efficiencies of the building process, they added methods of marketing and closing that accelerated occupancy and thereby shortened the term during which they carried construction loans.[36] The largest companies, like Levitt, achieved further control through vertical integration, in which the company owned its own lumber mills and appliance manufacturers.[37] By 1950, the large merchant builders, riding a mass market fueled by the ease of obtaining VA loans and the demand for a house in the suburbs, controlled more than two-thirds of all new housing production.[38]

Levitt and Sons began acquiring property for Levittown on Long Island in 1946. The first houses were offered for sale in October 1947. By the time the project was completed it contained 17,400 houses. The basic Levittown house was a Cape Cod model, built on a concrete slab, with a first-floor area of about 750 square feet. An important feature was an unfinished attic, ready for the time when the family would need an extra bedroom.[39] The first Cape Cod models sold for $6990, with no down payment, closing costs, or hidden fees. Levitt not only built the houses, but also provided community swimming pools, recreation fields, and a series of large "village greens" (linear park strips). Thousand of trees from the company-owned nursery lined roads laid out in the curvilinear patterns favored by contemporary planning theorists. Prefabricators sought to provide housing; Levitt tried to provide community.[40]

The performance of merchant builders compared favorably with that of efficient prefabricators. In 1949, for example, one prefabricator offered a Cape Cod model for $5500–$8500, exclusive of land and site preparation, compared with Levitt's ready-to-occupy model at $6990. It was often argued that an advantage of prefabrication was the increased speed and reduced labor with which a project could be completed, but if speed were measured in the time from land acquisition to occupancy, the record of merchant builders was hard to beat. To be sure, prefabricated housing was more efficient in small-scale and in-fill developments, but even this advantage was lost when a lengthy approval process was required to allow it to be permanently sited in a community.

Large-scale merchant builder developments could be considered "conventional construction" only in the sense that 2 x 4 framing was used and the houses were designed in a traditional style. In all other respects, they represented a new form of construction: genuine mass production, with Ford's principles of "power, accuracy, economy, system, continuity and speed" well in evidence.

Spartan Trailers and the Silver City

In the final scene of the movie, *The Best Years of Our Lives* (1946), the hero, a disabled war veteran, visits the site of a mothballed fleet of fighter planes. He encounters a workman disassembling a plane and asks him what he is doing. The man replies that he is salvaging the planes to convert the materials into houses. For the veteran, unemployed and disillusioned by life in postwar America, this act reaffirms his hope. As the music swells, the camera pans back to reveal acres of planes, no longer useless scrap, but a symbol of a new future. The viewer is asked to imagine the planes transformed into houses spreading across the landscape in a silver suburb.

While there is no evidence that any attempt to turn planes into homes was actually made after the war, several aircraft manufacturers made proposals to construct prefabricated houses. A widely publicized design by R. Buckminster Fuller, the Wichita House, was to be produced by Republic Aircraft. It consisted of lightweight standardized aluminum elements. Though far more sophisticated in design than the Lustron House, the extensive skilled labor required for its site assembly would probably have made it too expensive for a mass market. In the end, only two Fuller houses were constructed. Beech Aircraft and Douglas also developed models, but neither went into commercial development.

After World War II, Spartan Aircraft turned to trailer manufacturing; pictured here is the "Spartan Manor" of 1947.

Spartan Aircraft, of Tulsa, took a different approach and began to manufacture house trailers. The models Spartan offered incorporated the structural technology of aircraft. They were constructed of aluminum sheets riveted to deformed ribs, forming a structural membrane. The front window wrapped around the sides like a windshield, and was held in place by a rubber gasket. The edges of the trailer were rounded both to reduce wind resistance and help shed water. Spartan was not the first to employ this type of construction. Wally Byam had used many of these features in his Airstream trailer. Whereas the Airstream was at the upper end of the travel trailer market, Spartan designed for a house trailer population. Like most of the house trailers of the postwar period, bathrooms were included. Since the trailers would still have to be towed by car, lightness remained a consideration, but new emphasis was placed on interior accommodations, particularly those that provided more privacy for year-round family living.

In 1951, Spartan received a $2 million contract from a construction company, for four hundred trailers for workers building the McNary Dam near Umatilla, Oregon. The only site preparation necessary was laying utility lines and roads. The workers soon dubbed their community "Silver City."[41] When the dam was completed the trailers were sold, many to the same workers who had first occupied them.

The Spartan Company was innovative in areas other than engineering design. It was among the first to offer insurance and wholesale and retail financing. Through a subsidiary, it made sixty-month loans available at 5 percent with a 25 percent down payment. Comparable terms were offered on used units. At the time, these terms were more attractive than those offered by financial institutions. At $5000, exclusive of site preparation, Spartan Trailers were more expensive per square foot than Levitt's houses or those offered by many prefabricators, but they were designed for a particular market that still required mobility.

The Trailer Advantage

Unlike prefabricators, who enjoyed, though briefly, the largesse of government loan programs, or merchant builders, who based their market on subsidized mortgage programs, the house trailer manufacturers thrived after the war because their product fell between established categories of housing. Since it was clearly not a house in form, in the way that most prefabricated housing tried to be, it was not supported by government postwar housing programs.[42] At the same time, because it did not beg comparison with conventional site-built housing, it did not provoke the resistance from real-estate interests and building unions that the prefabricators were up against. The house trailer nevertheless was considered housing under special circumstances and for special populations. Thus, the industry was able to succeed during the postwar housing boom, while prefabrication efforts stagnated or failed.

The trailer's competitive advantage lay in its combination of mobility, affordability, and availability. Mobility was not just being mounted on wheels, but having a widespread network of parks where units could be set up. Affordability was a function of the economies of mass production, as well as flexible distribution and financing systems that could accommodate the cyclical variability of the housing market. A network of dealerships, as well as parks, made the mobile home a visible, if not always desirable, housing alternative.

Mobility

Of all the experiments in prefabricated housing during the 1930s and 1940s, only the trailer evoked ideals distinctly outside the realm of conventional housing; the combination of mobility with shelter seemed to touch a vital chord. The first associations with mobility had been with vacationing and the ideal of returning to the wilderness and "basic principles." The wartime and postwar housing experience evoked images of the pioneers whose perserverance had opened the frontiers and whose spirit, in the modern trailerite, would help build the new dams, highways, and factories that would assure America's continued greatness. A 1945 editorial in *Trailer Travel* magazine explicitly called on trailerites to take pride in their mythic lineage.

Who is it today, like the pioneers in their covered wagons, feels the desire to dip over the horizon—who but the trailerite? Like the pioneer he, too, is hardy and self-sufficient—he can live and thrive wherever he goes. Why not? His house and his home go with him. . . . He solves the manpower problems and housing shortages of the nation. He is independent, entirely democratic.[43]

A more romantic, if less heroic, appeal of trailer life was celebrated in the 1951 novel *The Long, Long Trailer*, by Clinton Twiss. Two years after its publication it was made into a successful movie starring Lucille Ball and Desi Arnez. In the movie, Desi is a band leader who must be on the road much of the year. His new bride, Luci, suggests that one way for them to stay together is to tour in a trailer. While the movie was predictably peppered with mishaps,—Lucille Ball could make an ordinary kitchen look like a mine field—it presented an appealing image of trailer life and of the people in trailer parks, as Luci and Desi saw America firsthand.

Another contemporary traveler through mobile home land was John Steinbeck, who wrote about families he met living in trailers in *Travels With Charley*. "Don't you miss some kind of permanence," he asked the father of one family?

Who's got permanence? Factory closes down, you move on. Good times and things opening up, you move on where its better. You got roots and sit and starve. You take the pioneers in the history books. They were movers. Take up land, sell it, move on.[44]

Further along on their trip Steinbeck thinks aloud to his dog Charley.

In the pattern-thinking about roots I and most other people have left two things out of consideration. Could it be that Americans are a restless people, a mobile people never satisfied with where they are as a matter of selection? The pioneers, the immigrants who peopled the continent, were the restless ones in Europe. The steady rooted ones stayed home and are still there. . . . Perhaps we have overrated roots as a psychic need. Maybe the greater urge, the deeper and more ancient is the need, the will, the hunger to be somewhere else.[45]

Whether transient by occupation or choice, 60 percent of year-round trailer residents interviewed in a survey in the

Many trailer manufacturers hoped that with the resumption of peace their market would again be the vacationing family. These lakeside trailers featured site-built cabanas.

mid-1950s reported they had moved within the previous twelve month.[46] The typical trailer household was a married couple without children. They were employed in transient jobs (as craftsmen, machine operators), earned an income higher than the national average, and had a higher than average level of education. When asked if they would move out of their trailers if offered a house at a reasonable price, fourteen out of fifteen said no. The survey concluded that "even though the mobile dwelling may never be moved . . . the fact that it can be moved is a positive factor in the popularity of the mobile home."

Mobility depended on having places to park. The restrictive zoning practices of the late 1930s that had been relaxed temporarily during the war reappeared with a vengeance after the war. Restrictions assured that trailer parks within city limits would be confined to commercial and industrial areas: along railroad tracks, or next to car dealerships and junk yards. Despite the zoning restrictions, parks were being developed at a rapid pace, with larger and more lots than their prewar predecessors. By 1953 there were approximately twelve thousand parks across the country, which could accommodate 50 to 75 percent of the trailers in use. The rapid and largely ad hoc development of trailer parks was essential to the house trailer's success. Without them, sales would have been dampened significantly and trailer life would have been considerably less affordable.

Affordability

The assembly line, crucial to the economy of house trailer production, had been introduced in the late 1930s, when it began to be used by larger manufacturers such as Covered Wagon and Silver Dome. Early factories were usually organized in an end-to-end layout, with units moving through the plant past stations where components were sequentially attached.[47] Large government contracts during the early part of the war and in the postwar period continued to provide enough work that the assembly line could be used efficiently by the major manufacturers.

When significant cost savings were realized by reducing hours of labor and using unskilled labor, critics of the industry suggested that its production economies amounted to little more than cutting corners, using cheap materials, and generally disregarding safety. Free from building codes, trailer manufacturers could follow practices not allowed in conventional building or prefabricated housing. Industry old-timers recall that some postwar manufacturers used garden hose for water supply lines, lamp cord for electrical wiring, and 2 x 2 lumber for wall

An end-to-end trailer assembly line at the International Fleetwood factory.

framing. While such abuses led to the establishment of voluntary and eventually mandatory standards, the lack of codes also invited innovation. Manufacturers, for example, were able to use plastic pipes for plumbing and fast-drying glues to attach sheathing to frames. Such labor-saving innovations were resisted by local building trade unions and building officials, delaying their use in site-built housing.

An important aspect of the economy of trailer manufacturing was the way in which payments to suppliers were handled. Suppliers extended credit, so manufacturers were often able to delay their payments until after units were sold. This meant running production lines based on orders in hand and shipping units as soon as they were completed. By selling their units for cash, manufacturers had necessary capital for further production. Manufacturers also tried to schedule production so that they could maintain a minimal inventory of materials and components. They located near suppliers, who stored orders till needed. Northern Indiana and southern Michigan, with their concentration of suppliers to the auto industry, became ideal locations for trailer manufacturers.

Suppliers also provided the industry with new materials and technology. The aluminum industry engaged in research and passed the results on to manufacturers in an effort to expand aluminum's use in trailers. Suppliers of appliances, heating systems, and other building materials from insulation to glues, all assumed the costs of developing product lines for the industry. There was little incentive for manufacturers to be technologically innovative, aside from incorporating new power tools into their assembly lines.

This flexibility in the industry's relationship with suppliers is paralleled by its accommodation to the seasonality of housing sales. In theory, factory-built housing has the advantage of year-round production. Manufacture, which takes place inside, is not slowed by inclement weather, and a steady rate of production is supposed to help amortize capital development costs, such as plant and equipment. In practice, however, sales have seasonal cycles, reflecting when buyers prefer to move. Stockpiling units during slow sales periods, to maintain employment and utilize equipment, is financially risky. Industrialized housing efforts, such as Lustron, that had high equipment costs, were particularly vulnerable to seasonality. Trailer manufacturers, with low equipment costs and good relations with material suppliers, were in a better position to cope.

The industry responded to seasonality by structuring a flexible labor force. Most of the factories were located in rural areas or small cities, where they hired semiskilled and unskilled laborers, willing to endure seasonal work schedules and less inclined to unionize. Manufacturers also tried to keep their labor force small by contracting out parts of production through a "contract payment plan." As described by Carlton Edwards,

> The basis of the plan is that one man would contract with the
> manufacturer to do work for a certain department, such as cabinet
> work. The contractor would then hire men to build the cabinets
> for which he was paid on a per trailer basis. The owner of the
> trailer manufacturing plant had quality control of the product
> through the contractor for each department. If the trailer did not
> meet the manufacturer's standards when the trailer was ready
> to leave the factory door, the contractor had to do whatever was
> necessary to have the work in his department satisfy the owner.
> The work contractor usually made a handsome profit on the differ-
> ence between the amount paid to him and the amount he paid
> for labor.[48]

The contract payment plan, initiated in the late 1930s, was used through the 1960s, when it was replaced by an incentive plan. The plan was similar to the auto industry's practice of contracting out the manufacture of components, and the merchant builders' practice of contracting out the construction of specific parts of the house: foundations, framing, or roofing. With contracting, the role of manufacturers and developers became one of coordination and assembly.

The industry was also well structured to accommodate recessions in the national economy, which typically occur every four to seven years and last one to two years. The relatively low cost of starting a factory in the early 1950s, when demand was strong, encouraged the formation of new firms. In 1955, plants could be started with as little as $10,000 to $15,000. By 1966, the average start-up costs were only $150,000. The ease of entry also resulted in cyclical "shake outs," when economic recessions caused marginal companies to go under. In 1959, there were 268 manufacturers with 327 plants; in 1964 the number of manufacturers had fallen to 200 with 261 plants.[49] Arthur Bernhardt observes that sales in the industry have generally been countercylical to site-built production: when house construction is down because of recession, more people seem to turn to a trailer/mobile home.[50]

Since the mid-1930s, most of trailer/mobile homes have been produced by the fifteen to twenty largest firms, while hundreds of smaller manufacturers produced the rest. This mix gave the industry a flexibility well suited to the inevitable cycles of the housing economy. The small new firms were often innovative by necessity to develop market recognition and generate orders. A new firm's eye-catching model at a regional trade show was likely to develop a market, but by the end of the circuit of shows around the country, other manufacturers would have incorporated the idea into their own models. A bay window or a raised living-room ceiling might be one year's fancy. Another year, island kitchens or vanity sinks might be in. Unlike the auto industry, where new model tool-up costs are significant, the low-tech character of the trailer industry permits rapid design changes without major delays and costs.[51]

The ease of changing designs meant that manufacturers could build to individual customers' specifications. Since units were manufactured based on orders in hand, a customer could request a model with a different wall arrangement, rather than settle for whatever was on the lot. Customers more typically chose furnishings and finishes rather than rearranged floor plans, but it was possible nonetheless.

The affordability of the house trailer, then, resulted from the industry's flexibility and loose structure. Production took advantage of factory assembly, using simple technology and requiring little capitalization or skilled labor. With the low start-up and production costs, manufacturers could accommodate economic cycles that crippled more technologically sophisticated forms of industrialized housing. And inexpensive park space assured that affordability would not be lost after the trailer left the factory.

Availability

Factory-built housing is generally most cost-effective when the plant is located within a day's drive of a building site, usually three to five hundred miles. This means having a network of dealerships within that radius capable of generating enough business to keep the plant profitable. General Houses Corporation's demise in the mid-1930s resulted, in large part, from its failure to develop an adequate dealership network. Lustron also suffered from a lack of dealerships, though that failing was eclipsed by its problems with capitalization. The trailer industry, by contrast, developed an extensive network of dealers early on. It was less sensitive to travel radius limitations, so dealers could represent even far-flung factories. Many dealers also secured park space for their customers, often by developing parks themselves. This was especially important after the war, when the explosive growth of sales exceeded available park space.

In the 1930s, many trailer dealerships were combined with car sales or service lots. Distributors, contracted by manufacturers, sold trailers to individual dealers. In the postwar period, distributors were replaced by a franchise system to assure that dealers in the same town would not directly compete with each other. A franchise might give a dealership exclusive sales rights for a fifty-mile radius. Dealers displayed different models, either by the same manufacturer, or several manufacturers. In the early 1950s, an individual could open a dealership for as little as $5000.[52] By 1953, there were an estimated 3500 dealers across the country.[53]

Initially the trailer industry expected to market its product like cars, changing styles yearly and fostering loyalty to specific manufacturers. A 1951 industry-sponsored marketing report, however, found that people wanted to comparison shop rather than go for a specific brand. The report recommended that dealerships be established in a "trailer row," similar to car dealerships, so that comparison shopping would be easier.[54] Such trailer rows, which were already developing spontaneously, became the dominant pattern until the mid-1970s. Another typical location for a dealership was in the trailer park, which the dealer often also owned and lived in. The dealer could sell units to prospective tenants and also provide for the resale of units of tenants who wanted to move without their trailers.

Where park space was scarce, buying a trailer from the dealer might be a requirement for getting a space.[55] Today about two-thirds of all dealerships are in parks, or have sales offices in other types of mobile-home developments.[56] The others continue to operate as "street dealers," many of whom also sell recreational vehicles.

Since dealers became acquainted with new models through annual regional sales shows, organizing such shows became an important function of the first manufacturers' associations. Manufacturers would build special models, and then, if dealer interest was strong, put them into production. Shows were also a convenient way to inspect the models other companies offered, and a quick way for information about consumer preferences to circulate through the industry.

Dealers paid manufacturers upon receipt, financing their inventory through bank loans. Under this arrangement, dealers tried to limit their inventory to display models, relying on manufacturers to provide timely delivery of new orders. Since dealers assumed the risk in carrying an inventory, they had to know their market. The manufacturer, in turn, read market preferences through dealers' orders. In the early 1950s, the manufacturers' associations began to commission market studies to get an overall picture of where their sales were and could come from. Such studies, however, only supplemented what could be learned from dealers at the trade shows.[57]

One of the services dealers provided was to arrange financing for purchasers. Whereas conventional homes could be financed with twenty to thirty year fixed mortgages at 4.5 to 5.5 percent and little or no down payment, a new house trailer typically required a one-quarter to one-third down payment. Bank or finance company loans for the balance had terms ranging from twenty-four to sixty months, at interest rates applicable to automobile loans. Postwar trailer sales also were subject to an excise tax, which was not lifted until 1953. The buyer then had to absorb a discount charge, usually 6 percent of the face value of his loan, further inflating the cost, so that the simple interest on a postwar trailer purchase might be 11 to 12 percent; more than twice the rate of a conventional home mortgage.

Dealers were not only a source of financing, but of services to make the house trailer system work: if a buyer needed a park space, the dealer might have some on reserve; if a unit needed to be transported, or if an owner preferred professional towing, the dealer could arrange it; if a family needed to sell their old trailer to buy a new one, the dealer might take it in trade or offer to sell it on commission; and if a unit needed repairs, the dealer was often the person to contact. Dealers sold skirting to hide the chassis, stairs to make it easier to enter, and even add-on rooms like cabanas, porches, and carports. In short, the dealer made sure this form of factory-built housing was accessible and liveable.

The House Trailer Industry as a System

By and large, manufacturers of industrialized housing tried to achieve affordability by rationalizing the production process following the principles of mass-production. In theory, production under controlled factory conditions would yield housing of superior quality at reduced prices. Manufacturers had an abiding faith that such a product would create its own market, and so considered the problems of distribution and location only secondarily. In getting their product from the factory to a site, however, much of their advantage was lost. Without adequate marketing, economical levels of production could not be sustained; and without visible local dealers helping to provide zoning approved locations where prefabricated housing could be sited, markets could not be sustained.

The merchant builder and many prefabricators could produce a less expensive product on a square-foot cost basis, but the trailer's advantage was in the performance of the industry as a system, which consisted not only of manufacturers, but of park owners, dealers, suppliers, and transporters. Arthur Bernhardt, in his comprehensive analysis of the industry, observed:

> The "product" of the mobile home industry is housing, which
> is not just a physical artifact. Housing includes not only the dwell-
> ing unit as produced by the production system but the physical
> and community framework and services provided by the mobile
> home park system.
>
> When compared to other systems of the building sector, the
> most notable feature of the mobile home industry is the separa-
> tion of [these] . . . three functional systems. . . . While most
> firms in the mobile home industry specialize in only one of these
> tasks, these functional systems are clearly interdependent: the
> success of one relates directly to the success of the others.[58]

In the mid-1950s becoming part of the system had a relatively low entry cost: $10,000 to $15,000 to become a manufacturer, $5000 to start a dealership, and $300 to $500 per space to start a park. Consequently when markets were strong, more people would enter the business, and, in economic downturns, they could turn to other pursuits without crippling the industry as a whole. This same flexibility characterizes each part of the system. Manufacturers, using a simple assembly technology, readily modified designs in response to consumers' preferences. Consumers made their wants known through dealers. Dealers, in turn, developed the local contacts necessary to finance units and find space for them in conformance with local restrictions. The availability of parks across the country allowed units to be moved or sold in place. Where parks were not available or suitable, single siting could usually be arranged, so a trailer/ mobile home could be located virtually anywhere in the country where it wasn't specifically excluded.

The "looseness-of-fit" between the elements of the system[59] allowed each part to develop in response to local needs and specific requirements, and encouraged ad hoc innovation that kept the industry vital. For the next two decades, these characteristics continued to propel the industry's success. Ironically, much of this vitality would be lost as the mobile home gained official recognition as a form of permanent housing.

Blindness and Invisibility

Many of the advocates and theorists of industrialized housing, from the 1930s through the 1960s, were blinded by their own theories, which, influenced by the great success of mass-produced automobiles, fixed on a specific image of what industrialized housing ought to be. Transferring that idea too literally, however, produced an image of streamlined houses of steel, coming off of an assembly line with clock-like precision. In 1929, for example, Theodore Morrison wrote in *House Beautiful*,

> Until our houses can be made in the factory, by machine, we shall have no true economy of housing comparable to the economy prevailing throughout industry generally. Until they can be installed, not built, we cannot expect them to be truly efficient and rational adaptations of means to ends.[60]

In 1935, half a million people rushed to see the exhibit of Motohome, a panelized prefabricated house built on a steel frame with an integrated mechanical core, sold complete with appliances. The home was exhibited in stores, demonstration models were built, and there was extensive press coverage. By 1936, one hundred and fifty Motohomes had been sold, and the line was abandoned for a more conventional house with clapboard siding and a peaked roof.

A dozen years later, an article in *Fortune* magazine bemoaned the lack of industrialization in housing.[61] Ignoring the examples of factory-built housing that had been successfully produced and used during the war, it pointed instead to a more exotic experiment: the aluminum stressed-skin house designed by Buckminster Fuller at Republic Aircraft's factory in Wichita, Kansas. *Fortune* proclaimed that Wichita was destined to become "the Kitty Hawk of housing." Fuller emphasized the lightness of his house, which would make it easy to transport, and the fact that there were relatively few parts, making it easier to assemble. One year later only two houses had been built, and Republic withdrew its support. *Fortune* blamed the failure on insufficient capital,[62] but given the fate of the highly capitalized Lustron House, that alone would have been only one among many obstacles: local codes, unions, the cost of on-site skilled labor (which appears to have been considerable), mortgage approval by lending institutions, and so on. In short, the Fuller House would have met the same obstacles as did other postwar attempts at industrialized housing.

Fortune's choice of the Fuller house as an example of the future of industrialization illustrates the belief that the correct application of mass-production techniques would produce a specific style of house: modern and streamlined in some vaguely understood way. On the one hand, critics were blind to other alternatives, like the trailer, which looked different but did not present themselves, per se, as innovations. On the other hand, they were blind to the pervasive effects of convention. They chose to dismiss the public's desire for conventional looking houses as the result of inertia or lack of education, rather than a response to the integral relationship between form and meaning.

Part of the blindness industrialized housing theorists suffered came from their conception of what the manufacturing process would be like. It seemed clear to them that anything resembling the way houses were currently being made was wrong. If housing was to be a modern industry, then it would have to exhibit the characteristics of modern industry, such as Ford's assembly line. Behind this image was a conception of industrialized organizations themselves as machine-like. The different parts of the organization would have to interact with a high degree of precision. This would mean determining markets through sophisticated studies, defining human needs through research, and extending control over the process through increasing vertical integration. A basic assumption behind all this was that a "universal man" could be defined, for whom a "universal dwelling" could be designed.

From this perspective, it is not surprising that Levittown's significance as a demonstration of industrialized housing was largely ignored. With Levittown there was no factory in evidence, yet the whole site was a factory. Its conventional design helped mask its innovation, and assure a market, while its unfinished attic displayed a genuine understanding of how people improve housing over time, and make it into a home.

The genius of the trailer/mobile home industry was also ignored. Here was a production system that consisted of small businessmen, unsophisticated in the methods of corporate industry, producing housing that wasn't even recognizable as such. As an object, the trailer contained all the characteristics of the theoretic industrialized house: light, portable, factory-made, and easily scrapped. It didn't look like a conventional house, yet it enjoyed a strong and expanding market as housing. The industry's manufacturers, dealers, park operators, material suppliers, and transporters functioned as a loosely organized but efficient system, capable of responding to changing market demands and the vicissitudes of seasonal and economic cycles. In addition, its product was easily modified, whereas Lustron, the house of steel, was beyond the weekend handyman's expertise.

The trailer industry, despite remaining largely invisible to theorists and advocates of industrialized housing, did not suffer. Indeed, inattention may have been fortuitous, in that there was none of the resistance that stifled the development of other forms of prefabricated housing. The blindness of the theorists, however, had a counterpart in the industry itself. Even though the majority of its production effort was being used for year-round housing, the trailer industry in the immediate postwar era did not see itself as being in the business of housing. Rather, it saw itself producing for a special population needing temporary dwellings while it waited for the automobile vacationing market to resume. It was the consumers, through their buying decisions, that lead to changes in production and industry perceptions. It was the industry's flexibility and loose structure that allowed it to follow this lead without fully understanding its implications. Not until the advent of the ten-wide units in the mid-1950s would the change in use be fully accepted and the house trailer become a mobile home.

Mobile Homes:
Form, Meaning, and Function

Birth of the Tenwide

The 1954 Florida Mobile Home Exposition in Sarasota was like other annual trade shows held around the country for years. Manufacturers seeking sales in the large Florida market brought models to the show. Some units were built especially for the event. If sold, they would go into regular production; otherwise, they would disappear forever. For the first few days, the show was open only to dealers; then on the weekend the general public was allowed in. When business was slow exhibitors had the time to check out the competition, especially those models customers had told them were really worth a look. Orders taken at the show determined whether it would be a good or bad year. For new manufacturers that could mean the difference between survival and failure.

The trailer industry had enjoyed impressive growth since the end of World War II. In 1953, 76,900 trailers had been shipped. Sales were up $2 million from the previous year, a record to date. The number of units manufactured, however, was almost 7 percent lower than in 1952. Manufacturers were concerned about their market growing soft. The surge of construction of new dams and AEC facilities had subsided. The Korean War was winding down, and, with it, the demand for trailers for military personnel. This seemed an opportune time to appeal to the growing vacation market and focus on smaller units with more convenience features; or perhaps it was a time to make further inroads into the housing market, with units that were bigger and better suited to year-round living.

The trailers exhibited at Sarasota that year included the diminutive Zollinger, only 10 feet long including the hitch, and the Cal-Craft, with two-tone siding designed to look like waves being parted by the prow of a boat. Nearby was the more experimental Comstock, built in Parsons, Kansas. Its whole roof pivoted up so that more headroom was available once the unit was parked. For the weekend vacation market there were 15- to 16-foot units, designed with a single door and an unpartitioned interior. Aside from the more extensive use of metal for exterior sheathing, these models were essentially indistinguishable from those produced in the 1930s.

More serious innovation had taken place in the design of the longer units, over 25 feet, that were suitable for year-round living. A 1953 survey revealed that the typical mobile home family consisted of 2.9 persons.[1] Approximately one fifth of the two thousand trailerites surveyed had lived in a trailer for more than five years, and another 30 percent had done so for two to five years. The full-time trailerite wanted space and privacy without forfeiting mobility. The manufacturers' problem was to meet these criteria within the restrictions established for towable vehicles. In 1954, most states specified that house trailers could not be more than 12½ feet high, 8 feet wide, and 35 feet long. Twenty-one states allowed somewhat greater lengths, and Maryland permitted a 55-foot unit. Since the trailers were still highly mobile, moving an average of every twenty months, the common minimum dimensions became the standard. Although limitations easily allowed interior ceilings of 8 feet, the added height produced greater drag and instability in side winds and could create clearance problems when driven off the main roads. Consequently, the most common ceiling heights remained 6½ to 7 feet.

Making the trailer more attractive year-round housing meant squeezing more livable space into a shell that had to remain mobile. One approach to the space problem was the Stout folding trailer, which continued to be offered by its wartime manufacturer, the Palace Corporation.[2] The postwar popularity of the folding trailer, however, was limited due to its cost as well as the technical problems associated with setting up units so that their extensive joints did not leak water and let cold air in. The difficulty of towing such a unit behind a car, or finding space for it on the standard rental trailer lot, also may have limited its appeal.

Another approach to expansion that had premiered in the

The exterior of the bilevel Pacemaker featured action lines characteristic of trailer design since the mid-1930s, while its interior suggested the appointments of a conventional house.

1930s and found a new market in the postwar period was the two-story unit. Variations of Corwin Willson's 1938 bilevel "mobile house" were offered by three manufacturers in the 1954 trailer show. Whereas Willson's design had a blimp-like shape with porthole windows, suggestive of an aerodynamically designed object, the 1954 bilevels were more restrained in their lines. Their sides were flat and their curves confined to the roof line. Portholes continued to be favored details, but not on the duplex units.

One solution to the limited headroom in the typical bilevel design was a pop-up or telescoping roof. In 1946, the Liberty Company introduced a unit in which the second story tele-

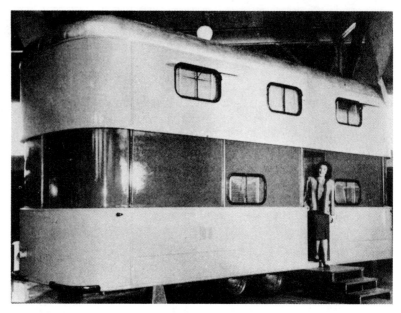

A novel approach to increasing the size of the house trailer was introduced by Liberty in 1947. The second story telescoped out from the first.

scoped out from the first, raising the ceiling while keeping the profile of the towed unit within restrictions. Even so, the unit set up on a lot would have presented a high profile to the wind. Although the Liberty model was exhibited in the 1947 trade shows, there is no evidence that it went into production; by 1954, no manufacturers seemed interested in pursuing this approach to expansion.

1953 saw a more practical approach to the solution of telescoping a unit. Budger introduced its "Expando" model, which measured 24' x 7'6" when towed. Once at a site, three sides and the roof telescoped horizontally, and the floor for the expanded area folded down from the inside. The result was a unit almost doubled in size, with significantly fewer joints and hinges than in the folding house.

Models with smaller expandable sections were offered by many manufacturers. In 1947, Elcar had introduced its SunCar, which featured a screened rear porch that folded up for transport. In 1949, Road King brought out a model with a rear room that folded out of a tapered aft section styled to suggest mobility. Four years later, Transahome introduced a model with demountable rooms that appear to have been foldable additions. This line of design development was still being worked on in 1954. Prairie Schooner, for example, offered a fold-out porch on one of its new models, and Flagship had a "pooch porch" that could be assembled on the roof of its deluxe unit.

For the dealer attending the 1954 show in search of something to satisfy the year-round trailerites' demand for more space, there were many approaches vying for consideration; but the most controversial was a model offered by Marshfield Homes. In general appearance this model did not seem a departure from other larger units displayed that year. Its sides were flat and sheathed with unpainted aluminum. In the living room was a large picture window with fixed central panes and upper and lower windows that could be opened. A pair of smaller windows at the front of the unit had rounded edges looking like train or bus details. Only the rounded ends of the roof and the slight taper of the lower front end evoked the motion symbolism that had been so pronounced in earlier periods of trailer design. Even these gestures were countered with a pair of tendril-styled brackets beside the front windows. What made this model unique was its 10-foot width, a feature that gave it its name— the "Tenwide."[3]

The Tenwide was the brainchild of Marshfield's president, Elmer Frey. Like many industry pioneers, his first experience with trailers had been building one for his own use.[4] After World War II, Frey tried his hand at a number of businesses, but they all failed. He returned to his father's Wisconsin farm, in 1946, where he began to build another trailer for himself. Instead, he

A modest application of the fold-out method of expansion was Elcar's "Sun Coach Model," which featured a folding rear porch and sunscreen.

sold it for a profit and began to think about going into commercial production. The next year, he formed a partnership with his three brothers and a brother-in-law. The Rollohome Trailer Coach Company was established in the barn. By the end of 1951, the company had grossed over $1.5 million and was producing about thirty-five coaches a week.

In 1952, Frey developed a new product called Lakeside Cottages. They were 10 feet wide and up to 50 feet long, and built on a wood frame rather than a chassis. When a prospective customer asked about cottages for his construction company, with chassis and wheels attached, the dealer explained that a permit for such a wide trailer would be impossible to get. The customer replied: "Oh we don't have a problem with that. We'll get a permit for it as a 'construction shack.'" Several years later Frey recalled:

> This set me to thinking. It was not really the size of the object
> that highway officials objected to, it was the matter of what it was
> called. I could clearly see it was discrimination against the
> Gypsy ring of the, as they called it, house trailer industry, and dis-
> crimination in the first degree, and it made me very angry. We
> took the order for the LAKESIDE COTTAGE with a chassis
> attached under it and wrote the order up as a "construction
> shack" . . . It was after that when I decided that some day I will
> take on a fight with those discriminating highway officials and
> show them how to use the overwidth permit when the item is
> called a MOBILE HOME.[5]

Apparently Frey's partners were not equally eager to go into battle over the transport of wider units. In 1954, he resigned from Rollohome and took over Marshfield Homes with the intention of developing a new type of mobile home. Frey immediately went to work on building a pilot model for the Sarasota show.

The new Marshfield Home was not simply wider, it used its additional width selectively to provide privacy for the bedrooms. In the typical house trailer, all but the end bedroom served as corridors; the bedrooms of the Tenwide featured sliding doors that separated them from the corridor. There was also space along the corridor for additional storage, and the furnace, refrigerator, and washer could be moved out of the kitchen, leaving more space for the dinette. Despite pending battles against state highway departments, dealers began placing orders. The response of other manufacturers at the show, however, was quite different.

> Suffice it to say [Frey recalls] that competing manufacturers and
> dealers became very angry, so much so that at the show in
> Sarasota, five manufacturers came at me planning to "clean my

clock." But I did have enough friends near enough to me that with some explanation, I cooled them down. They were still angry but the affair ended peacefully. Dealers were giving me orders for my Tenwide but they [the manufacturers] felt I was going to upset the industry.[6]

Enraged manufacturers were concerned that their battles to win approval for longer trailers would be complicated by new efforts to permit the transport of wider units. At first, California manufacturers lobbied the highway department to deny permits for the wider units. Only a few years later they would try to influence the opposite decision. Manufacturers were also concerned about the effect that wider units would have on existing inventories. Some may have recalled how in the mid-1930s the industry giant, Covered Wagon Company, had been left holding the bill for a large order of chassis that had become obsolete when wider models became fashionable. The sudden obsolescence of 8-foot-wide models could pull many companies under. Besides, many of the older trailer factories were not large enough to accommodate construction of wider units. The Platt trailer factory, which had been founded in 1936, for example, was organized on two stories. The wider and longer units that were being designed by the mid-1950s simply could not make their way down the ramp between the floors.

The Tenwide had to be shipped to the Sarasota show on a railroad flatcar because Frey could not get permits to transport it by highway. After that experience, he spent several years lobbying highway departments to allow road transport of ten-wides. He distributed a flier, "Out of the Frey-ing Pan," which argued that permits for oversized vehicles such as tractors, boats, and combines should also be offered for ten-wides. Infuriated, the sales manager of Spartan Trailers wrote:

> For you to arbitrarily decide that 2 feet or more is the needed additional width for your customers is beyond any reasoning as far as I am concerned. . . .
>   If it is possible for mobile homes to be legal at the ten foot width then it should certainly be legal for moving vans, freight trucks and other vehicles of this type to increase their pay load by having 10 feet wide vehicles. . . .
>   When you have completed defying the laws of every state I think your only claim to fame will be that you have thrown the mobile home industry back at least 10 years with regard to highway legislation. You should be very proud as I know of no other industry where so small a part of the industry could have such a wide-reaching effect.[7]

One year later, Spartan was also producing ten-wide models and lobbying with other companies for highway department

A Marshfield Homes "Tenwide" being shipped to Palm Springs, California in 1954.

acceptance. By 1957, many states permitted ten-wides on their highways, with the provision that the towing vehicle be adequately insured, have permits from each of the states it passed through, and be moved only during daylight hours.

With a growing demand for longer and wider units, manufacturers were faced with the choice of remaining in the travel trailer business, to produce larger mobile homes exclusively, or manufacturing both products, essentially for different markets. In 1963, the two industries formally split, with travel trailer manufacturers identifying themselves as the recreation vehicle industry. They formed their own lobbying group, the Recreation Vehicle Association (RVA). As if to make the split more final, Paul Abel, who founded the RVA, scheduled its annual industry shows on the same days as the mobile home trade shows. Many manufacturers were forced to choose which show they would attend and which industry they would affiliate with.

The Mobile Home Market

By 1954, the worst of the postwar housing crisis had passed and the use of trailers as stopgap housing had diminished; yet industry sales continued to grow. Between 1954 and 1955 the number of units manufactured increased by more than two-thirds, the new growth apparently owing to people seeking affordable starter housing. Whereas a California study in 1948 showed that the mobile home population was somewhat more affluent and better educated than the U.S. population as a whole, a 1959 market survey revealed that a mobile home household tended to be less affluent and educated than the national average.[8] The earlier sample reflected the dominance of construction workers and military personnel, while the later sample suggested a population of recently formed families with young children, who were saving to buy a site-built home. An analysis of 1960 census data confirmed this shift. The greatest concentration of mobile homes was at the fringes of rapidly growing urban areas, particularly in the West and the South:

> The largest group of trailer dwellers are young lower middle-class working families who are looking for a better way of life but cannot yet afford to buy a permanent home in the suburbs. The residents of trailer housing, thus, may view their home on wheels as an inexpensive escape into suburbia which will enable them to save for a permanent home while being able to immediately get a foot into the suburban door. Thus, the attractiveness of mobile home living lies not in its "mobileness" but, instead, in having a place to call one's own home and perhaps a small garden and a lawn on which the family barbecues can be held.[9]

The ten-wide appeared on the market just as this shift was beginning. It provided the "new" mobile home family with a unit well suited to its objectives: more space and less mobility. A year after it was introduced, four other companies were showing ten-wide models. By 1957, approximately a dozen manufacturers, out of the more than three hundred comprising the industry, offered at least one ten-wide. In 1960, the ten-wide dominated production, but it was already being challenged by a 12-foot-wide unit introduced the previous year.[10] By 1969, a 14-foot-wide, as well as double-wide, models were available.

The Question of Form

The distinction between the mobile home and the house trailer involved a shift in attitude, as well as use. Manufacturers no longer made trailers that could also serve as dwellings, but dwellings that happened to be mobile. In 1952, *Trailer Park Management Magazine* changed its name to *Mobile Home Park Management*. The following year, the industry's key association changed its name from the Trailer Coach Manufacturers Association to the Mobile Home Manufacturers Association (MHMA). All this had occurred before Elmer Frey's Tenwide.

The currency of the name identified a need still searching for an appropriate form. That search was carried on simultaneously by both manufacturers and users.

The shifting sentiments of the industry were well expressed by Frey, writing in *Trailer Dealer:*

> I believe that products should be called exactly what they are. . . . If you saw a truck and a semitrailer loaded with a bulldozer, would you say, "There goes a trailer?" No—you would say, "Look at that bulldozer!" By the same token, when you see a man towing his home, why do you call it a trailer? Why not say, "There goes a man towing his home!" Why not call it exactly what it is—a home which is mobile—hence a MOBILE HOME.[11]

The name change, which dealers, manufacturers, and owners were slow to assimilate, was only part of the effort to shift identity. A stronger expression of what manufacturers thought about their product and where its market lay was reflected in the models they offered. Each manufacturer faced the problem of deciding what the mobile home, as distinct from the house trailer, should look like. Prefabricated builders faced a similar problem relating their products to a market, but they approached it from a different angle. From the start they knew that they were making site-fixed houses, whereas the mobile home manufacturers were discovering this after the fact. Many prefabricators also perceived themselves as theorists of industrialized housing and the pioneers of modern design. They had read the tracts and assimilated the rhetoric. But the mobile home manufacturers, excepting a few pioneers of the 1930s, seemed virtually ignorant of these views.

From the 1920s through at least the 1950s, the theorists of industrialized housing were concerned with the relation of form and function to the appearance of the industrialized house. Function meant not only how the dwelling was used, but the way it was manufactured. The issue was, should housing produced by new methods, particularly factory prefabrication, reflect those methods in its appearance? In a 1935 symposium sponsored by *House and Garden,* Raymond Parsons, an engineer with Johns-Manville Corporation, expressed the prevailing ideology:

> It can almost be taken for granted that when good prefabricated houses become a fact their architectural style will be different from the quaint English cottages and Cape Cod Colonials that are the present favorites of the speculative builders. The idea that we should take new and better building materials and mould them into the lines and textures of old materials possessing any number of short comings is abhorrent. . . .
> And still I think, that even among prefabricators, there are a

few who feel that the public is not going to accept anything new or revolutionary. They seem to think that we should soften the shock of change by inserting a transitional period combining new construction methods and old materials. And so they are trying to make or insert, tapestry brick finishes on sheet materials and things of that sort. The result must always look like what it is—a cheap imitation.

At the same symposium, Howard Fisher, president of General Homes, added:

> The final decision in the matter of design will of course depend on what the public wants. But in everything else the public has shown a preference for the best modern design, and I doubt that it will pay extra for fake imitations of the past when they buy their houses. . . .
> The public's conception of style has heretofore been much more advanced in the case of their automobile, for example, than in the case of their house; but I believe that they are going to develop an equally advanced taste in houses.[12]

The other side of this debate allowed for a degree of independence between method and form. It argued, in effect, that the method of production has a form independent of its products.[13] Therefore, form could respond to public tastes even if it was inclined toward imitations. On more pragmatic grounds, it sought to avoid the opposition of regulators and a tradition-bound public. Massachusetts Institute of Technology Professor Burnham Kelly later wrote:

> Today it is principally the houses of unconventional materials such as steel and aluminum and those of unconventional architectural appearance that are apt to arouse suspicion and opposition, although many communities try to exclude prefabricated houses simply because they are small and inexpensive, and therefore likely to give little aid in meeting local tax burdens. In regard to appearance, there has been a strong tendency to make the prefabricated house indistinguishable from the conventional house and to abandon flat roof and battens.[14]

Within the mobile home industry itself, the important design issue was not the relation between production methods and product form, but rather the more mundane, but vital, issue of the relation between the purchasers' concept of the product they were buying and the industry's idea of what it was producing. If the product was a trailer, shouldn't it look like something made for travel, with features commonly associated with cars, ships, and trains? But, if the object was a dwelling, shouldn't it resemble a house? These questions were answered through the designs manufacturers exhibited and customers purchased. Every manufacturer had to take a bit of a gamble here, working from an accepted model, but pushing at its boundaries to distinguish its unique product. Adding to the complexity of this process were the actions of others who could indirectly influence design. There were the highway authorities determining if wider models could be transported; park developers establishing lot sizes; lenders deciding on what was a good risk; town zoning boards; and neighbors, all of whom might have something to say about the form of the mobile home.[15]

Looking at the modern mobile home and reflecting on its evolution it is tempting to conclude that its form, as well as use, were clearly heading toward a simulation of the site-built house. But from the perspective of the 1954 trailer show, plurality was more evident than consensus. The distinctions between travel trailers, house trailers, and mobile homes were not yet very clear. The forms and features of each were still relatively interchangeable. The introduction of the ten-wide and the emergence of a new mobile home market only began to clarify the lines of development.

On Being House-like vs. Vehicle-like

The obvious advantage of the ten-wide mobile home was its increased floor area. Less apparent, but no less significant to manufacturers, was that the cost of producing this added space was not proportionally greater. One could have more space at a lower cost per square foot, and without the worry of movable joints and complex set-up. How to use the increased space, however, was not immediately apparent. The Marshfield Homes' first Tenwide featured a corridor, but the initial floor plans of other wider models were essentially the same as those in narrower units. The additional width was used for more storage, kitchen, and living-room space. In the 8-foot-wide house trailer, space had always been at a premium, and circulation area had to be reduced to a minimum. As units got longer, and included separate bedrooms and complete bathrooms and kitchens, circulation simply occurred through the middle rooms. If you slept in the end bedroom this didn't pose a problem, but for those in the middle bedroom it was a different story. In the travel trailer, the secret to creating livable space was to make a convertible area to fit several uses, and to tolerate a lack of privacy among family members—the accommodations were only temporary. In the house trailer, livability still demanded a capacity for transformation, but a high priority for the newly gained space was greater privacy. Privacy would seem to be most easily achieved with bedroooms at opposite ends of the unit, yet though such designs were available, they never achieved the popularity of the rear bedroom models.

Cutaway view of a typical eight-wide showing a walk-through middle bedroom.

This 1957, "ten-wide" by Peerless still retained the walk-through corridor in the bathroom, but placed the kitchen at the front end of the unit.

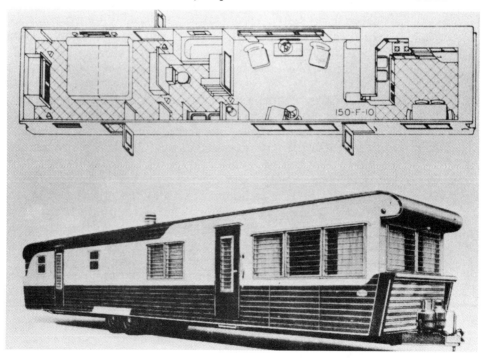

By 1960, there was a consensus on the proper use of the ten-wides' increased area. The corridor scheme had become the standard plan for such models. Consumers' preference for more privacy over increased storage was telling. If the philosophy behind the design of travel trailers and house trailers had still been current, a storage wall would surely have occupied the new space; but the mobile home was evaluated on different criteria: by comparing it with a conventional house floor plan. In this language, storage walls said "mobility," while a corridor meant "dwelling." This interpretation was further supported by a preference for bedrooms clustered at the rear of the unit, rather than at opposite ends. The latter arrangement has the advantage of eliminating the need for any corridor, but it was not a plan common in either homes or apartments.

The clustering of bedrooms at the rear of the mobile home was not the only element that reflected cultural ideals. In 1959, several manufacturers began to offer models with a front-end kitchen, an arrangement they called the "galley plan." The typical house trailer floor plan placed kitchen and bathroom back to back, or as close together as possible to shorten plumbing runs and reduce the possibility of pipes freezing. In the galley plan, the kitchen faced the street, where a woman preparing meals could presumably spot approaching visitors and keep an eye on children playing. Typically, the front kitchen was separated from the living room by a pass-through counter. The door opened into the living room rather than the kitchen, making the entry area of the house the living room, an arrangement common to the suburban tract homes of the 1950s and 1960s.

Beginning with the house trailer, a second door became a standard safety feature. In the mobile home, the second door was primarily an emergency exit, often with no stairs leading to it. Following the curbside orientation of trailer design, both doors, and the corridor to the rear bedroom were on the left side of the unit. As length increased through the 1960s, the corridor scheme resulted in a "shotgun" type plan: one entered the unit, turned left and looked straight down the hall some forty feet or more into the rear bedroom. Such a plan was rare in conventional houses, and it exaggerated the linear proportions of the single-wide. It made the person entering aware of the thin-wood framed wall that separated exterior and interior. In a site-built house, the flatness of the exterior wall is broken by window sill, door frame, and overhanging eaves. In the mobile home, the flatness is unrelieved. Consequently, the view down the corridor is accelerated by the smooth unbroken surface of plywood sheathing and window glass. It was not until the early 1970s that a few manufacturers saw the shotgun plan as a feature that

The bay window, a modest but important pop-out detail, was featured on 1955 Ventoura models, along with higher ceilings over the living room. Although Ventoura at the time was experimenting with a ranch style model, most of its production consisted of shiny metal-skinned boxes.

exposed the boxiness of the single-wide unit. So they introduced models with the second door opposite the entryway and placed the bedroom corridor there as well. Soon, with double-wide models, the floor plans would be borrowed directly from conventional house designs.

Other details of the mobile home which distinguished it from the house trailer and reflected the buyers' changing preferences were more house-like doors and windows. The trailer door was, at most, 6 feet high, and swung outward, like vehicle doors. House doors are around 7 feet high and swing inward, allowing a storm or screen door to be attached. With increased ceiling height in the mobile home living room, it became possible to use taller doors. They still had to swing out, but screen doors could be attached inside. Many manufacturers introduced doors with jalousie windows, and Trailorama's 1955 pull-out double-wide unit featured a sliding glass patio door.

Along with house-like doors, many manufacturers were featuring more house-like windows. The awning-type, popular in trailers of the 1930s, were replaced by casement-type windows beginning in the late 1940s. Some models, like the 1946 Spartan, the 1950 Pacemaker, and the 1952 PanAm, had wraparound

By the mid-1950s more curtains were being added to soften the shiny wood
paneling of trailer interiors. Many built-in pieces of furniture remained,
especially in smaller models.

front windows, suggesting a hybrid of the bay window and a
windshield. In the early 1950s, several manufacturers offered
picture windows, usually with a large fixed pane and sections
that opened on the sides. By 1955, genuine bay windows were
introduced. Ventoura offered an optional bay window that slid
in for transport and popped out when the unit was at a site.
Among other advantages, the bay window had a sill for plants, a
lamp, or knickknacks, a feature absent from the typical trailer
or mobile home window. These seemingly insignificant details
were the main focus of full-page advertisements, suggesting
that the shift from house trailer to mobile home had to do with
more than increased width and area.

The changing treatment of windows and doors reflected the
fact that these features were meant to be seen from the interior,
as part of a home rather than as part of a vehicle. This shift was
also evident in other aspects of interior decor. The cafe curtains
common in railroad passenger cars and yachts were replaced
with venetian blinds by the mid-1940s and, a decade later, by
floor-to-ceiling drapes tucked neatly behind valances. Interiors
of this period were often finished in a light colored plywood

such as birch veneer. The same material often covered the ceiling, and all surfaces were lacquered. Built-in furniture was usually made of plywood, often from left over scraps of wall panelling sheets. Floors were covered with linoleum. The result was an interior as shiny and hard as the metal sheathed exterior. In such spaces, the use of draperies must have had a visually softening, as well as a sound-deadening effect.

In the late 1940s, trailer buyers began expressing a preference for units with detached rather than built-in and transformable furniture, especially tables and chairs that could be rearranged. Unlike built-in furniture that could be regarded as "equipment," loose furniture could be made or purchased in an identifiable style. The "Early American" style, upholstered in the same fabrics as the drapes, was a favorite. In small rooms, however, trailer furniture had to be scaled down to fit. With the introduction of the wider mobile home, full-size furniture was introduced and promoted as another selling point. Other interior details featured as "flash" (a term in the industry for showy details that help sell a unit), were built-in TV cabinets and fake brick fireplaces.

Just as furnishings initially had to be scaled down to fit the trailer, kitchen and bathroom fixtures were typically smaller than those found in houses. By the late 1940s, most units were equipped with electric refrigerators and bottled gas stoves. Hot and cold tap water was delivered by pumps, and a forced-air

"I wouldn't give up my home on wheels for anything."

Larger kitchens and bathrooms were an important selling feature for people considering year-round mobile home living. Especially important were full-sized appliances and house-like rather than yatch-like cabinets.

furnace in the kitchen circulated air through floor ducts. The house trailer bathroom was small, but more fully equipped than that of the travel trailer. The bathroom floor no longer doubled as a shower pan, as it had in travel trailers, with the addition of a separate stall shower in house trailers, but bathtubs were still rare.[16] Flush toilets were now common, but in some parks, sewage lines were not adequate to permit their use. In California outside toilets were required until the late 1940s, even for independent units (i.e., those containing their own bathrooms). Some units throughout this period also continued to use Pullman-type lavatories in which the sink and toilet seat could be folded into a single cabinet.

In the mobile home, larger, better-appointed kitchens and bathrooms were expected. Many ads focused on kitchens finished with attractive cabinets, double sinks, built-in stoves, clocks, and knickknack shelves. Even small details, like a set of canisters displayed on a counter, suggested more space and greater conventionality. In bathrooms, tubs became more common, along with vanity sinks and mirrored walls. To reduce humidity in this space, separate vent fans were also introduced.

If there was a lingering question whether the mobile home could serve as a comfortable year-round home, the appearance of larger and more completely appointed kitchens and bathrooms was probably the most important feature to assure the hesitating prospective buyer.

As house-like interior details became more popular, vehicle details faded out. The clever placement of storage areas above cabinets or below beds, and the use of collapsible or transformable furniture, such as Pullman berths, had become associated with the spartan nature of the travel trailer and the house trailer. Mobile home owners wanted to identify with a different image and way of life. Often this meant giving up features that remained eminently practical in the enlarged but still restrictive confines of the mobile home.

The Split Imagery of Interior and Exterior

Even though house trailer and early mobile home interiors were becoming more house-like in plan and decor, exterior design remained tied to a vehicle-based imagery. Taylor Meloan, professor of business at Indiana University, observed in his 1954 study of the industry:

> Now that mobile homes are used almost exclusively as semipermanent and permanent housing one would surmise that manufacturers would make the external appearance of their products more homelike. This is not the case. Generally speaking, the larger companies have not tried to make their homes look like conventional homes.
>
> Illustrative of an exception is a manufacturer of 30- and 35-foot mobile homes that resemble small clapboard cottages with shingle roofs. The interiors are similar to their other coaches. These cottages may be purchased without running gear for permanent installation or with undercarriages for use as mobile dwellings. In spite of their resemblance to conventional homes, they have not been popular. The majority of mobile home buyers apparently prefer aluminum or steel structures designed and painted so they appear more like automotive equipment than like conventional dwellings.[17]

Meloan's observations were made before the ten-wide was introduced, and before the demographic shift in mobile home occupants had become apparent.

Manufacturers of the immediate postwar period still thought of the exterior of the mobile home as an object to be seen with a car. The sleek, silver 1946 Spartan Glider had rounded edges, a forward canted front, and a wraparound windshield-type front window. A band of three stripes made a lightning-like streak from front to rear. Motion symbolism, in the form of lightning

Exploded view of a Skyline mobile home showing the interior corridor arrangement that became an industry standard by the late 1950s.

stripes or waves, was as common in trailer design as it was on automobiles. The 1946 Terra Cruiser, for example, featured a tail-like protrusion on the rear of its rounded body, suggesting a fin. This model was offered in two tones with whitewall tires. A family could select its house trailer to match the colors of its car.

Although streamlined, vehicle-like bodies dominated the market, other approaches were being tried. The 1947 Elcar Sun Coach featured a screened-in porch and sunscreens over a horizontal ribbon strip of windows. The streamlined design was still emphasized when in motion, but the porch and sun screens unfolded at the site to transform the exterior into something more livable and more house-like. The smaller windows of the Sun Coach were bracketed by shutters. The 1954 Prairie Schooner also featured a screened-in, fold-out porch that served as an entry area.

During World War II, when strategic materials such as metal were scarce, hardboard, homosote, and other forms of pressboard were used as exterior sheathing. Often they were covered with a canvas skin, painted to provide waterproofing. By the early 1950s, metal had become the standard sheathing material, especially aluminum because of its light weight. The metal sheeting was either tacked onto the wood frame or laminated to the exterior plywood. Some manufacturers, such as Spartan and Airstream, however, continued to use the metal skin as an integral part of the structure, riveting it to metal ribs as in aircraft construction.

The use of metal sheathing undoubtedly influenced the form of the house trailer shell. The metal, delivered in large rolls, was more easily attached to flat sides than to curved surfaces. Decorative patterns, usually corrugations, diamonds, or fan shapes, could be crimped into the sheets as they were drawn off the rolls. Roof shapes were simplified so that curves occurred at the front and rear only, rather than on all sides. The resulting "squared-off" look also simplified interior detailing and made it easier to apply plywood sheets. Unlike the house trailer, the mobile home looked more boxy; still shiny, but less streamlined or sculptural.

Experimentation with the external appearance of mobile homes concentrated primarily on two images: one derived from the trailer aesthetic, which treated the unit as part of a car/trailer ensemble, the other based on a house aesthetic, which promoted the image of a permanent dwelling in a park setting. However, a third approach, which sàw little success, promoted the mobile home as an industrial product. In the mid-1950s, the design firm of Raymond Loewy was commissioned to develop a new line of mobile homes, though apparently none were manufactured. In 1963, Marlette Company commissioned a Chicago industrial design firm to develop a new image, which resulted in models that looked like they might have been designed by the architect Mies van der Rohe. Both the interior and exterior design was modularized. Exterior elevations were made up of standardized glass or sandwich panels joined with matte black metal channels. The top and bottom lines of the elevation were also detailed with black metal strips. When set up on the site, the front entrance was to be completed with a platform capped with a canopy. The hand of the professional designer was evident in the way joints matched up: floor tiles and counter edges, partitions and windows, wall panel and counter widths. These were units conceived at the drafting table rather than on the factory floor. Despite, or perhaps because of, its novelty, the line died rather quickly. In less than a year Marlette went back to producing more conventional units. Buyers might accept that their homes were made in factories, but apparently they didn't want them to look that way.

More curious even than the Miesian-styled model Marlette

In the early 1960s, Marlette Homes decided to treat the mobile home as an object of industrial design. It hired a Chicago firm, which produced the model shown here among others in a new line. The public didn't buy the idea, and the line soon went out of production.

offered was a prototype developed by the Taliesin Architects of the Frank Lloyd Wright Foundation. In 1970, National Homes commissioned a model using "prairie style" principles: long, low horizontal lines and projecting eaves that reflect the "earth-line" of the Midwestern landscape. National's final version was used only for display and never marketed as a commercial model.[18]

The differences between the vehicle and house approaches to exterior design are well illustrated in Ventoura models of the mid-1950s. In 1954, Ventoura introduced its duplex "Land Yacht," with an exterior sheathed in shallow, horizontally ribbed aluminum siding. It had a dark strip at the base and below the roof. The roofline itself rippled back in two curved-edged steps defining the higher ceiling over the entry area and the second level of the unit. The smaller awning-type windows had rounded edges, and large picture windows on all three sides of the living room provided a view. One year later, Ventoura

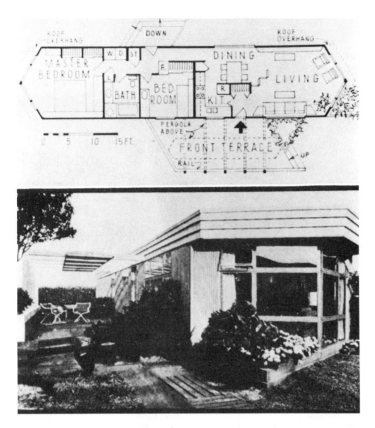

In 1970, National Homes commissioned the Frank Lloyd Wright Foundation to design a mobile home using Prairie style principles and avoiding objectionable box-like shapes. The Foundation also developed designs of units and parks for the Wisconsin Department of Natural Resources.

In 1955, Ventoura offered a duplex model that was intended to be house-like in its exterior, as well as its interior. This model was soon replaced by a more trailer-like design.

unveiled a radically restyled duplex trailer which made no visual references to yachts or boats. The lower main section was defined by a broad pediment, half of it being the actual roofline of the unit and the other half consisting of an appliqué. The rounded edge transition to the second story was replaced by a slight overhang terminating in a flat roof section. The dark horizontal band at the base was retained, but with vertical ribs, intended, no doubt, to emphasize the height of the unit (12½ feet). The most curious detail of the elevation was a brick patterned section that looked like a chimney. It rose above the first floor pediment, tucked under the face plate of the second story roof, and ended a few inches above the top. Since there was no fireplace in the unit, the detail was purely cosmetic. A company advertisement of the model showed its base masked by planter boxes sprouting flowers, and a fenced-in patio area. The caption beneath the rendering boasted "A Real Home."

Ventoura was not alone in approaching the single-wide elevation as a house in its design. In 1958, Midwest introduced the "Cozy Cottage," which had lap siding, a saddle roof, double-hung windows with attached ornamental shutters, and screen doors. In 1960, West-Wood produced the "Park Estate," which did not emulate cottage detailing so much as "contemporary" house styling. It had a slightly recessed house-type doorway, a simulated fieldstone wainscot at the front end, and a pitched shed roof. Several manufacturers began to change the ceiling height over the living room, both to enhance the spaciousness of the interior and to provide more house-like lines to the exterior.

Strategies of Accommodation

The evolution of the mobile home from vehicle-like to house-like was not an unquestioned development. Although the industry's main association had changed its name from the "Trailer Coach" to "Mobile Home" Manufacturers Association, most of its members and the public still informally referred to mobile homes as trailers. The house trailer had established a place for itself as a special form of year-round housing for a particular, but limited, segment of the population. The mobile home was an attempt to enlarge the market by moving beyond this group. Even among manufacturers who were pursuing this market, however, attitudes toward design differed. As recently as 1976, the year the Housing and Urban Development construction code went into effect, some manufacturers at the regional show in South Bend were displaying "shiny metal boxes" while others were trying to make their units look indistinguishable from site-built homes. Possibly the makers of the shiny boxes were simply suffering from inertia, failing to see that change was necessary. Yet experimentation was active, with different design approaches reflecting different tacit strategies for assimilating a new type of housing.

Out of the various design experiments which characterized the mobile home's development, two general strategies are evident. In the first, vehicle-like features and house-like features are combined freely on the exterior. A model might have streamline detailing—two-tone horizontal corrugated siding with the front end tapered upward, but also shutters flanking a picture or bay window. The interior features would be almost exclusively house-like, except for the floor plan, which would be constrained by the vehicular envelope. Here the hybrid character of the mobile home is openly expressed in its features. Anthropologist Homer Barnett calls this strategy of assimilation syncretism.[19]

Syncretism draws on the positive associations of the different elements which make up the innovation. In the case of the mobile home, there are positive associations with vehicles, especially cars, that can be used as selling points. The trailer built like a yacht connotes luxury, while features associated

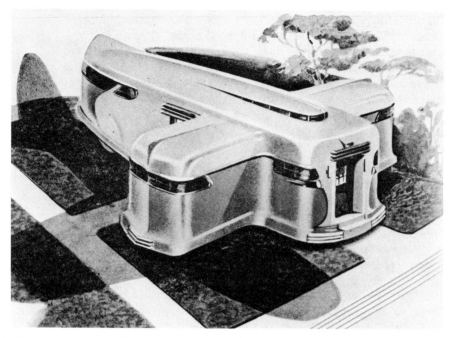

After World War II many manufacturers hoped to return to vacation trailer production. A series of advertisements by Palace Corporation, published during the war, showed units whose designs were inspired by advanced technology. In this artist's rendering, a none too subtle reference to an airplane is the basis for a streamlined trailer shown hovering above the ground.

with planes may suggest technological sophistication. The theorist/practitioners of modern architecture often employed syncretism in developing a style which they hoped would be appropriate to the "Machine Age." Le Corbusier, for example, took features directly from ships, planes, and trains in some of his buildings. Syncretism asks the adopter to think cross-categorically; to accept that a mobile home, for example, can be reasonably categorized and treated as both a vehicle and as a house. As a strategy, it stresses function over form, suggesting that meaning should be based on how a thing is used rather than on conventions associated with form.

The alternative strategy of assimilation is conventionalization in which the innovation is made to look more like the object it is replacing. Since the mobile home is offered as an alternative to the site-built house, through conventionalization its features become more house-like. Conventionalization usually occurs as an incremental transformation; there is a search for the features most salient to the desired identification.

From an institutional perspective, syncretism requires that

different and formerly unrelated institutions coordinate their efforts. If the mobile home is a hybrid of both vehicle and house, then the institutions concerned with regulating each must coordinate their efforts constructing for it a new common category. By contrast, with conventionalization, regulation falls primarily to a single institution or closely related institutions, which still must struggle with the question of standards encompassing form and meaning, as well as use.

Both the strategies of syncretism and conventionalization are evident in the transformation of the house trailer into the mobile home. They play off of each other in a kind of gigantic game of Mr. Potato Head, in which institutions and individuals vie with each other to attach that part which gives the object its recognized identity and ultimate acceptability.

Modifications by Owners

Among those deciding what the mobile home should look like are the owners themselves.[20] They often have been responsible for determining how their units would be placed on a site, expanded, modified to accommodate local weather, and decorated. Many of their changes and additions were to make their homes more comfortable, particularly by providing more space for activities and storage; others were to make their homes more attractive and socially acceptable.

Just as the mobile home manufacturers were guided by different images of their product as they tried to style it to meet market needs and avoid local resistance, the modifications users made suggest similar images and strategies. On the one hand, there were owners who saw the mobile home as part of a park/trailer ensemble. They did not mind if their homes looked like trailers, with hitch and lights attached, while surrounded by house-like, site-built additions. On the other hand, there were those who seemed to have had a house/subdivision image in mind. Their modifications were clearly intended to make their dwelling indistinguishable from a site-built house.

The most obvious features identifying a mobile home as a vehicle is its undercarriage, or chassis, and hitch. Consequently, camouflaging these became an important way for owners to change its appearance from vehicle to dwelling. Since mobile homes often were used at a site for several years, they were set on blocks, the tires removed and stored so that they would not be damaged by weather and sun.[21] Once mounted on blocks, the unit sat about two feet above the ground with its chassis and utility connections fully exposed. Skirting, typically consisting of sheet metal or hardboard, was used to hide the undercarriage as well as the bicycles, lawn mowers, and hoses that might be stored under the unit. Writing in *Trailer Topics*, Jane Liebetrau cautioned that:

> One of the greatest eyesores and one which can defeat even the most carefully planned gardens and patio arrangements is the black vacant space beneath the trailer. Not only is this black space downright unfriendly looking but it makes a heavy trailer perched several feet above the ground look ridiculous, not at all reflecting the homelike efficiency and comfort of the interior. For the sake of good design this gaping space should be skirted with something giving the appearance of equal weight with the trailer. . . .
>
> The front of the trailer with its [propane] bottles is always unsightly. Two planted boxes tall enough to hide the bottle, can be placed together with both ends meeting at an arrow-like point.[22]

Griffith and Lillian Borgeson, in their 1959 book *Mobile Homes and Travel Trailers*, devoted a chapter to ideas for landscaping the mobile home lot. It included pictures of flower-lined entryways, concrete steps, and awnings that extended the length of the unit. The effect of these recommendations, like those of Jane Liebetrau, was to hide the undercarriage and hitch, while making the home look more permanent. Better parks required that all units be skirted, and some charged a landscaping fee which might include such additions as storage sheds, carports, and awnings. By the 1960s, many municipalities required skirting.

Another problem with the mobile home set on blocks was entering and leaving it. The typical solution was a set of metal pipe framed steps, not unlike the kind pilots use to get into fighters. The cheapest of these had no top stoop on which to stand or place groceries while opening the outward swinging door, nor space for chatting with a neighbor, or sitting to observe street traffic. For a stoop to be adequate it had to be larger and preferably covered for protection from the weather. A more desirable entry would have room for plants, porcelain cats, plastic ducks, pinwheel daisies, and other regionally fashionable doodads. In the early 1970s, several parks came up with a more radical solution to the problems of the undercarriage and the elevated front door. They dug a shallow trench and backed the mobile home into it, so that its final height was one step above the walk. This also improved the proportion of the unit, bringing the height–width relationship closer to that of a ranch house.

Even when the mobile home was skirted and provided with a stoop, the hitch projecting out in front announced to all that this

Example of a single-shed type addition in Crawford, Colorado. The original unit here is an 8' x 45' house trailer; the added room is used as a workshop by the potter and jeweler who live here. On the extreme left is a green house used for growing vegetables. Hay bales have been piled on the North to provide insulation.

was a towable dwelling. Making the hitch more prominent were the bottled gas units typically mounted on top of it. A 1966 article in *Trailer Topics* listed five basic solutions to the problem: cutting off the hitch (if legally permitted), hiding it with plants, placing a planter on top of it, running skirting around it and, finally, building a bench over it (it was suggested that the bench not be too inviting, "lest neighbors park themselves under your window for leisurely hours of conversation"). The ultimate solution to the unsightly hitch would come in the mid-1970s, when manufacturers began to offer an optional hitch that could be unbolted.

In their attempt to find more room, owners frequently built additions. The most common of these was a shed, attached to the entry, that served as a mudroom and utility porch. A 1940 article in *Trailer Travel* commented on a vacation cottage consisting of a trailer completely enclosed within a shed, with a porch running along its entire front side.[23] Although an apparently exotic development for the time, within a year the use of trailers as temporary housing for workers during the war would make shed additions commonplace. At Willow Run, for example, a typical weekend project was to build sheds.

After the war, shed additions became more elaborate and permanent. If a family expected to stay in a park for a long time, or if it owned its lot, it usually added some kind of shed. Several manufacturers, such as Alum-O-Room and Add-A-Room, began marketing prefabricated sheds. Along with their recommendations for landscaping mobile homes, the Borgesons suggested adding a shed-type porch or cabana. "Mobile home dwellers" they wrote, "are not Gypsies. They put down roots, build picket fences, plant."[24] By the early 1960s, shed additions were popular enough for *Trailer Topics* to feature articles like "Immobile Mobile Homes," without intended irony. Details were offered, for example, on how H. B. Ellis added a 14' x 20' living room with a fireplace onto his mobile home. "At first glance," the article observed, "the casual passerby wouldn't notice that this pleasant home is really a mobile home."[25] Farris and Lorraine Bynum's "House With a Trailer Inside" consisted of a 41' x 8' trailer with a 12' x 48' site-built addition on one side. Since Farris, an itinerant electrician, had retired, he and Lorraine could enjoy "the conveniences of a mobilehome [sic] and a conventional home as well. That is kind of like having their cake and eating it too."[26]

Often a shed addition started as an awning-covered, concrete pad carport. Later, part or all of the area would be enclosed, forming a long, narrow, unpartitioned space. In warm climates this space might be left screened, while in colder regions, it would be insulated and warmed with a stove or some other source of heat. The floor level of the slab and the main unit were usually two feet apart, and when the shed was enclosed, the difference in levels was rarely rectified. The metal siding of the unit was usually left exposed as one of the walls of the new interior space, and exterior details such as attached shutters, skirting, and lights, become part of an interior space with little if any modification. While in most respects the shed additions on mobile homes were not unlike ones tacked onto site-built houses, the final ensemble often looked as if the mobile home was the addition rather than the shed.

A variation of the shed addition has spaces on both sides of the home, with one side an activity room and the other a carport and utility area. A common Southwestern version of this double shed consisted of one large roof covering the entire unit and additions. Open space between the roof and the mobile home allowed air to circulate in the summer. The resulting ensemble often looks something like a box car tucked in a hay barn.

A mobile home with double-shed additions outside of Phoenix, Arizona. The high roof over the mobile home provides shade and air circulation for cooling.

More elaborate than the double shed was an arrangement in which two or more mobile homes or trailers were connected with site-built sheds and breezeways into what might be called a compound unit. In some cases the compound consisted of two units joined longitudinally, with new doors cut for circulation, effectively forming a double-wide. Other units were arranged in an L- or H-shaped configuration. In the L-shaped arrangement, a new entry was usually constructed at the crux of the two units. In the H-shaped arrangement, the connecting piece might be a site-built room or a separate trailer which served as an entry.

The compound unit took advantage of the low cost of used trailers. They provided instant space complete with wiring, plumbing, and a waterproof exterior all at a low cost and without too much labor. Owners often attempted to make all floor heights the same, with entry porches and shed additions elevated as well. And they might put a new roof over the ensemble, preventing leaks and giving the whole more visual unity. Compound developments were more common in rural areas where occupants owned their lots, neighbors were more tolerant, and building regulations were not enforced.

A literal example of a seed unit. The house trailer is being used to live in, while a conventional house is being built around it.

Owner-built additions to mobile homes illustrate what the Danish architect Peter Stephensen calls the "seed analogy" of building.[27] He noticed that Danes building a second or vacation home often started with a very small unit, just big enough for immediate needs, and as the family and income grew, added rooms to the house. In later years, as children left home, additions were torn down and the house reduced to a manageable size. Many theorists of modern architecture and planning have suggested that the ideal prefabricated dwelling would consist of standardized parts flexible enough to allow for, and even encourage, alterations and additions.[28]

In an ad hoc fashion, the modification of house trailers and mobile homes illustrates the seed analogy of housing. It extends a rural tradition in site-built homes of building a small cottage as the original dwelling, onto which shed additions are successively added. A walk down the alleys of most older communities reveals a variety of additions in striking contrast to the uniformity of the facades along the street.

The way in which people modify their units, working within site and budget constraints, produces a rich and varied form of housing. The contrast between site-built additions and the factory-made core can be provocative and at times humorous. Often it is the site-built shed that looks like the original core and the mobile home like the addition. Sometimes there appears to have been a literal collision, in which a trailer has smashed into a site-built house and stayed there. Ironically, these kinds of modifications, which demonstrate better than anything else the capacity of the mobile home to evolve into a genuine dwelling,[29] are often disparaged by manufacturers, who fear they will provoke images of trailer camp slums.

Complexity in the Experience of Living in Houses

It might seem easy to dismiss the changes which both users and manufacturers made to the form of the mobile home as superficial mimicking of features on traditional, site-built housing. Borrow a window detail here, a roofline there, and before you know it, Mr. Potato Head is starting to look like a house. Certainly some of the models designed upon such casual borrowing were silly if not ugly; yet, there was something else carried over in this process. Changes in the layout of the mobile home, particularly of public and private spaces, suggest a response to the experience of living in houses. Two important dimensions of this experience identified by psychologists are complexity and adaptability.

Complexity[30] is experienced, in part, in the differentiation of interior from exterior. One aspect of the complexity found in the ordinary house is that its floorplan cannot be read from the outside. Ask people who live in a site-built house to describe it, and they will often begin by telling you the number of bedrooms it has; but ask people in a mobile home and they will tell you its exterior dimensions.

In the single-wide mobile home with a shotgun corridor, the interior organization can be read from the external elevation, and the shape of the exterior is apparent from inside. There is a transparency, or thinness, which is more than physical. The double-wide and single-wide with extensive shed additions, by contrast, restore the complexity of the typical site-built house. The desired independence of interior from exterior may have to do with the public and private faces of the house, what occupants show to their neighbors, and the image they give themselves.[31]

In modern housing in general, much of the complexity of dwellings has been lost. The "free plan," advocated since the 1920s by architects of the modern movement and adopted by builders because it reduced costs makes tighter living areas seem more spacious by eliminating partitions between rooms.

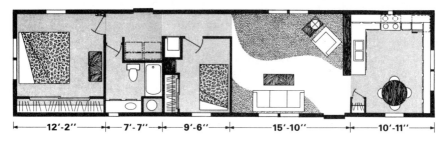

MODEL: 6014-2K   NET EXTERIOR FLOOR SIZE: 56'-0" x 13'-8"

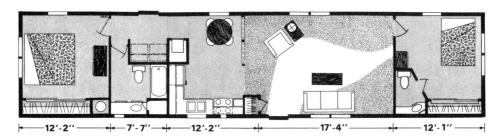

MODEL: 6514-2D   NET EXTERIOR FLOOR SIZE: 61'-4" x 13'-8"

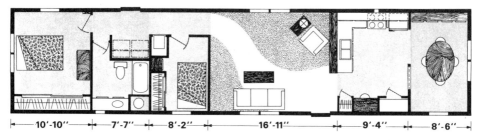

MODEL: 6514-2B1   NET EXTERIOR FLOOR SIZE: 61'-4" x 13'-8"

One of the ways in which the mobile home tried to shed its image as a trailer was to abandon the shotgun corridor-type plan. These 1976 floor plans of models by Nashua Homes attempt to break up circulation patterns, providing the interior with a feeling of greater complexity.

But the free plan also requires combining functions and accepting an informality which may not always be desired. Another change dictated by construction economics and technology has been the disappearance of attics and basements. The basement, which was once needed for the furnace and its bulky fuel, can now be eliminated because furnaces can be placed in closets and fed by gas. Similarly, the attic, which provided dusty storage and extra play space, has been replaced by the garage, which is often too stuffed with items to leave room for the car. These spaces not only had specific purposes, they also invited unintended activities and meanings (the attic as a children's clubhouse, the basement as the dark and mysterious place where children often fear to go).[32] Both the owners of sparse modern homes and of mobile homes seem to prefer house forms with greater complexity and hence modify their dwellings to achieve it.

The transformation of house trailer into mobile home also suggests the importance of adaptability in the experience of dwelling. By adding to and changing the form of their housing, mobile home users were not only attempting to make their homes look more acceptable, they were also personalizing them. The act of dwelling involves what environmental psy-

Starter home, by Cardinal, designed to receive add-on rooms.

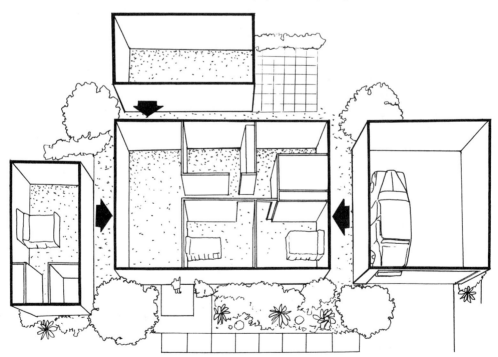

chologist Perla Korosec-Serfaty calls appropriation—taking control of, becoming familiar with, investing with meaning, cultivating and caring for, and displaying identity with a place or object.[33] Mobile homes' inexpensiveness encouraged modification and thereby helped to assure that owners would be satisfied.

Thinness

The changes in mobile homes—whether through conventionalization or syncretism—resulted in objects of unmistakable thinness. This quality is most apparent in the physical structure of the mobile home: in its lightness, shallow cross section, and the tactile experiences of living in it—the way walls bellow in the wind, floors deflect under foot, and roofs resonate with the sound of falling rain drops. Its thinness is evident in the shallow recesses and the characteristic appliqué look of details, whether structural or ornamental. "Thinness" is also apparent in something more subtle and figurative: in the imitative borrowing of elements, such as the photographed grain of an expensive wood laminated to the surface of cheap paneling, or details borrowed from different styles collaged on a single object. The figurative thinness of the mobile home consists of the way it casually borrows characteristics from other often unrelated objects. Both the literal and figurative aspects of thinness are indicative of how meaning, form, and use are associated with one another in the mobile home, and in American vernacular design in general.

The physical thinness of the mobile home is not without precedent. A tradition in American domestic architecture is the wooden house designed to be light, disposable, or portable. Among the earliest of such structures was the slab house, used in seventeenth-century Virginia, consisting of vertical boards nailed to a horizontal sill. The most common example of light wood-frame construction is the "stick-built" house, a colloquial term for buildings made with 2" x 4" wood studs and wire nails in either platform or balloon frame structures. Despite the lightness of the frame and the typical nonchalance with which it is nailed together, such structures have a great deal of rigidity. This construction technology was an early and significant American contribution to industrialized building. Developed in Chicago in 1833, it made possible the rapid and cheap erection of buildings using relatively unskilled labor. Contemporary descriptions of Chicago marveled at the speed with which buildings were put up. Whole walls could be nailed together on the ground and lifted into place with just a few men. By contrast, heavy timber-frame construction and buildings with masonry-

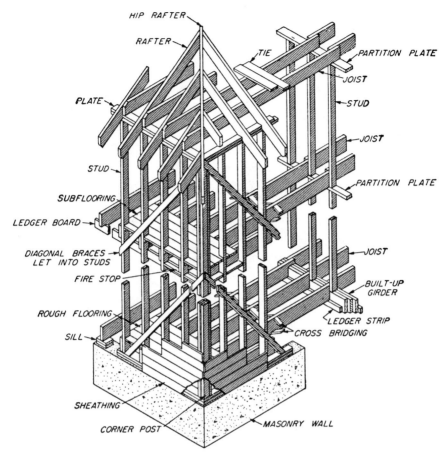

The Balloon Frame: lightweight construction using standardized 2' x 4' studs and wire nails.

bearing walls required skilled labor and work with heavy materials.

The thinness of stick-built construction is temporal as well as structural—buildings were meant to be used for a relatively short period of time. Historian J. B. Jackson, in an essay on the "moveable dwelling" in America, observes that the early balloon frame house

> was quick and simple to build, it was indifferent to local and folk architectural traditions, and it was seen as temporary; not that it would collapse, but that it would soon be sold and passed on to newcomers. Solon Robinson and other writers on western pioneering thus advised families to build their balloon frame houses as impersonally as possible so that they could be acceptable to any prospective purchaser.[34]

Building as appliqué analyzed by Robert Venturi, Denise Scott Brown, and Steven Izenour in "Learning from Levittown."

Twentieth-century advocates of industrialized building have frequently cited disposability as an important characteristic of modern house construction because it allows technological improvements to be easily introduced. Yet nineteenth-century stick-built construction already provided an economical form of disposable building. The framing members of a 2″ x 4″ structure could be easily shipped throughout the Midwest, especially to areas where timber was scarce. Before long, prefabricated houses were available through mail-order and catalogues and were widely distributed. The mobile home clearly falls within this tradition of building, its thin cross-section a strong confirmation of vernacular standards.

The need to build quickly and cheaply, which propelled the diffusion of stick-built construction, promoted an architecture that was not only physically thin, but figuratively thin. Figurative thinness, as suggested earlier, refers to the relationship between the physical features of a building, their meaning, and the way they are used. The figurative thinness of stick-built architecture is well illustrated in what architects Robert Venturi, Denise Scott Brown, and Steven Izenour call the "decorated shed," which occurs "where systems of space and structure are directly at the service of program, and ornamentation is applied independently of them."[35] These ornaments may be expensive materials or they may be painted on. The simplest form of the decorated shed is the western frontier town Main Street building with a false facade, suggesting a structure larger than the actual one found behind it.

Decorating the shed is just one technique for applying meaning to stick-built architecture. The ample houses of Walnut and Elm require a somewhat different approach, one which uses the structural elements of the house decoratively. The shingles which are applied to enclose the stud frame, for example, can be cut and placed in various geometric patterns. The trim facing over the ends of rafters can be shaped with a scroll saw into playful curves. The battens that seal the seams of exterior wall boards can be used to accentuate vertical lines. These structural elements can be used decoratively to articulate a flat surface, but they also can be used to evoke associations.

In *Architecture of Country Houses*,[36] the prominent nineteenth-century architect Andrew Jackson Downing advocated the use of appliqués on houses to evoke associations appropriate to their owner. The house of a pastor, for example, might be decorated with Gothic appliqués, while a banker's would be suitably finished with Italianate flourishes. The philosophical, and protopsychological, foundation for this approach to design rests in the eighteenth- and nineteenth-century belief that aesthetic sensation does not arise from the innate properties of materials or things but from their association with other objects that have meaning for us.[37] Thus, if the Gothic style is associated with Christian morality, Gothic features applied to a house are expected to evoke an association between that morality with the occupants of the house.

In the hands of practitioners like Downing, the theory of association suggested that the functional requirements of a house could be satisfied with a fairly generic box, whether of balloon frame or masonry construction, then ornamented with the appropriate appliqués. Historian George Hersey describes Downing's approach, and that of many of his contemporaries, as one which treats the house as "an appliance wrapped in a jacket."[38]

The predisposition to accept such an aesthetic is itself a manifestation of modern society's search for a way to manage change and, in America, to cope with constant migration and expansion. It was a way of taking an architectural kit of parts and by applying the pieces to new forms and a new landscape, to achieve a sense of familiarity and, hence, bring the environment under control. The result is an environment of borrowed, standard elements in a familiar yet individual collage.

The mobile home is composed almost entirely of materials that make allusions to other materials: metal siding with a wood grain pattern printed on it, interior paneling laminated with the photographic image of decorative wood, ceilings made of a material that looks like stucco but is actually foam padding, plastic hardware finished as if it were antique brass. Architect and critic Steven Izenour confirms the lineage of this characteristic of design from colonial times to the modern mobile home.

> One mobile home for sale in Virginia . . . featured a sunken living room which was sunken all of two inches. "The effect becomes totally two-dimensional, a paste-on look" . . . but this thin and conspicuous veneering is, in itself, a tradition in Ameri-

The house as an "appliance wrapped in a jacket."

The mobile home as an "appliance wrapped in a jacket" with paste-on portico.

can architecture: what appears to be stone facing on Mount Vernon is, in fact, ground up oyster shells cemented to wood.[39]

As transparent as these imitations are, they are necessary for the acceptance of the object as a whole. Imitative ready-mades brought together to form an essentially new object is characteristic of many of the most original artifacts of the American environment: the fast-food franchise, the gas station, and the speculatively built suburban house. On a larger scale, it is the method underlying the merchant builder's subdivision, the enclosed shopping mall, and the mobile home park.

Mobile Home Land:
The Search for Community

Trailer Estates

In the same year that the ten-wide mobile home made its debut, a new community was being planned in Bradenton, Florida. It had been conceived by Syd Adler, a young lawyer whose only previous experience in building was selling construction materials while working his way through college. Upon graduation, Adler went looking for opportunities in Florida. On a visit with a friend in Bradenton, he encountered one of the largest concentrations of trailer housing in the country. Most trailer households were of retired people, many of them "snowbirds" who moved South for the winter and returned to more substantial homes back North for the summer. Adler's friend was in real estate, selling lots for the American dream. "I drove around here," recalls Adler, "saw all of those trailers, and being ignorant to the industry, I said why not sell lots for trailers. People down here thought I was crazy because they felt that people in trailers would want to move."[1] One experienced hand, Franklyn McDonald, was willing to listen. McDonald's career in the industry had begun in the 1930s with a trailer dealership in Michigan. Many Northern dealers had found that the seasonality of sales could be offset by moving with the trade and opening a second dealership in the South for the winter. McDonald went to Florida, and like other dealers, saw the need to get into land development to be able to offer customers a

Trailer Estates, opened in 1955 in Bradenton, Florida, was the first mobile
home subdivision in the United States. Many lots back on to canals and
have individual docks. The development also has a central marina.

place to set up their new home. Usually, this meant buying or
developing a park, but Adler's idea of selling lots appealed to
him.

Adler and McDonald's Trailer Estates was a 160-acre subdivision where people bought, in addition to a lot, a community
with planned recreation and facilities. Following the advice of
gerontologists at the University of Michigan, a full schedule of
social activities was developed, including square dancing on
Tuesday, potluck suppers on Wednesday, hobbies on Thursday,
cards on Friday, and, to round out the week, ballroom dancing
on Saturday night. Shuffleboard courts, thirty of them, were
provided, and within four years, a marina was added, together
with a post office, grocery, laundry room and finally, a 1400 seat
auditorium.

Lots at Trailer Estates went on sale in March 1955. Five
months later the first resident moved in, and by the end of the
year 250 lots had been sold. The initial price of a 40' x 60' parcel
was $898. Within four years, most of the 1451 lots had been sold,
at prices ranging from $1300, for inside lots, to $4500 for lots
bordering canals leading to Sarasota Bay.

The site plan of the development, a gridiron composed of long narrow blocks with utility lines running down the center, was not significantly different from contemporary rental parks. The monotony of the streetscape was relieved by the rapid growth of tropical shrubs, and by a herringbone layout of lots. The pattern was successful, but at first sales were better on one side of the street than the other. Apparently people preferred to look out of their front door onto the street, rather than face the side wall of a neighbor's house.

The first units in the development were eight-wide house trailers, but ten- and twelve-wides soon followed, along with site-built ramadas, carports, and storage sheds. All additions had to be approved by the developers, and covenants also reserved them the right to restrict the size of clothes-drying racks, approve the on-site storage of boats and boat trailers, restrict the use of individual TV antennas (a master antenna was provided by the subdivision) and, if a resident fell behind in keeping up the lot, the right to do it and bill for the service. Pets were restricted to a three-block section, and families with children to a four-block area, both tucked into a far corner of the community. While most of these restrictions were characteristic of well-managed contemporary parks, they went beyond those of typical stick-built subdivisions. Adler felt that the rules were necessary to maintain the appearance of a community with the density of Trailer Estates.

Another aspect of management was overall upkeep. Trailer Estates was legally a subdivision but upkeep of roads, utilities, and recreation facilities was not turned over to the City of Bradenton. Instead the developers planned to maintain them on the $10 per month fee assessed on all lots. Inflation soon diminished the real value of the fee, and the developers were faced with increased operating costs. At first they tried to raise the assessment, but residents objected, and in 1968 the developers offered to sell out to the property owners if they would form a recreation district with the power to assess taxes and make rules. In 1971, what had been the nation's first trailer subdivision became its only recreation district comprised exclusively of house trailers and mobile homes.

Today, Adler will enthusiastically take a community planner through the subdivision he started. Touring the development in his car, back seat stuffed with files, he points to the care and community pride evident in the maintenance of the area.

> In terms of appearance, after thirty some odd years, it's as clean and as nice as any community you can find.
> Here you can see old eight-wides and ten-wides right next to a new twenty-wide, and they all work together. It's a renewable

community, because old units can be removed and new ones installed.

Where the unit has become part of the land, and the neighborhood built up, there has been a noticeable appreciation in values. Today a lot with a home could sell for $20,000 to 35,000, and that's with a trailer that's thirty years old.

The first factor in choosing the mobile home is the economy of providing comparable housing. The other significant factor is community. For some reason, and the only one that I can think of is management, the stick builder has never been able to equal, even if they provide the amenities, the lifestyle of the mobile home park. They build the clubhouses and all this stuff, but for some reason it just doesn't seem to work. And so there is still that intangible of the lifestyle that these parks provide.

That intangible lifestyle includes close-knit neighborliness and the surveillance of strangers. Walk through the community on your own, and residents will stop to inquire about your business; express an interest in where they live, and you receive a short history of the place.

Trailer Estates shares one border with the Sara Bay condominiums, and another with a 1950s FHA stick-built development of ranch houses. It is, Adler claims,

the perfect example of a lot of different kinds of housing put together compatibly. Here you see an expensive condominium development overlooking Trailer Estates and you find the boats from both developments looking at each other across the canal.

[As for the FHA development, however] I once told a HUD official, who I was giving a speech with, that his houses were depreciating my property. Retired people don't want to live right across the street from houses with children.

Five years after Trailer Estates opened, Adler started another subdivision, Tri-Par Estates, a few miles south in Sarasota and, several years later, a development in Palm Springs, California, and one in Tuscon, Arizona, built around an eighteen-hole golf course.

For thirty years I've been advocating the idea of mobile home subdivisions and condominiums, but the idea has never really caught on. We wondered why people in mobile homes were more inclined to rent than to buy. We found many reasons. In the retirement market people seem to feel that if their home is personal property rather than realty they don't want to tie up their estate with property. We also found that, psychologically, people moving into a mobile home liked the idea of mobility, even if they didn't move. This way if they didn't like the community they could leave it. Even when you tie the land to it, people don't see the mobile home as housing, but it is real housing. Young families see it as interim housing. Subdivisions have not done as well in family markets as in retirement markets. It may be that the smaller lots do not work with families with young children.

Trailer Estates was an attempt to invent a new form of community using trailers and mobile homes as permanent housing. It was a successful and innovative response to a particular market segment, the retired household, for whom community amenities rather than cost alone was the main appeal. More characteristic of the households which began to swell the mobile-home market in the late 1950s were young families who wanted a taste of a suburban lifestyle that they would otherwise be unable to afford. In the mobile home they saw a way of building equity while experiencing some of the advantages of home ownership in a miniaturized version of the American dream—objectives that could not be adequately met by the typical trailer court, with its transient, vacation-oriented housing. It required new organizations of land and alternative forms of tenure and management. Trailer Estates is one example of the search for a community structure appropriate to the emerging market, a structure that would be at once both new and familiar.

Developing Mobile Home Land

Although sales have always depended on the quality and availability of park space, trailer and mobile home manufacturers largely steered clear of the land development aspect of the industry. "It's a real Catch-22," Syd Adler suggests.

> The industry has the ability to provide the housing unit, but its a single-level industry. The manufacturers are interested in making the unit, the dealer is interested in selling it, and so on. You don't have too much vertical integration.[2] There has never been an overall view of the industry, a concern for what the total industry has to do to make it work. The manufacturer has rarely gotten involved with the land, and the end use of his product.
>
> Even though traditional developers, like U.S. Homes, have been in this business, they have gotten out of it because the bottom line is that the manufactured home loses all its efficiency when you have to tie it to land. The cost advantage comes in the lack of foundation and less costly plumbing and electrical requirements. You're looking at a $4000 to 5000 difference right there. That's why the manufactured home will only serve as permanent housing for retirement-level people and as interim housing for younger families.

If manufacturers felt they could afford to be independent of land development, dealers could not. After the war, many

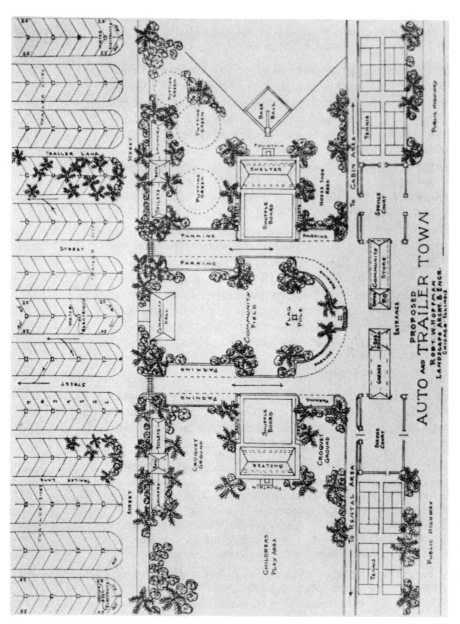

Proposal for a franchised system of "Auto and Trailer Towns," featuring extensive recreation facilities that would act as a buffer to the highway.

dealers set up sales lots in the parks they owned and many park owners found that operating a dealership was a natural adjunct of their business.[3] The relatively low cost of developing a park allowed supply to respond quickly to demand, though it typically lagged behind. In 1937, Al Sweeney, writing in *Trailer Travel*, complained that:

A little over a year ago, the dearth of trailer parks was a source of querulous comment by new converts who sallied forth with trailers only to have a hard time finding havens in which to stop with electrical, sanitary and other facilities that go to make the modern conveniences so necessary to the comfort of many people these days.[4]

Between the Winter and Spring editions of the 1937 *Official Directory of Trailer Parks and Camps*, the number of trailer parks doubled to a total of 3300, a remarkable increase, but still lagging behind the growth of trailer sales. Migration to remote rural areas during the war years, followed by record-breaking postwar trailer sales exacerbated the supply problem. Between 1950 and 1959, the number of trailers increased by 140 percent. In 1953 the manufacturers' annual *Park Directory* listed 4000 approved parks out of a national total of 12,000; a year later, 5000 parks had been approved, and by 1959, 13,000.

Periods of rapid growth steeled local communities' resistance to trailer parks. Alexander Wellington, in *Survey* magazine, expressed the sentiments of many municipal officials when he warned of

a new kind of slum, the permanent trailer camp, offering all the bad features of the urban "blight area," none of the vacation adventures for which trailers were made. . . .
  Trailer camp slums are a very real, if as yet unrecognized, menace to our American way of life. They should be eradicated *now*, even in the face of an acute housing shortage, for the creation of more slums is not the solution to the problem of housing shortage.[5]

While manufacturers did not wish to develop parks themselves, they realized the threat community and institutional resistance posed in the form of restrictive zoning. Just as they had encouraged construction regulations to counter the potentially paralyzing effect of local and state regulations on manufacturing, they moved to encourage park standards to assure communities that mobile homes were a compatible land use.

After World War II, the Trailer Coach Association of California developed and operated several model parks, featuring such amenities as on-site parking, patios, and landscaping. Simultaneously, the Trailer Coach Manufacturers Association (later the Mobile Home Manufacturers Association) established a park division, which produced *The Trailer Park Guide,* rating parks on a hundred-point scale. The division also published *Trailer Park Progress,* a magazine it hoped would promote improvements in park management and development. By the early 1950s, the division had developed model park standards, and, in 1957, it issued a model park zoning ordinance. A year later, the Land Development Division was established which, over the next fourteen years, produced designs for more parks than any other firm in the nation.

Private and public organizations also established land development standards. From 1937 to 1976, Woodall's published a popular directory of trailer parks based on personal inspections and a five-star rating system. Since only half the parks in the country typically qualified for a listing, Woodall helped set standards for park design. In the mid-1950s, it briefly maintained a park planning service. Another source of design standards was a two-volume manual published by the Trail-R-Club of America, which offered advice not only on design, but management.[6] Park standards were also being developed by federal, state, and local agencies. In 1952, for example, the Federal Housing and Home Finance Agency established minimal development standards as a basis for making loans. While few agency loans were actually issued, the standards helped banks evaluate park loan applications.

The widespread effort to establish criteria for park design was a counterpart to manufacturers' attempt to define the form of the year-round house trailer *cum* mobile home. Just as the trailer had to be rethought to fit its new function, so the trailer camp had to evolve into a mobile home park that fit the ideals and images associated with single-family housing communities. At the same time, the parks had to preserve what was unique about mobile home living, both to accommodate the requirements of a lifestyle and to avoid excessive and costly regulation. Freedom Acres, whose residents were described briefly in the first chapter, is representative of attempts by many dealer/park owners to invent the physical and social form of the mobile home community.

The Evolution of Freedom Acres

Woodall's Mobile Home and Park Directory of 1974 awarded Freedom Acres three and one-half stars, and considered it one of the better parks in the city of Muncie. Founded in 1951 as Muncie Trailer Park, it has expanded twice, in the early 1960s and again in the early 1970s. The original park had thirty-six lots and was built in conjunction with a dealership. When the park opened, it was outside the city boundaries, but the city has since expanded and incorporated it. The park's location is still regarded by locals as "the wrong side of the tracks." The old working-class section of the city, with its now abandoned glass works, is not far to the east.

Phyllis Yohey, who with her husband Paul built the park, recalls their original objectives:

> Paul was trying to sell quality permanent homes, and not just temporary housing. At the time we started out the park situation was not really good enough for a permanent home, so he designed this. Our idea was to provide permanent housing for those people who wanted a small home without any worries.
>
> When we started this park there was White's, which has since been rebuilt, and a few other parks that were just rat holes. So when we came in there wasn't any kind of planned park in the area, there wasn't even a place where anyone cared what it looked like. I have a picture of the park that goes back, and even then we had little white picket fences. It was just an entirely different idea.
>
> We sold awnings. We tried to get rid of the oil barrels by burying them and using pumps. . . . Whenever there was a zoning case against putting in a new park, the park people would always come here to use us as a good example.[7]

Muncie Trailer Park consisted of two blocks, each with a double row of trailers. Parking was along the curbless streets, and utilities ran down the center of each block. The park office, which sat by the entrance, also housed the mail room, laundry, and dealership office, while the area in front served as a sales lot. Individual lots were 35' x 80', with units parked perpendicular to the street, resulting in a density of about thirteen units to the acre. As wider and longer units were introduced, the open area of the lot shrank, so that the setback from the street became little more than the depth of the hitch.

Most of the open space was to the side, a long narrow yard with boundaries sharply defined by neighboring units. A red 1957 Landola with silver appliquéd fins might face the turquoise and silver side of a 1959 New Moon and the back end of an old Troutwood. From the windows of one you could see through the living room of the other, and so on right down the row. The close spacing of the units had the effect of amplifying noise as well as the view. Someone walking along the linoleum covered hall in one home could be clearly heard next door. Fortunately, there were few babies in the park.

Although it was intended for relatively permanent homes, the park still owed much of its form to the campground. The per-

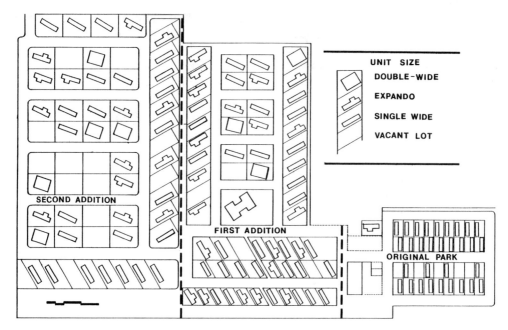

Site plan for Freedom Acres Mobile Home Park in Muncie, Indiana. Its population heterogeneity is characteristic of many housing-oriented parks.

pendicular alignment of lots expressed both economy in utility layout and the requirements for moving units in and out. Until the early 1960s, most of the units were indistinguishable from larger vacation trailers and, in fact, vacant lots were rented out for traveling trailerites' temporary use. What really distinguished the early park from the campground or trailer court, then, was not appearance so much as the intention of management and tenants to be part of a more permanent community.

The first addition to the Muncie Trailer Park attempted to respond to the changing character of the mobile home. The twenty-six lots in the front part of the addition were set diagonal to the street, and the typical unit there was an "expando," usually with a pullout living room/foyer section. When sited on a diagonal lot, the room expansion helped create a more conventional sense of frontality with the street, an effect often reinforced by a site-built entry porch. Other blocks featured 50' x 100' lots, with alleys and carports complete with built-in storage closets. The largest lots were 120' x 90', located on the three blocks behind the Yoheys' house—an H-shaped modular structure that looks somewhat out of scale with its neighbors.

When the addition was opened, a pool was built where the sales lot had been and, in recognition of the fact that people who don't move accumulate more possessions, a central storage area was built. The larger lots and increased amenities were designed to attract more families with children. One of the main selling points that Paul now emphasized was that the mobile home was a good starter home: an ideal way to build equity toward ownership of a site-built home.

The second addition to Freedom Acres opened in 1972. It contained three long blocks laid out in diagonal lots and was designed for units that could still be recognized as mobile homes. But the central section, with 120' x 150' lots and two-car paved parking pads, was prepared for bigger homes. A few modular units now occupy this area along with double-wides, both looking much like the site-built ranch houses across the road. With the last addition, the Yoheys' original idea of "permanent housing for those people who wanted a small home without any worries" had evolved from a campground-like setting into a subdivision. Today Paul Yohey reflects that "as far as I'm concerned, what this [park] is, is a housing development. It's just like a builder would come out here and build a housing development."

The original Muncie Trailer Park was laid out in narrow lots with units placed perpendicular to the road. The larger ten- and twelve-wides which now occupy these lots have virtually no front or back setbacks.

Mobile Home Land

Just as the mobile home is a hybrid of vehicle and dwelling, mobile home land—whether park, subdivision, or individual site—combines various aspects of land use: auto campground, site-built subdivision, rural retreat, urban apartment, and transient motel. Its hybrid character also is evident in the status of its occupants and its categorization by institutions.

Specific types of mobile home land can be distinguished in terms of spatial organization, community structure, and form of ownership. In the trailer court, whose form is rooted in the automobile campground, lots are small, units oriented perpendicular to the street, and streets are narrow, laid out to achieve the greatest economy of utility lines. At the other extremes are luxury subdivisions and mobile homes scatter-sited in residential areas, with lot size, unit orientation, and street layout indistinguishable from site-built housing. In between are parks and subdivisions with modest lots and a mixture of units ranging from shiny boxes parked perpendicular to the street, to conventionalized double-wides set frontally to the street. Community structure also has distinct extremes: the full-service retirement park, where residents are more concerned with social life and services than with basic costs, and the bare bones rental park, where little is offered beyond utility hook-ups, a kind of horizontal apartment house, where socialization is encouraged by the close proximity of units.

Spatial Organization

Trailers and then mobile homes were perceived as a threat not just to real estate values, but to a community's moral character. By restricting mobile homes to parks, then relegating parks to undesirable nonresidential areas, zoning officials tried to confine the "blight" while confirming their own prejudices. A 1971 report by the American Planning Association, reviewing zoning practices across the nation, concluded:

> Regulatory negligence has contributed to the development of the kinds of parks that have given the mobile home a bad image. In the case of the mislocation of parks in commercial or industrial districts . . . there is both abuse and negligence—abuse in the sense that persons living in mobile home parks are forced into an unsuitable environment; negligence in that parks are allowed to locate in such areas.[8]

Although the main purpose of zoning is to extend the greatest protection to residential developments, by the end of World War II, parks provided primarily year-round housing, yet they were still relegated to commercial and industrial zones, where the nearest neighbor might be an auto junkyard. Even when parks were recognized in zoning regulations, their development could be limited by "constructive exclusion," a practice which allowed parks, but only on land where they already existed.[9]

The practice of confining mobile homes to parks and restricting parks to undesirable areas illustrates adaptation through what anthropologists call independence.[10] Its effect is to accept the mobile home as housing, but to confine its use in such a way that the housing system in general does not have to assimilate it. The mobile home and park effectively become a special category of use. The industry itself, through the MHMA, endorsed the idea that mobile homes are properly confined to parks. It argued, however, that parks be allowed in residential areas. In its *Suggested Model Ordinance Regulating Mobile Home Parks* (1956), the MHMA stated that "parks may be permitted in any district where multiple dwellings are permitted." Similarly, Florida planners Ernest Bartley and Frederick Bair, Jr. advised that "generally speaking, and certainly in urban and rural areas, the mobile home belongs in a good mobile home park." They went on to observe: "A great deal of public hostility toward mobile homes arises from their use as residences on individual lots in conventional residential areas, either in connection with a conventional residence or independently."[11]

Benevolent restrictive practices, such as those suggested by the MHMA, would have increased park development costs. Malevolent restrictive practices would have confined parks to undesirable areas or excluded them altogether. Not surprisingly, many park developers chose to locate adjacent to town or city boundaries, where there were more lenient building and zoning regulations or none at all. Likewise, individuals who wanted private lots found rural areas less restrictive.

The result of these practices has been a continuing migration of mobile home development from central city to more rural locations. In the *1960 Census of Housing*, 50 percent of all mobile homes were located inside "Standard Metropolitan Statistical Areas (SMSA)," with a little over 20 percent of these inside central cities. By 1974, the *Annual Housing Survey* found that only 40 percent of all mobile homes were located within SMSAs, with the percentage in central cities down to less than half of what it had been in 1960. In general, mobile homes have followed lower land costs and restrictions.

Land use restrictions, in turn, reflect community values and characteristics. A survey conducted in 1977 by industry analyst Arthur Bernhardt found that mobile home placements were most likely to be restricted in communities that were wealthy, spent more on schools, were densely populated, and were growing rapidly.[12] Similarly, in an analysis of zoning practices in the Adirondack region of New York state, sociologists Charles Geisler and Hisayoshi Mitsuda found that communities with an economy based on tourism and second-home ownership were more restrictive than those with an agriculturally based economy.[13] These findings suggest that in communities where basic housing needs are a concern of most residents, there is greater acceptance of the mobile home as a housing alternative.

The confusion surrounding the classification of mobile home land was fostered by appearance. Parks continued to resemble campgrounds rather than permanent communities. But park design gradually changed, both to accommodate larger units and in reponse to a changing market and lifestyle. Much of the change was the result of independent developments such as Freedom Acres, but it was also influenced by a growing body of model ordinances, plans, and standards developed by government agencies and industry.

One widely available set of park standards was issued by the Federal Housing and Home Finance Agency. Its 1952 edition suggested that to prevent overcrowding parks should not exceed a density of 18 units per acre, that lots should not be less than 1250 square feet, and that minimum side-to-side spacing should be at least 15 feet. Three years later, the FHA issued a land-planning bulletin recommending that 90 percent of park lots be at least 1350, and 5 percent at least 1500 square feet. Other recommendations included off-street parking, a service building with a laundry and group recreation building, grouped tenant storage lockers, and a landscaped buffer area between the park and public streets. The MHMA offered similar standards in its model code. While the association hoped its ordinance would be adopted by municipalities, in many respects it was less demanding than the FHA's, and neither came up to the standards of the original Muncie Trailer Park, where the lots were 2800 square feet.

Perhaps the most important influence in this period was the MHMA's Park Division. It prepared free planning kits, which included suggested site plans and construction procedures for developers, and it offered an architectural consulting service for a nominal fee, refundable upon construction of the park.[14] One of MHMA's chief consultants was architect George Muramoto, whose designs exceeded the Association's Model Ordinance standards and gave a more complete image of what the modern park could be like.

An innovative aspect of Muramoto's designs was a planning

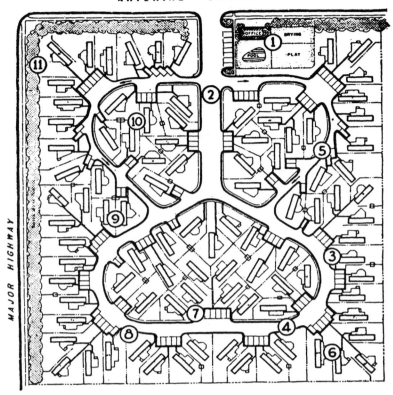

Mobile home park plans developed by George Muramoto for the Mobile Home Manufacturers Association. Muramoto based his plans on modular clusters of units.

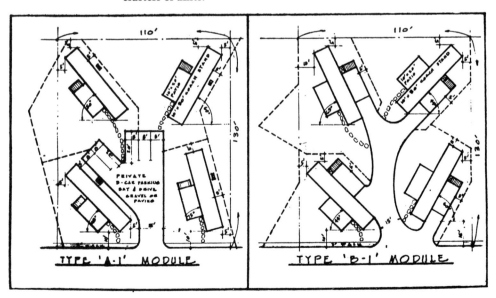

TYPE 'A-1' MODULE   TYPE 'B-1' MODULE

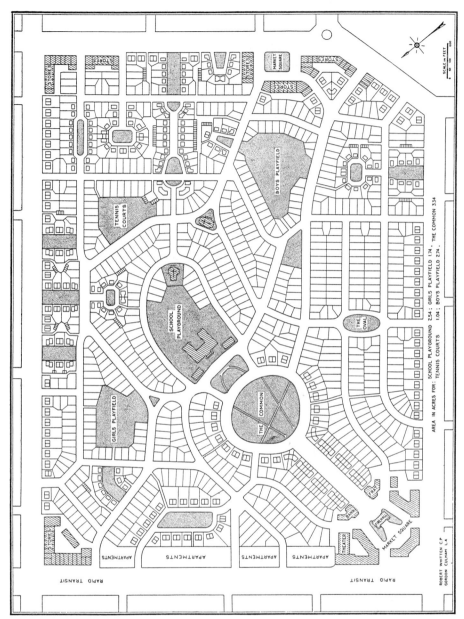

The neighborhood unit plan developed by Clarence A. Perry in 1929 provided a conceptual model for mobile home park design beginning in the 1950s, especially for the MHMA's model plans.

module, consisting of streets and utility lines and an arrangement of four 10' x 50' mobile homes complete with parking and patios. In the typical park arrangement of the day, every lot had street frontage, with units set perpendicular to the street. The modules allowed each street to serve a double depth of units, and created a more suburban setting and additional area for recreation. The savings from reducing the amount of paved street would be significant. Muramoto's plans also featured a landscaped buffer zone around the park boundaries, especially where they fronted city streets.

By 1958, the demand for consulting services had increased, and the MHMA began to create site plans and to draft engineering specifications—aided by consultants drawn largely from the landscape architecture departments at the Universities of Illinois and Michigan. By the time it was phased out in 1972, the association's Land Development Division had produced plans for more home sites than any other developer, site-built or mobile, in the United States. Herbert W. Behrends, chief engineer of the division, estimates that about 10 percent of all park developers utilized the planning service, and that approximately half of the plans produced were constructed.[15]

In many respects, the model plans from the MHMA and other groups bore a strong resemblance to the neighborhood unit plan which had been the pattern for much of the postwar suburban development.[16] The neighborhood unit featured curvilinear streets to slow down traffic and boundaries with buffers, including shopping strips between housing and major streets. The best mobile home park plans also clustered housing around shared open space and recreation facilities. But there was a big difference in the scale of the two types of development. The neighborhood unit assumed a population of about 5000, enough families to support an elementary school; the typical park contained 100 to 150 spaces, enough to support the salary of a resident manager. Both plans were intended to give form and order to areas with rapid growth and were meant to be modified to fit local conditions.

Behind the physical pattern of the neighborhood unit plan was a fundamentally sociological idea about meeting the needs of people in urban areas.[17] There was concern for the dynamics of neighborhood change, the need to form identity with place, and the importance of forming social bonds between neighbors. Little discussion of social organization accompanied the development of the model park plan, but by the time it emerged there was a clear sense of parks as social as well as physical organizations, and recognition that some care had to be taken in mixing household types and providing community facilities.

Suggested arrangement of lots from *Guidelines for Improving the Mobile Home Living Environment,* published in 1978 by the U.S. Department of Housing and Urban Development. Here the perpendicular arrangement of units is preserved, but the treatment of the front entry is more formal. From the sketch it is difficult to tell if any part of the lot is intended for the informal activities associated with a back yard.

If the layout of parks reflected, in miniature form, the organization of suburban neighborhoods, designs for individual lots used as their model the conventional house lot, but distorted it to fit the constraints of park density and the elongated shape of the mobile home. The traditional American house lot is divided into three distinct zones: semipublic, semiprivate, and private, each designating a different degree of the resident's control over public intrusion. The zone between the sidewalk and the front stoop is semipublic. It is the place for such formal displays as Christmas lights and ornamental flower beds, but it is not generally a place for any activity. The stoop or porch is a semiprivate zone, where the activities of the house extend out through its formal entry and where visitors are screened. Finally, the back yard is a zone of privacy, where the family barbecues, sunbathes, and grows vegetables rather than flowers. Even in the suburban tract house, where more often than not the functional entrance is through the garage, these zones are maintained.

Associated with each of these zones are certain rituals and

ways of behaving that people living in mobile homes try to maintain. The problem is how to map them on a lot that typically has only one side yard. Both park developers and home owners have tried to solve this problem, with varying degrees of success. For most residents, the front yard is the side of the lot which faces the street. Although this is usually a shallow area with a hitch projecting into it, it is still a place where ornamental landscaping is likely to be done, whether it be the small picket fences of Freedom Acres or Helen Norris's ceramic ducks. The definition of the area that is *front* often extends to the door, unless this area is used for parking. The "back yard" then becomes the area on the other side of the entry stairs: the zone where storage sheds are located. Although all three zones can thus be collapsed into the single side yard, it is an arrangement in which privacy is hard to control.

A recent variation on the single side yard arrangement that has appeared in Southern California is the "zero-lot line plan," where the unit is set perpendicular to the street but with one edge on the lot line; the effect is to add perhaps five feet to the width of the yard. A unit designed specifically for this lot plan makes the arrangement work. Often the plan includes a site-built garage fronting the street. The side yard then becomes a courtyard with the windows of the unit facing onto it.

Better quality parks, usually in the Sunbelt, often have lots with two equally wide side yards. Although one side serves as carport and the other as patio, the zone considered "front yard" is still the front part of each side. This plan encourages double shed additions by owners. With the introduction of larger mobile homes, especially double-wides, came another lot arrangement. Larger models tend to have more conventional floor plans, including front and back doors, suggesting more traditional front and back yards. Since this arrangement requires a large lot, it has been more common in subdivisions than parks.

In the evolution of the mobile home lot, then, there has been a clear, if not always self-conscious, attempt to restore the functional and symbolic characteristics of the conventional house-to-lot arrangement and, in doing so, to maintain the traditional rituals and behaviors associated with houses.

Forms of Community

The idea of a trailer community strikes many as a contradiction in terms. The very transience of trailer life, whether actual or potential, appears to deny a sense of community or a stable environment in which to raise children. In 1954, for example, the Girl Scouts sponsored a study of trailer camps with a

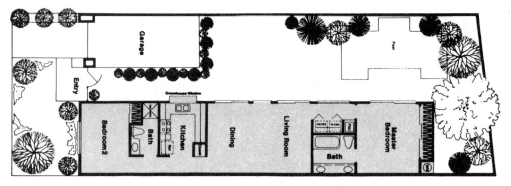

Zero-lot line arrangement in a California manufactured housing community by Kaufman and Broad.

Lakeside is a manufactured housing subdivision in Santa Ana, California. Households buy their house but the land is leased. Zero-lot line site planning and units designed especially for the site make maximum use of relatively small lots.

Establishing frontality with the site is important in demonstrating that the home belongs to the site and is no longer mobile. Typically the undercarriage is skirted, but units may also be backed into shallow trenches, lowering their entire profile. This unit, in Parkview Mobile Estates, Palm Springs, California, has a traditional perpendicular alignment with the street, but frontality is created with plantings, symmetrical additions, and a patio entry door.

particular interest in children. The study, conducted by sociologist David Hager, focused on construction workers living in Lower Bucks County, Pennsylvania. He concluded that trailerites

> possess characteristics that are generally prized by all American communities—sobriety, occupational skill, and a genuine interest in contributing to and improving the community in which they live . . . they take considerable pride in the important and necessary role they play in industrial development. They view themselves as community assets and are, therefore, extremely sensitive to charges that they are irresponsible trailer trash.[18]

Residents saw a distinct advantage in house trailers and mobile homes over apartment buildings, particularly as places to raise children.

> We've been in nice apartments, though temporarily, but it's not the same. I've always had a little lost feeling whenever I go into one. It's not my home. It's not my furniture and just try and keep a child's hands from things. No freedom there.
> Of course you may say, "But a child is so restricted in a trailer park. After all, you are renting your land." That's true, but neither

we nor our child are any more restricted in a nice trailer court than we would be in the close housing of the cities or suburbs. . . .

As to our bunching together, we love it. Rarely does any neighborhood attain the intimate friendliness, the camaraderie of a trailer park. . . .

For Heaven's sake, lose the idea that we're all poor unfortunates. Why, one of my neighbors owns a local skating rink. Another has bought a grocery. I've met doctors, bankers, and famous retired people.[19]

Even as the mobile home market shifted to a less affluent and less well educated population in the mid 1950s, there was a strong sense of social cohesion in park life. Rather than being a threat to community stability, parks with year-round housing often had a stronger sense of community than conventional housing, both apartments and subdivisions. Planner, Frederick Bair, Jr., concluded that "mobile homes may be the last genuine communities in America." In part, the sociability of park life naturally results from the physical organization: a relatively small number of households live in close proximity, share common facilities, and keep an eye out for each other.[20] Social cohesiveness also often results from the homogeneity of the residents, especially in adult-only parks, and those with separate sections for families.

Not all analysts have viewed the parks' homogeneity as an asset. In 1971, Elaine Kendall, in the *Happy Mediocrity*, described this situation with disdain:

In this whiskery age, it is possible to drive through forty-seven parks without ever seeing a beard, mustache, or even a set of sideburns on any male, young or old. And when one realizes—of course—there are no students in the parks, no blacks, no urbanites. Nobody in communications, advertising, show business, the arts, or the sciences. No one, in fact, who even approves of these categories.[21]

Despite Kendall's exaggerated conclusions, residents often prefer the homogeneity of a park, just as people living in site-built subdivisions do.

James Gillies, professor of business at UCLA, concluded in a study of parks for the Trailer Coach Association in 1965 that there were two kinds of parks, housing-oriented and service-oriented.[22] In housing-oriented parks, like Freedom Acres, residents have chosen to live in a mobile home primarily because of the cost of housing; whereas in service-oriented communities, like Trailer Estates, residents are more concerned with ease of upkeep and amenities such as golf courses and clubhouses.[23] These types of parks generally correspond to the two most

A home in Blue Skies developed on an "Egyptian theme" has attached pylon and lotus capitaled columns flanking the carport. A single-wide mobile home can still be distinguished underneath.

common types of households in mobile homes: young couples with no children and retired people. Service-oriented parks appeal to the more affluent retirees who can afford a second home and the cost of a high-quality park. Some housing-oriented parks also cater exclusively to retired persons, but usually to those with fixed or limited incomes.

One of the most celebrated of the early service-oriented parks was Bing Crosby's "Blue Skies" near Palm Springs, California. The park, developed on 26 acres with 152 trailer sites, featured a swimming pool, billiard and card room, shuffleboard courts, pitch and putt golf course, and a recreation building hosting performances by name entertainers. The park also provided a security force and optional maid service. Tenants have been encouraged to make additions to their units. Typically these are double-sheds with a carport on one side and an enclosed ramada on the other. Such additions are now common in luxury parks in the Sunbelt, and often are provided as a part of the lot. At Blue Skies, however, they are exceptionally elaborate, including one in an Egyptian pylon motif. In 1960 the average single-wide mobile home in the park cost $15,000, with site-built additions costing that much and more. Yearly lot rental ranged from $720 to $1200. While these prices were at the high end of mobile

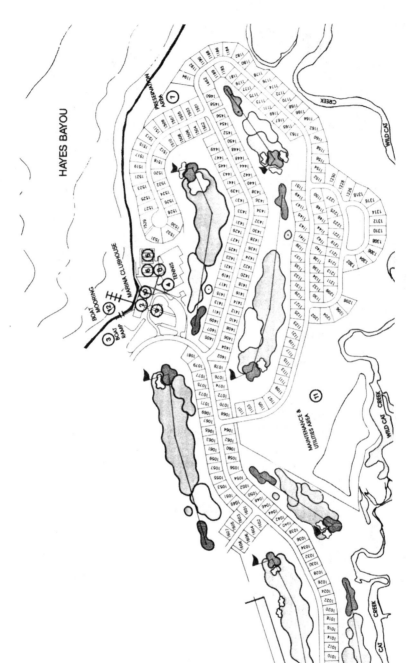

Many of the service-oriented mobile home communities being developed today are organized around a golf course. The site plan shown here is from The Moorings of Manatee in Ruskin, Florida. It is marketed extensively to Canadians interested in second homes.

home living at the time, Blue Skies was a relatively affordable, free from real estate taxes way to live in a resort community.

Today most mobile home land developers seem to favor service-oriented communities. They provide a better return on investment and, when they cater to adults only, are less likely to rouse local opposition. The "Moorings of Manatee," north of Sarasota, Florida, is an example of a high-quality contemporary development. Its marketing is directed primarily at Canadian retirees. The community is built around a golf course and water inlets, and for the most part is indistinguishable from a site-built community. Developing housing-oriented parks, by contrast, has become less attractive because of smaller profits, greater local opposition, and more difficulties in management. Yet it is the housing-oriented park which is most needed to fill the gap in affordable housing so evident in most metropolitan areas. Developer Syd Adler suggests that "the problem with affordable housing is that it often involves the tenants who are most difficult to deal with, so the entrepreneur/developer really doesn't want to take on the responsibility if there's another place to make a buck. Yet the real need for manufactured housing is in the industrial centers rather than in retirement centers." With good management, however, housing-oriented parks have been exceptionally stable businesses as well as communities.

A third type of development, one which does not fit neatly into Gillies' service/housing-oriented typology, is the company park. This is a community built by a company to temporarily house workers, usually in a remote rural area. The parks built and run by the federal government during the war were among the first of this type. After the war, major contractors building for the Atomic Energy Commission often provided parks, like Silver City, for their workers, and even supplied the trailers for some. More often, skilled construction workers who migrated with construction projects, like Mel Schlicter, owned their own trailers, and referred to themselves as "tramps."

For "tramps," a house trailer or recreational vehicle (RV) was a familiar and comfortable place to live; and for a tramp with a family, it offered the means to keep the family together. Kay Peterson, in *Home is Where You Park It*, writes of the enduring attraction of the tramping way of life:

> some of the construction men who begin tramping through necessity find they enjoy moving around and continue traveling even when it is possible to work in the home local or union hall. The so-called supertramp is a man who suffers from the same malady that attacks people from other walks of life. He is one of those who is plagued by the wandering itch. However, unlike most of

us, he works at a trade that permits—in fact encourages—him to scratch his itch.

Recessions take their toll on everyone, but the RV [trailer] tramp has it easier than his buddies who live in a more conventional style. Without deep roots and the commitments that house owners have, the tramp who lives in an RV home can take both his family and his home to wherever work is available. He does not have to worry about finding an apartment. Nor does he have to wonder about the vacant house he left behind as a temptation to vandals.[24]

The tramping life, as David Hager observed in Lower Bucks County, Pennsylvania, produces a close-knit community.

Battlement Mesa, near Parachute, Colorado, is a modern mobile home company town. Built to house construction workers for Exxon's Colony Oil Shale Project, it was designed to be converted into a permanent housing subdivision when regular mining operations began. The problem with large-scale construction projects like Colony is that more workers are needed during construction than operations, resulting in a boom/bust cycle of growth. The first housing phase in Battlement Mesa consisted of company-owned mobile homes, including three-bedroom single-wides, and a special section of single-wides divided into efficiency apartments complete with maid service and a dining hall. Another part of the community was for people living in RVs. At the height of construction, there were over 2000 residents in Battlement Mesa, making it the largest park in Colorado. When the oil shale construction phase was completed, every two mobile home sites were to be converted into a single-family site; thus, as population declined density would decrease. In the early 1980s, oil prices plummeted and the Colony Oil Shale Project shut down. Today, the stick-built housing of Battlement Mesa is being marketed as retirement housing, and the temporary mobile homes have been sold off and shipped elsewhere.

Owning and Renting

The mobile home has proven to be adaptable to a variety of communities ranging from conventional subdivision developments to special purpose worker camps. Residents' general satisfaction with mobile home living often depends on whether they own or rent their homes and lots, since ownership frees residents from arbitrary rules and regulations and protects them from sudden sizable rent increases or eviction without due process and reasonable cause.

Under common-law traditions home ownership confers clear and significant rights, whereas renting either a mobile home or

Some companies responsible for creating boon-town conditions take responsibility for providing housing and amenities for their workers. Shown here
is an aerial view of the Monument Creek Village section of Battlement Mesa,
Colorado. The village was designed so that when construction of the oil
shale facility was completed, two mobile home sites could be converted into
a single conventional house site.

Double-wide mobile home in Battlement Mesa, Colorado. When the oil
shale development was mothballed, Exxon converted the community for use
by retirees.

lot throws residents into a grey area of the law. Their historically ill-defined status is evident in the 1974 edition of Hodes and Roberson's authoritative *Law of Mobile Homes*. It only briefly discusses the role of park operator as landlord, observing that while some states prescribe maximum rents and all regulate evictions for tenants of conventional dwellings, few specify the applicability of landlord/tenant law to mobile home occupants.[25]

In the 1950s and 1960s, a tenant could expect to be required to comply with a specific set of park rules, without the protection of a lease or state laws to prevent eviction on frivolous grounds. In a few states, statutes protecting tenants in other forms of permanent housing were interpreted to apply to park renters, but in most states tenants were regarded more as motel or hotel occupants than as residents of rental housing. Hodes and Roberson advised, at that time, that

> in the absence of specific legislation, a mobile home park operator may assert a landlord's lien or, arguably, an innkeeper's lien on property of the tenant. In common law, an unpaid innkeeper has the right to seize and retain possession of personal property brought upon the premises by the guests and remaining thereon, until the amount due to the innkeeper shall have been paid.[26]

Under this interpretation, a mobile home owner in a rental park is like a hotel guest whose dwelling may be seized, like a piece of luggage, for failure to pay rent.

One of the conditions that favored landlords' abusive practices was, and remains, the scarcity of park space. A 1977 survey found that 47 percent of a national sample of parks had no vacant space, and 41 percent had waiting lists.[27] Where there was high demand and few vacancies, an operator could run a "closed park," forcing prospective tenants to buy a unit from the operator or from selected dealers. Residents might be charged a landscaping fee, even if the site had been occupied, or if the buyer bought a home that was already in the park. Some operators charged tenants an "exit fee" when they removed a home from the park or sold one that would remain there. Park operators could also control who might deliver gas and oil, make repairs, or provide skirting and landscaping.

Besides extra fees, park operators might make rules that could infringe on other rights. For example, parks often required that tenants register guests staying for more than a few days. Although this practice was justified as a way of controlling the use of utilities, such as water that ran off of a master meter, its indirect consequence was to infringe on privacy.

Arthur Bernhardt, in his study of the mobile home industry, suggests that explicit and excessive rules arose at a time when parks were changing from vacation facilities into year-round communities:

> the need arose for a new image of parks as stable, ordered communities of responsible citizens. Owners and operators extended their authority to include not only the physical setting and maintenance of the site but also the behavioral and social interactions of the residents.[28]

Carlton Edwards, an industry historian, offers a different and perhaps more plausible explanation.

> The early park owners commonly regarded their property like a kingdom and often exercised harsh regulations toward tenants. These owners were usually experienced in construction techniques or were those possessing available land and were not adept at human relations.[29]

As Edwards suggests, many park owner/managers were paternalistic, feeling that tenants needed strong rules or their park could become "trashed out." Tenants generally agreed that rules were necessary, but not always democratic. In Freedom Acres, residents were asked if they wanted cable TV. When the majority voted yes, all tenants were charged for the service. Tenants who didn't like the decision could leave; exceptionally disruptive tenants might find their homes towed out of the park within a day.

Many states now have mobile home landlord/tenant ordinances. In general, the protections accorded to apartment dwellers have been extended to park renters, and practices such as closed parks are now illegal. Even with such protection on the books, many tenants are unaware of their rights and, in areas where vacancies are low, intimidated against exercising them.

Parallels Between Theory and Practice

Just as the mobile home embodied theoretical principles of industrialized housing which more deliberate attempts failed to realize successfully, mobile home land was the hybrid of dwelling and land that theorists had proposed, but which they largely ignored when it developed with the mobile home. One idea, remarkable in its parallel with the evolution of mobile home land, had its origins in the city planning schemes developed by the architect Le Corbusier in the early 1930s. His sketches for high-rise housing in plans for Algiers, Sao Paulo, and Rio de Janeiro showed reinforced concrete platforms, which Le Corbusier called "artificial land." The idea was to allow people to build their own individually designed units on the artificial land as they would along a city street. The framework provided not only utilities, but a full range of community services from schools to parks. More than twenty years later, when Le Corbusier was planning the Marseille Block apartment structure, he revised his idea, using the metaphor of the "bottle and wine-bin."

> We have taken a momentous step, introducing an entirely new concept into the theory of housing—and into practice. The dwelling is regarded as a thing in itself. It contains a family. A thing in itself, with its own reality, its own criteria, its own requirements. It's a bottle.
>
> And, having made our bottle, the dwelling, we can plump it down under an apple tree in Normandy or under a pine tree in Jura. We can equally well shove it in a pigeon hole, that is to say into a space on the fifth or seventeenth floor of a steel framework. It won't make any difference to the thing in itself or to the way we make it.
>
> Yes, we can put it anywhere we like in what might be called the supporting skeleton. Or more simply, a wine-bin. We just stow the bottle away in the bin.[30]

Although the Marseille Block was not built as a wine-rack, Le Corbusier's illustrations were highly provocative and influenced the thinking of many young designers. Among them were British architects Peter and Allison Smithson. In 1959 they wrote an article entitled "Caravan: embryo appliance house," in which they speculated that the proper dwelling for modern times was already evident in the form of the caravan (the British term for travel trailer).

> Against the standard solution to the permanent dwelling the caravan is neat, like a big piece of equipment, has a space for everything like a well run office, has miniature appliances in scale with the spaces like a toy home, is as comfortable as this year's space heated car. And like the car, the caravan represents a new freedom. It has become a sort of symbol as well as a sign of 'population in flux.' It has something of the cheerful, safe, transient feeling one gets driving along in a car.[31]

The Smithsons carried Le Corbusier's bottle analogy a step further, insisting that the bottle remain mobile. They were not convinced, however, that they had seen in the trailer a new idea of community. Under a picture of a project for a high-rise mobile home park is the caption: "This is what happens when caravaners start putting down roots. Rape of the idea of caravan, concreted in."[32] The idea they objected to was one being developed by Elmer Frey, Father of the Tenwide.

Several years later, the British group of architects, "Archigram," proposed schemes which continued to explore the bottle and wine-bin theme. One plan, conceived by Ron Herron and

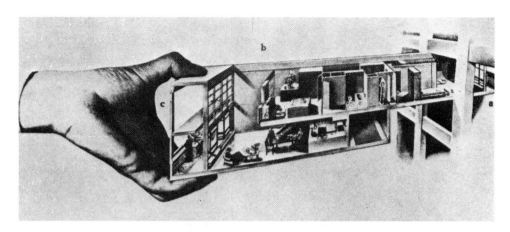

Illustration of the "bottle and wine bin" idea, from Le Corbusier's Marseille Block. In theory the building was to consist of prefabricated, factory-built apartments, which would be shipped to the site and slipped into a site-built concrete frame.

The bottle and wine-bin form underlay the "Freetime node: Trailer cage" proposed by Archigram's Ron Herron and Barry Snowden, but here the plug-in modules are recreation vehicles.

An unintentional realization of the bottle and wine bin in Vadnais Heights,
a suburb of St. Paul, Minnesota. SkyeRise was the nation's first multilevel
mobile home park. The president of the development company was Elmer
Frey (standing to the left), father of the Tenwide. He conceived of the idea in
1958, but it was not realized until 1971.

Barry Snowden, consisted of a high-rise frame into which caravans could be plugged. Archigram saw the caravan as a ready-
made object in the inventory of modern cultures, one that could
be used to achieve instant villages.

> The trailer home is a moveable container used for living in for
> extended periods. It requires a high-powered prime mover. . . .
> Extensive style ranges are available, purchasable ready for living.
> Hook up on the site of your choice.
> Villages of trailer homes like this are relatively immobile and
> their major concern, usually is to imitate straight suburbia as
> closely as possible. This is achieved by a comprehensive inventory
> or purchasable stick-on extras to make their trailers look like
> real houses.[33]

In another proposal, Archigram's Ron Herron described a
moving city in a kind of spaceship structure on telescoping
legs. Presumably when the members of the community decided
that they wanted to go somewhere they could simply move en
masse. Peter Blake, the editor of the journal *Architectural
Forum*, suggested that the feasibility of Herron's proposal had
been demonstrated in the moving platform which transported
the fifty-story high Saturn Rocket to its Cape Kennedy launch

pad. Ironically, a closer parallel would have been the mobile home parks dotting the highway approaching the Cape.

The 1964 General Motors Futurama exhibit at the New York World's Fair included, in its model of the future city, a high-rise framework on which suburban type plots of land were stacked one above the other, a private house set on each. In 1968, American architect Paul Rudolph proposed constructing high-rise housing composed of mobile-home-like units suspended from a mast containing support utilities.[34] Rudolph's scheme was resurrected by Arthur Bernhardt in *Building for Tomorrow* as one of the future alternatives for mobile home development. The bottle and wine-rack analogy was again revised in 1972 when the Dutch architect and planner John Habracken proposed a system called "supports." Though more detailed than Le Corbusier's schemes, "supports" essentially was that vision revised.

These various images circulated within the high cult of design in a search for a new hybrid form of housing and community that would meet the needs of modern society. They recognized the mobility of the population and the desire, at least as demonstrated in the demand for other consumer goods, for a type of "renewable" housing that could be updated as new technological advances and styles became available. At one level, these schemes appeared to be hopelessly utopian, but, at another, they were simply attempts to give visual form and order to lifestyles that were already highly evident.

The Future of Mobile Home Land

The challenge that had faced the mobile home industry beginning in the mid-1950s was to develop adequate, quality park spaces to keep pace with the increasing sales of homes. By the early 1970s, that challenge was being met, and in some urban areas there was a surplus of spaces. The situation today is quite different. In 1984, 46 percent of the units purchased were in parks; by 1987 park placements had declined to 40 percent. While this trend reflects a preference for owning land, it also reflects a decline in park development. The formation of new rental parks has not kept pace with sales, and older parks are being sold to make way for more profitable land uses. The impact of this trend has been felt particularly by people with low and moderate incomes for whom the mobile home is one of the few available forms of nonsubsidized affordable housing. The challenge for the future of mobile home land clearly rests in keeping it affordable. The main obstacles are not technology or alternative designs, but barriers which prevent new housing-oriented development or raise its cost so high that it is prohibitive.

Park development costs are being affected by increased regulation, higher standards, and escalating fees. Water and sewer tap fees in many areas have taken an enormous jump in the last few years, rising from a few hundred dollars to several thousand, in an attempt to pass on the costs of extending new service. Development standards for parks are being written with new requirements intended to improve parks' appearance and safety, but which also increase costs—costs which are passed along as higher rents. And even though some communities now allow mobile homes in residential areas, the developments must bid against other uses for the more expensive land. The effect of all this is to increase the cost of parks and, of course, their monthly rental.

Park development is most active in the Sunbelt, especially in the service-oriented market, but not in housing-oriented communities, a market few developers seem inclined to enter. At the same time, older, less expensive parks are disappearing. A case in point was a group in Englewood, Colorado, called WHERE (We'll Have Equitable RElocation) formed in 1980 when their homes were threatened by the proposed widening of a four-lane commercial artery into a six-lane highway. The area affected was a twelve-mile strip in southeast suburban Denver. Although zoned for commercial and industrial uses, it contained twelve small, old parks. The highway expansion threatened about 180 rental lots. No new park space had been built in Denver since 1974, the vacancy rate in the metro area was less than 1 percent, and newer parks did not want to accept old units. When first confronted with the problem, planning officials confessed that, since mobile homes are mobile, they assumed they could simply be moved. They did not regard park residents, many of whom had lived on the same lot for twenty years, as permanent residents of the city.

WHERE was organized to convince the State Highway Department that the homes they planned to remove were not particularly mobile, especially since there were few places to move them. After months of negotiations, plans for the highway were modified: one interchange was eliminated from the design, and a right-of-way was shifted. As a result, only a few home sites were destroyed. With its initial objective met, WHERE turned its efforts toward finding a more secure location for members' homes. It began working to establish a new cooperative park. Assisted by the Highway Department and the State Land Use Commission, WHERE identified possible sites. The Commission had been instructed a year earlier to use state lands

Elm Park on South Santa Fe Drive in Englewood, Colorado, was deemed an expendable commercial development at the time the highway was being widened. Residents helped form a protest group, WHERE, which eventually got the city to redesign the highway and avoid destroying most of the existing parks.

to alleviate the affordable housing crisis. With a long-term lease on public land, establishing a cooperative appeared more realistic. Although WHERE found an acceptable site south of Denver, county officials refused to rezone. Eventually the group turned its attention to gaining cooperative ownership of the parks in which its members resided and succeeded.

The Cherokee Mobile Home park in Anaheim, California, is another case of cooperative development. In 1986, residents inadvertently discovered that their park was about to be sold. Fearing that a new landlord might hike up the rents, or convert the land to another use, they organized a cooperative to buy the park. With help from the Los Angeles Community Design Center, a nonprofit development firm assisting low- and moderate-income community groups, they were able to work through the difficult process of securing financing, and completed purchase in 1986.

Over one million California residents, many of them senior citizens, live in mobile home parks. Out of approximately 5000 parks in the state in 1986, only twenty were owned by residents, but that situation is changing, at least in San Diego County. In 1984 the county initiated the Mobile Home Occupant Assistance Program (MOAP), providing financial assistance to lower-income households in mobile home parks so that they could convert their parks to resident ownership. County officials recognized in the early 1980s that the rapid escalation of park space rental rates was eliminating an important source of low-cost housing. MOAP was created to help stabilize rents and thereby preserve a crucial dwindling source of affordable housing.

Qualified families are given 30-year, 5 percent loans on which the maximum interest and principal payment is limited to 3 percent of the household's income. When participating residents sell their home, the balance of principal and all accrued interest becomes due. MOAP is financed through a combination of federal Community Development Block Grants, county, state, and private lending. In its first six years, MOAP has provided financing to assist the conversion to resident ownership of eleven mobile home parks with a total of 2030 spaces.

Converting parks to resident ownership is one approach to preserving the inventory of existing affordable rental space; another is slowing the sale of parks for other uses. In 1986 the city of Sunnyvale, California became the first in the state to enact an ordinance protecting residents from the impact of park conversion.[35] The ordinance recognizes the mobile home's important role in providing housing for people with lower incomes, especially senior citizens, and acknowledges the lack of alternative affordable housing and the scarcity of vacant park space. Developers proposing to convert a mobile home park to other uses are required to determine the impact on residents and, if necessary, compensate owners based on in-park value or help them relocate. This provision is critical, since the value of mobile homes with no alternative space to locate can be 25 percent of their in-park value.

In the late 1980s low-income housing advocates began focusing attention on the looming threat to the low-cost rental housing inventory posed by "expiring use."[36] Expiring use refers to the expiration of mortgages and rental assistance contracts that have been used to build and maintain public housing and to keep their rental rates low. As mortgages are paid off, many housing authorities are disposing of their properties rather than doing costly repairs or picking up subsidies to keep rents low. The problem of expiring use will affect 523,000 units of rental housing by the mid-1990s. Experts estimate that it will cost approximately $18 billion to preserve 90 percent of these units over the next fifteen years, roughly $38,000 per apartment.

While the problem of expiring use is real and significant, the attention it has been given in contrast to that given the loss of mobile home park space occurring around the country at the same time demonstrates again the essential invisibility of the mobile home. San Diego County's MOAP program has effectively preserved 2030 mobile home spaces as a form of affordable housing for less than $4.4 million, or a cost of about $2,200 per household. At a time when the affordable housing stock is in danger, efforts like MOAP and the Sunnyvale ordinance are essential. The rate at which such programs are being adopted by other states and localities, however, suggests that thousands of mobile home rental spaces will be lost over the next decade, and with them one of the nation's most significant privately developed sources of affordable housing.

Threats from the Feds

As if local opposition and economic pressures were not enough, existing parks and new developments now face threats from federal agencies. The Federal Emergency Management Agency (FEMA), which is responsible for preparing for natural and man-made emergencies, proposed, in 1986 as part of its National Flood Insurance Program, that mobile home park spaces in floodplains be made safe against flood. Occupied park spaces could remain in use, but once a unit was removed it could not be replaced unless the lot met flood requirements. Compliance would require constructing levees around an affected park area, elevating lots, or creating an elevated foundation. In many cases, these measures would be prohibitively costly, creating an incentive to leave spaces vacant. If enough spaces became vacant, it might even be reasonable to convert the park to another use.

A letter from the Florida Manufactured Housing Association suggested that compliance with the rule could produce absurd results.

> If the only option available to the park is to build the home on pilings, the home could become vulnerable to wind damage because it will extend 5 to 8 feet above the other homes in the park, thus losing the natural buffer afforded by the continuity of homes sited at the same height. This situation seems to create conflicting directions from FEMA since they also admonish the public to go to secure areas when wind turbulence is imminent. . . . The aesthetic created by 5 to 10 homes jutting high above the other 300 or more homes in the park is itself a reason to give pause. Unfortunately, while it may sound like a good idea in Washington, the practical effect will not escape the enterprising media types who will be quick to point out the myopic source of the debacle.[37]

Cartoon by Gil Richards portraying the consequences of the FEMA ruling.

The proposed regulation, while not directed exclusively at mobile homes, had the potential of significantly affecting parks. Many older parks were zoned into less desirable areas, including floodplains. The reasoning at the time was that, since parks catered to transient trailerites whose homes were moveable, they could be towed away in case of emergency. Such an option clearly does not apply to the modern immobile mobile home. To assesss the impact of the new rule, the National Manufactured Housing Federation (NMHF) surveyed its members and petitioned FEMA, protesting that more than 2000 mobile home communities and over 100,000 park spaces would be affected.[38] FEMA was unmoved, but several members of Congress added wording to the 1987 Supplemental Appropriations bill mandating suspension of the new rule for a year.

In September 1989 FEMA sent Congress an alternative to its previous rule on flood-prone mobile home sites. It recommended that existing parks be "grandfathered" for ten years; existing homes that were unmoved could remain without being elevated, and new homes moved to existing sites need only be elevated if the home previously at that location had suffered high water damage.

An interesting aspect of the FEMA case is that it had the industry calling for a federal agency to recognize that mobile home communities are not like site-built housing communities. In a petition to the agency, asking it to alter its proposed rule change, NMHF argued that mobile home communities are unique because they are designed so that homes can be moved in and out regularly. While hardly inaccurate, the impression is contrary to the industry's promotion of the idea that modern manufactured housing in parks is virtually site-fixed.

Despite the industry's attempt to fight the FEMA ruling, the most muted voice of all in the effort to maintain and increase rental park availability in general has been that of the industry, particularly the manufacturers. Faced with a dearth of park space in the period following World War II, manufacturers strongly encouraged development and improved design. They saw it as a necessity for their own economic survival. Today the industry is experiencing a protracted period of declining sales stretching back to the mid-1970s, yet the manufacturers have made little organized effort to encourage community development that would support affordable housing, and hence improve sales. At the same time, the type and size of parks built today is beyond the capacity of most dealers. The economics of the situation have changed, leaving a gap for others to fill. While there are some hopeful signs in efforts to create cooperative parks, or to utilize municipal assistance, successes are few and far between. The mobile home industry may be able to survive with sales for private lots and service-oriented developments, but its market will continue to shrink if it fails to meet the needs of the low-income household it has historically been most successful in satisfying.

Institutionalization:
The Price of Visibility

A Presidential Pardon

In his 1970 message to Congress on national housing goals, President Richard Nixon made what to some must have been a rather startling announcement. The president, who had lauded the virtues of small-town life and with them the merits of home ownership, had to acknowledge that "for many moderate-income American families, the mobile home is the only kind of housing they can reasonably afford."[1] He was therefore including mobile homes in the count of new housing units being produced. At the time of Nixon's message, mobile homes accounted for approximately one third of new housing starts in the nation, and over 90 percent of all new housing selling for under $15,000. Despite mobile homes' prominent contribution, the Department of Commerce had not included them in its housing production figures; until the 1960 Census, they had been lumped in with "other" types of housing, a category containing houseboats, tents, and converted railroad cars. The mobile home, to many federal agencies, was still "temporary" housing at best, and totally invisible at worst.

The president's message to Congress was a requirement of the Housing and Urban Development Act of 1968. The act had established a housing production goal of 2.6 million units per year for a ten-year period. Without including mobile homes in the production figures, the president would have had to report that the nation had fallen 17 percent short of its goal. By including mobile homes the target would be exceeded. In addition to the goal of increasing available housing, the mobile home helped to meet the objective of affordability—and without the use of subsidies—that Nixon was intent upon reducing. According to a study by the Center for Automotive Safety, the mobile home industry agreed with the president's position. "Mobile home manufacturers, struggling for years to shed their public image as housing's bastard son, were delighted. Since that time, the Mobile Home Dealers National Association . . . has written to Department of Housing and Urban Development secretary James Lynn, asking that he end all federal subsidies and allow mobile homes to fill the housing gap."[2]

The president's message went further than simply recognizing the contribution of mobile homes. He seemed to want to encourage their development. Since an increase in the use of mobile homes depended on the availability of land, Nixon urged local governments to reform restrictive land use regulation and eliminate other forms of discrimination. His message was also intended to signal to various federal agencies that the mobile home was henceforth to be officially treated as primary and permanent housing. Such recognition could significantly improve mortgage terms and the secondary market for mobile home paper. Recognition, however, could also invite increased regulation and a new visibility that could cost the industry some of the advantages it had enjoyed.

The Housing Act of 1968 and Operation Breakthrough

The Housing and Urban Development Act of 1968 was fashioned in response to the urban riots of 1965–67. Violence in Detroit, Los Angeles, Cleveland, Chicago, and Newark challenged the capacity of municipal authorities. Firefighters feared entering areas of unrest, as did ambulance drivers, and even the police. In Washington, D.C., flames destroying homes and businesses in black neighborhoods could be seen from the steps of the Capitol. Two task forces, the President's Commission on Urban Problems and the National Commission on Urban Housing, were established and charged with studying the sources of unrest and suggesting plans for action.[3] One of the key problems both commissions identified was inadequate housing. They called for the construction of massive amounts of new housing, affordable by the lowest income groups. Whereas the landmark Housing Act of 1949 had intended to provide dwellings for the middle class, a new program was proposed to address urban redevelopment for the lower classes.

To reach the desired production and afforadbility goals, the Commission on Urban Problems recommended establishing a government-sponsored program to mass produce housing. Many of the recommendations of its report were incorporated in the Housing and Urban Development Act of 1968. A section of that act authorized the secretary of HUD to plan for the development and demonstration of new technologies for producing low-income housing. HUD was to sponsor the construction of 5000 dwellings per year, using five different technologies, for a period of five years.[4]

In May 1969, Secretary of HUD George Romney announced "Operation Breakthrough," a program designed to sponsor the development of experimental housing prototypes. In presenting the program, Romney boasted "We are now just in the first stage of the industrial age in housing production. . . . Before the Seventies are over, industrialized housing will dominate the market."[5] The enticement of Breakthrough was the potential aggregation of the housing market. A corporation like General Electric, which normally would have salesmen selling appliances to individual developments, might now find itself selling entire subsystems, comprising kitchen, bathroom, and the mechanical core of furnace, air conditioner, and water heater. If Breakthrough could aggregate the market for industrialized housing, it would be possible for manufacturers to sell the same housing throughout the country, thereby creating a large enough market to attract major corporations' participation. Such market aggregation requires uniform specifications, describing how the housing must perform, as well as uniform regulations, without which the product could be subject to different codes in every locality.

Breakthrough was organized in three phases. In the first, proposals would be solicited and reviewed; in the second, selected proposals were to be developed on demonstration sites; and in the third, larger-scale developments were to be built. Two hundred and thirty-six firms answered HUD's request for proposals, including five of the top ten Fortune 500 companies. In August 1971, HUD awarded twenty-two contracts for the development of a total of 2796 units, to be constructed on eleven demonstration sites. A year later, however, many of the contractors were in serious trouble, and some had already gone under.

A major problem was the lack of uniformity in local building codes; precisely the problem Lustron had encountered some twenty years earlier. Obtaining variances to codes resulted in extended and costly delays because of the lengthy reviews, hearings, and design modifications required. Ironically, the difficulties that codes might present had already been identified by

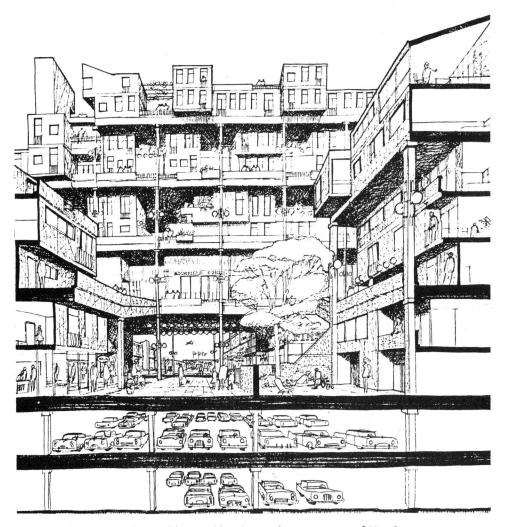

Example of a system submitted for consideration to the Department of Housing and Urban Development's Operation Breakthrough.

the Commission on Urban Problems, which had also suggested developing a demonstration program like Breakthrough. A survey the Commission had conducted in cities with populations of over 5000 found little uniformity of code or enforcement. The Commission concluded, "This chaotic condition prevents the effective application of modern mass-production methods and the adoption of new products and techniques. It is localism, provincialism and so-called home rule gone wild."[6] Rather than showing a way around the obstacle of differing local codes, Breakthrough demonstrated their intractability.

To help stimulate production of the volume of units the last phase of the demonstration called for, Section 236 (mortgage subsidies for rental apartments) funding was to be used. In January 1973, however, President Nixon declared a moratorium on new allocations of these funds. The loss of subsidies, the delays produced by dealing with local codes, and the onset of a deep housing recession combined to kill Breakthrough. Secretary Romney's promised "revolution in housing construction unmatched since men came out of the caves," had come and gone with no greater success than that of its predecessors, dating back to the Depression.[7]

Between 1969 and 1973, Operation Breakthrough produced approximately 25,000 housing units at a total federal cost of $72 million. During that same period, the mobile home industry produced almost 2.5 million housing units at no direct cost to the federal government. Inglorious and technologically primitive as it might appear to many, the mobile home again was vindicated as the only affordable unsubsidized form of industrialized housing in the United States. It was the beginning of the institutional recognition, at least at the federal level, of the mobile home. From the late 1960s on, the mobile home would increasingly be accepted, at least on the federal level, as permanent housing, enjoying all of the rights and privileges accorded that categorization.

Legitimacy and Institutionalization

Nixon's recognition of the mobile home as a legitimate form of permanent housing marked a significant shift in its acceptance by American society. Up to this point, a tacit policy of segregation had kept the mobile home confined to parks. Even though it served many of the functions of permanent housing, the agencies and institutions that made up the housing system largely ignored it. Its control fell to other authorities, such as motor vehicle bureaus.

By the late 1960s, the popularity of the mobile home had increased to a point that segregation alone was inadequate. If it remained officially invisible, the institutions and agencies of the housing system would not be able to impose requirements on its use. Extending institutional controls would require categorizing the mobile home in terms used for recognized forms of housing. It would require an evaluation of barriers to siting mobile homes in residential districts: a reconsideration of limits on the duration of stay; and an extension of legal and technical meanings associated with house and home to include the mobile home as a legitimate alternative.

From the late 1960s to the present, the housing system's treatment of mobile homes has moved increasingly from a strategy of segregation to one of integration, yet mobile homes continue to be treated as a special type of housing in many places. Their integration can most accurately be described as separate but equal: as an alternative that is recognized within the housing system but falls into a special class.

Legitimation has been a mixed blessing for the mobile home industry and its consumers. It has removed some of the stigma from living in a mobile home, provided a basis for fighting restrictions against discriminatory siting, and made financing easier to obtain. At the same time, institutional recognition has removed the protective shield of invisibility. Whereas the incongruities between mobile homes and other forms of permanent housing formerly were ignored, institutionalization has brought closer scrutiny and attempts to eliminate them. Institutionalization has also made the mobile home an easier target for a growing number of opponents, who are now able to plead their case through the housing system of which they are also a part.

Perhaps the most significant effect of institutionalization has been to make the mobile home less affordable. Higher standards for land development and construction have increased costs, reducing the availability of this form of housing. As a result, the industry today faces another transition, one no less significant than that which transformed it from a producer of house trailers to a manufacturer of mobile homes.

Federal Institutionalization: The HUD Code

The political advantages of recognizing the mobile home as permanent housing were not the only considerations in the early 1970s working to foster institutionalization. Safety and durability were becoming serious concerns. Fire-related deaths in mobile homes were reported frequently in local newspapers, and hurricanes and tornadoes seemed to single them out for destruction. Insurance companies and consumer groups lobbied for action to reduce the risks of mobile home living.

At the time, consumers' complaints about mobile home construction were being gathered by Ralph Nader's Center for Automotive Safety. Complaints spoke of inadequate and unsafe wiring, plumbing that froze, and walls that bellowed in the wind. One woman wrote that a frozen turkey had slipped from her hands while she was removing it from the freezer and had crashed clear through the particle-board floor of her kitchen. A man described how he sank through the floor of his home while sitting in his bathtub as it filled with water. The industry, for its part, was not unaware of these problems and attempted to monitor production in the hope of avoiding piecemeal regulation by different states and localities.

In 1963, the MHMA contracted the American National Standards Institute (ANSI) to develop construction standards.[8] Initially, only manufacturers who were members of the association were required to build to the ANSI standard. They could affix a shield indicating that their products were in compliance. MHMA employed fourteen inspectors to make in-plant checks, but, at best, this was only a small sampling. By 1973, forty-five states had adopted the ANSI standard, making it virtually mandatory for all mobile home sales.[9] In most cases, a state agency took responsibility for design review and in-plant inspections, but in some states a third party was hired to do so. In North Dakota, for example, the MHMA conducted that state's inspections. The Federal Housing Administration (FHA) and Veterans Administation (VA) also adopted the ANSI standard to assure the quality of units for which they provided mortgages. The FHA conducted no field inspections, relying on states to perform this function, while the VA conducted quarterly inspections of factories that supplied units for veterans.

In theory, since so many states had adopted the same standard, reciprocity of inspections, in which one state's certification of compliance with the standard would be accepted by another, should have been an easy matter. In practice, little reciprocity developed. In five of the states that had adopted the ANSI standard, no inspection system was ever established.[10] As a result, agents from one state would have to inspect units destined for their jurisdiction but built in another state.

In a review of problems related to compliance with the state-adopted ANSI standard, the Center for Automotive Safety concluded:

> Three factors contribute to the low quality [of mobile home construction]: poor design, cheap materials, and sloppy workmanship. State inspections of mobile home plants have helped to improve and standardize the engineering of mobile homes in recent years, but there are still notable examples of manufacturers having sold homes with defects that stem largely from poor engineering and design. The enforcement of an industry-promulgated construction code has also resulted in upgrading the quality of materials used in mobile homes. But in areas where the code is lax or ambiguous, many manufacturers still use the cheapest and shoddiest materials available. Poor workmanship by unskilled, untrained workers slapping together homes at a frantic pace, is an equally important cause of low quality. These three factors all too often result in shockingly bad products.[11]

State regulation had gone as far as it could go, and by 1972 Congress began seriously considering legislation of mobile home construction.[12] Not surprisingly, the first bill regulating construction was introduced by a representative from Florida, the state with the greatest concentration of mobile homes in the country. In 1973, Senator Proxmire introduced a bill influenced heavily by recommendations from the still unpublished report by the Center for Automotive Safety. Others in Congress supported bills that would create a preemptive federal code, while some wanted to establish a federal minimum standard, allowing states to impose more stringent requirements. One proposal called for including the mobile home, along with other "dangerous products," under a product safety bill. Mobile home manufacturers were generally supportive of federal legislation that would assure the public of the safety and durability of their product, but they wanted to avoid bills that would allow individual states to develop different requirements.

In 1974, Congress passed the Mobile Home Construction and Safety Standards Act, authorizing HUD to establish and enforce a code for mobile home construction.[13] The code would preempt local building regulations, but foundation standards would remain under local control. The act made mobile homes the first private-sector building type to be regulated by a mandatory federal code. It recognized the mobile home as a dwelling, but one that was separate and distinct, by virtue of being built on a permanent chassis. Modular housing was excluded from the legislation, so that the precedent set by a national code would remain restricted to a single building type. The legislation also stopped short of referring to the mobile home specifically as a consumer product, a categorization that would have raised the issue of warranties and questions about whether HUD was the right agency to be developing a code.

On June 15, 1976, the Department of Housing and Urban Development implemented its new standards for mobile home construction, commonly referred to as the HUD code. The code was based heavily on the ANSI standard of 1963. It contained two singularly important provisions. First, it was a preemptive national standard, and, second, it was based on performance. The need for a preemptive standard had been demonstrated by the failure of efforts like Lustron and Breakthrough, which had run aground trying to negotiate through a maze of differing local codes. By establishing a single standard, a manufacturer was assured that the electrical system built for a mobile home in Indiana would also meet the requirements of any other state to which it was shipped. Although the HUD code was preemptive, it took into account different regional requirements; specifically, those concerning insulation, roof strength, and wind loads.

That it was based on performance rather than on the traditional form of specification was another important feature of the HUD code. Most building codes are written on a specification basis, setting out precisely how something is to be constructed or designed. A ventilation standard, for example, might state that a room must have an openable window area equivalent to at least 10 percent of its floor area. (The calculation of 10 percent is based on the desired rate of air changes per hour.) In a performance standard, the rate of air changes is specified but the means of achieving it, whether by windows or ventilation fans, is left to the designer. Similarly, a specification-based code might require that wood frame walls in residential construction be made of 2" x 4" studs spaced 16" on center. A performance code might simply indicate the strength that the wall must have, allowing other spacing (such as 2' 0" on center with glued plywood facing). Performance-based building codes had been advocated for decades as a way of encouraging innovation in the building industry but had met with stiff opposition from state and local building inspectors. Although the ANSI standard had been performance based, most states did not have the necessary testing capacity to support this approach. HUD, by contrast, would be better able to test construction innovations.

The adoption of the HUD code furthered the institutionalization of the mobile home by bringing its construction and design under the review of the federal housing agency. Although the mobile home industry itself had lobbied hard for passage of the code, support for it among manufacturers was not unanimous. Larger manufacturers generally felt that benefits would result from this recognition, particularly in assuring a uniform national code. Smaller manufacturers, however, were concerned about the complexities of the new regulatory system, which, though similar to systems in many states, involved more inspections, more paperwork, and more review.

Recognition by Federal Mortgage Agencies

One of the significant disadvantages of buying a mobile home had been finding financing. Mortgages available for site-built homes were typically for a long term and at lower rates, benefits realized largely through federal involvement in the mortgage market. Federal agencies were both a source of loans and a secondary market for mortgages held by lenders. By assuming some of the risk of home loans, lenders could offer them at lower rates and with a smaller down payment. This kind of preferred treatment had not been extended to mobile home purchasers, even when a home was permanently sited on an owner-occupied lot, because the unit was still regarded as potentially mobile and because no one knew how durable it was. The HUD code's assurance of the safety and durability of mobile homes provided a basis for extending federal loans to purchase them. There was growing recognition that mobile homes were relatively immobile, especially when set up on a private lot.

Most households' primary financial yardstick in housing decisions is that the monthly cost not exceed 25 to 30 percent of their gross income. The benefit to a mobile home buyer of obtaining a loan at house rates, with its lower interest rates and longer terms, is obviously significant. If a household buying a $20,000 mobile home obtains a 13 percent loan, on 90 percent of the cost, for a ten year term, its monthly payment will be $276, whereas a ten percent loan, for a twenty-year duration, would mean a monthly payment of $176.

The equity requirements to purchase a mobile-home include down payment, title, transportation, and set-up fees. If the loan carries a large down payment, the total equity requirement on a purchase may be a significant hurdle for the prospective buyer. Again, with a government-backed loan, the lender is assuming less risk and can offer a higher loan-to-value ratio, resulting in a smaller down payment. As the equity hurdle is lowered, more households can consider owning a mobile home.

Before the HUD code, the federal government loaned money for mobile home parks only. Section 207 of the Housing Act of 1955 provided a loan insurance program to help finance the construction of new parks and the rehabilitation of existing parks. During the first twenty-five years of the program, almost $193 million in loans were made. Of that amount, about 84 percent was granted between 1970 and 1972, a period when mobile home park development was at its height, and when federal recognition began to broaden. By contrast, in 1980 no loans were made.[14] In all, no more than 4 percent of the total rental space in the country has been developed or rehabilitated with federal loan assistance under Section 207. Other federal programs, such as community development block grants, used to renovate older parks, and Section 8 rental assistance to low-income families, have been made available; but the extent of their application has been insignificant.

In 1969, Title I of the National Housing Act authorized HUD to make loans on mobile homes and lots for mobile home use. This allowed mobile home buyers, almost 90 percent of whom finance their homes, to do so at rates closer to those available to conventional home buyers. The original terms of Title I autho-

Multisection manufactured homes placed in subdivisions are eligible for a single mortgage financing on both house and land.

rized loans were relatively short, but after passage of the HUD code and testing for the durability of units manufactured under that standard, terms improved. In 1989 the buyer of a manufactured home could receive a maximum loan of $40,500 for the purchase of a home, or $54,000 for the combined purchase of a home and site under the FHA's special manufactured housing finance program. A minimum downpayment of 5 percent is required for the first $5000, and 10 percent on the balance. The maximum loan maturity for purchase of a home alone is 20 years, and 25 years for a home and site. Maturities on the VA's special manufactured home loan program are similar, but the maximum loan amount is limited to the lesser of 40 percent of purchase price or $20,000.[15] In addition to these special programs, a manufactured home permanently attached to an approved foundation may qualify for a traditional FHA or VA real estate mortgage for up to 30 years. Thirty-year mortgages are also offered by private lenders. As an additional incentive for private lenders to finance manufactured housing, the Federal National Mortgage Association ("Fannie Mae") and the Federal Home Loan Bank Board have been authorized to purchase manufactured housing loans from lending institutions, thereby creating a secondary market for loans, and reducing the risk of originating and holding such notes.[16]

It might be expected that with the more favorable rates

offered by federally guaranteed mortgage programs a large percentage of mobile home loans would be drawn from this source. During the first ten years of Title I lending (1969 to 1979), the FHA made loans for somewhat less than 3.5 percent of the total units shipped.[17] During the same period, VA programs made loans on only 1.3 percent of the total units shipped. Over the next eight years, however, 9.9 percent of new mobile home sales were FHA financed and 3.3 percent received VA loans.[18] While the growth in federal loan activity was significant, it has declined sharply since the early 1980s. In 1988 the VA made only 1674 mobile home loans; a year later it proposed terminating the loan program.

Working against the more extensive use of federal loans has been greater paperwork and the small fees offered to dealers and banks processing loans. As a result, the majority of mobile home loans are still financed as chattel though private banks, usually at rates one to two points higher than conventional home mortgages. Higher rates in the private market are justified by greater risk; yet, historically, the rate of mobile home loan defaults has been lower than that for conventional mortgages.[19] Because the private loan market remains lucrative, some of the larger manufacturers, such as Fleetwood, Skyline, and Champion, have established their own financial corporations. One dealer franchise, Ameristar, in conjunction with a bank, is trying to establish loan offices in K-Mart stores.

Institutionalization at the State and Local Level

In addition to the federal efforts to confer greater legitimacy on mobile homes and promote ownership, many states began trying to accommodate the mobile home as a permanent land use. Land use and building regulation are powers held by the states and transerred by them to local communities. The states, however, retain the power to modify this authority if they feel that it is being used discriminatorily. By 1989, twenty-two states had passed mobile home antidiscrimination legislation, or their high courts had ruled to that effect.[20]

Despite these actions, resistance persisted at the municipal level. In Colorado, for example, the state legislature passed a mobile home single siting bill in 1984. The bill requires that local governments provide for the placement of mobile homes on single lots. Partly to test the legislation, the Colorado Manufactured Housing Association (CMHA) purchased a lot in November 1987 and requested a permit from the Denver Building Department to place a mobile home there. A week later, the permit was denied on grounds that the mechanical systems of the home failed to meet building code requirements. This type of review would not have been required had the home been placed in a park, but CMHA objected that it should not have been required of a single sited unit either, as long as it was built under the HUD code. The Colorado legislation, however, is ambiguous. It requires that mobile homes meet HUD standards but, in addition, that they meet local codes on an "equivalent performance engineering basis," meaning that "all components and subsystems will perform to meet health, safety, and functional requirements to the same extent as required for other single family housing units." If a locality can insist on proof of equivalent performance, can the HUD code be regarded as preemptive?

One tactic used to exclude mobile homes in localities where they are technically permitted, is to add requirements that make them too costly to be competitive with site-built housing: expensive foundation systems, minimum floor areas, and minimum dimensions fall outside of the concerns addressed in the HUD code, and are properly controlled by localities within limits established by the state. The effect of such requirements is that combined home and land ownership is far less affordable.

Ironically, some of the states that have acted to reduce discrimination against mobile home placements have written legislation that discriminates against the most affordable mobile home, the single-wide. Many localities that allow single siting of mobile homes require that units be new HUD code models, of sectional design, with house-type siding and roofing. The average single-section mobile home in 1986 cost $18.84 per square foot, while the average multisection unit cost $22.08, and there is the extra cost of set-up and transportation. The minimum area of a multisection unit required in many single siting laws and ordinances is 24' x 36'. A single-wide 14' x 62' model could provide the same area for 15 to 20 percent less cost. Most affordable housing programs hope for savings in this range.

A new wave of litigation is now beginning, which attempts to remove the distinction between single-wide and multisection units in areas where multisection homes have been permitted. In a recent case, the Supreme Court of Pennsylvania ruled that a zoning ordinance permitting sectional mobile homes, but excluding single-wides, was unconstitutional.[21] The court found the ordinance arbitrary and capricious in its attempt to distinguish between single-wide and multisection units. It also found that there was no significant distinction between mobile homes and conventional single-family housing. In its ruling, the court recognized local government's responsibility to provide for a wide range of housing needs.

The designation "mobile home" still unofficially belongs to single-wides. This photograph, supplied by Schult Homes, was captioned: "Don't call this a trailer."

Manufactured Housing: A Rose By Any Other Name

At the same time that states began to fight discriminatory practices, the mobile home industry was revising an old tactic of its own. In the mid-1950s it found it useful and appropriate to change the name of its product from house trailer to mobile home, conveying a new pattern of use. By the mid-1970s it felt that mobile home conveyed the wrong image, and in 1975 the Mobile Home Manufacturers Association changed its name to the Manufactured Housing Institute (MHI). The renamed organization soon began lobbying in Congress for a legislative name change that would officially designate mobile homes as manufactured housing. This change was incorporated into the 1980 Housing Act, which mandated that "the term mobile home be changed to manufactured housing in all federal law and literature." Despite the revision, the general public continued to hold on to the labels trailer and mobile home. An interview during NBC's coverage of the 1988 Winter Olympics, for example, described how an athlete's family had made the financial sacrifice of continuing to live in a "trailer" to support his training. Within the industry itself, the term manufactured home is associated with house-like, sectional units, while mobile homes are thought of as single-wides.

Even as the public and industry worked on adopting the new name, the Reagan Administration began unofficially to broaden it to include other forms of factory-built housing. This broadening reflected the administration's desire to remove or reduce regulations which both defined and protected manufactured housing. Its new position first became evident in 1982 in *The Report of the President's Commission on Housing:*

> the term "manufactured housing" has come to designate what were once called mobile or modular homes, whether or not permanently attached to the site. More recently, large components of buildings, such as entire walls, have been manufactured in factories and shipped to the site for permanent installation. Such components, or the assembled building, sometimes have been designated manufactured housing. In this report, the term "manufactured housing" applies to dwellings formerly designated as mobile or modular homes, whether or not they are permanently attached to a site.[22]

By the mid-1980s officials at HUD began suggesting eliminating the HUD code entirely, which would have returned regulation to the states, sacrificing nationwide uniformity. At the same time, a report by the Office of Technology Assessment, an agency of Congress, lauded the HUD code as the only uniform national building code for factory-produced housing. Rather than returning regulation to the states, it recommended that other forms of industrialized housing and nonresidential buildings be included in the code.[23] Underlying these different recommendations at the federal level was the question of who would define the new category—manufactured housing—and what would be included in it. While the industry had promoted the change in name, it had little influence in the debate over its fate.

The Price of Visibility

Through the combined efforts of the federal government and states, the mobile/manufactured home was accepted and integrated into the institutional system of housing. Acceptance, however, was conferred on a more narrowly defined object—the manufactured home. Whereas the mobile home was by definition housing with the capacity to move and inherently independent of a specific site, built-in-a-factory manufactured housing was considered only incidentally mobile. Its mobility simply got it from the factory to the site, whether a park or an individual lot. Moreover, traces of mobility were to be removed from its form, and it was to be made indistinguishable in every way from a home built on a site. The result was housing that was more acceptable to public officials, as well as neighbors, but also less affordable and less accommodating to a broad range of users than the indecorous, shiny box, mobile home.

Institutionalization has integrated the mobile home into the system of housing, while still placing it in a special category of its own. Genuine and complete integration is still a long way off. The establishment of the HUD code headed off the development of conflicting state codes that would have threatened the growth of sales, but the status of sections of the HUD code is currently in jeopardy. It is no longer exclusively local interests fighting the battle of the codes, but powerful coalitions. The industry has gained increased recognition for its contribution to the effort to produce affordable housing, but it has also lost some of the flexibility which permitted innovation and a greater responsiveness to different segments of the housing market. Whether the benefits of institutionalization will outweigh its costs is yet to be determined.

The HUD code went into effect just as the mobile home industry, and the building industry in general, were pulling out of a major recession. In 1973, manufacturers shipped 566,920 units. In 1974, the number of shipments dropped to 329,300, and, in 1975, they fell to an eleven-year low of 212,690. Since 1974, annual shipments have not exceeded 300,000 units, even though dollar value of retail sales has shown significant increases, in part because of a greater percentage of sectional units. With immediate decline in demand during the recession, nearly 40 percent of the factories closed. In previous recessions, small manufacturers would go out of business and larger manufacturers would close some of their branch plants until the economy turned around. Coming out of this recession, however, small manufacturers were faced with a new set of regulations and a complicated design approval and inspection system. Instead of spot-checking units, every unit being manufactured now had to be inspected in the plant. For a small firm, turning out just a few units a week, the cost of filing drawings for approval and paying an inspector to come for a factory visit might mean the difference between being competitive or out of the market.[24] Many of the larger manufacturers bought out smaller companies that might otherwise have continued making it on their own. As a result, after the recession there were fewer firms, and an even stronger domination by the major manufacturers. In recent years, declining sales have been fueled by foreclosed units entering the market. Texas, once the center of industry production, is now a center for foreclosed homes. Because of their mobility, these units can be shipped to other regions, cutting into new sales and further dampening the industry's vitality.

If history is any indication, the cost of the industry's domination by the largest manufacturers has been less flexibility and innovation. Formerly, design innovations frequently came from small new manufacturers who had to make a place for themselves in the market. Although larger manufacturers rapidly adopted their successful innovations, a one-season sales advantage was often enough for small companies to establish connections with dealers and credit with suppliers. The mix of smaller and larger manufacturers also assured better coverage of a diverse market. New manufacturers had to look for potential submarkets untapped by the majors, meeting the demand for smaller units designed especially for parks, for example, or for the units with special features for the elderly. Since systematic market studies have not been done by the industry, this trial-and-error entrepreneurship helped assure that the emerging needs of the housing market would be met.

Along with the increased dominance of the major manufacturers, the industry experienced increased diversification. In the mid-1950s, when vacation trailers were differentiated from mobile homes, many manufacturers diversified by continuing to manufacture both. Again, in the 1960s and 1970s, manufacturers diversified by producing modular units along with mobile homes. In 1986, ten of the top twenty-seven mobile home manufacturing firms also produced or were part of companies manufacturing recreation vehicles and/or modular homes.[25] This type of diversification continues today, but with some new twists. Some of the largest manufacturers are now controlled by corporations with no previous ties to the industry. The nation's sixth largest mobile home manufacturer, Guerdon, is a subsidiary of City Investing Company, which also owns the merchant builder Wood Brothers. Kaufmann & Broad, a community developer, also owns a subsidiary that is the nation's twelfth largest producer of mobile homes. The new pattern of diversification is one in which corporations outside of the mobile home industry are diversifying by acquiring mobile home producers. In many cases, these acquisitions suggest an acceptance of the mobile home as permanent housing, whose manufacture is appropriate to the activities of community developers and housing manufacturers. Whether this pattern of diversification will bring new business practices and products to the industry is not yet evident.

Emerging Threats to the Industry

The effect of implementing the HUD code and extending other forms of federal control over manufactured housing was to consolidate the industry institutionally. For the first time since the war, manufacturers were obliged to follow standards defining not only construction, but aspects of appearance and use. The centralization of federal regulation was meant to assure uniform quality and safety, yet it failed to eliminate local discriminatory practices. With centralization, groups opposed to mobile/manufactured housing could more readily attack the industry as a whole, especially through the rule-making procedures by which federal agencies define standards and practices. When the National Home Builders Association, for example, found that manufactured housing was becoming an economic threat to its members who build traditional houses for the lower end of the market, it began to encourage rules and standards that would eliminate some of the mobile home's competitive advantage. Other strategies enemies of the industry have employed are to call for deregulation of selected sections of the HUD code—which by allowing state and local authorities to issue different standards would vitiate the power of a preemptive code—and to call for the elimination of protections which the industry, and particularly the parks, have enjoyed as a result of providing a unique type of housing.

All of these strategies—redefining standards, deregulation, and eliminating protections—have been used to attack the industry during the 1980s. The last two strategies, in particular, were consistent with the objectives of the Reagan Administration to deregulate all industry. In defending itself, the manufactured housing industry has found itself telling conflicting stories. In some instances, it has been to its advantage to argue for granting status to manufactured housing equal to that of site-built housing. In other instances, it has argued for special treatment, pointing out the ways manufactured housing and its communities are unique. At present there is no consensus in the industry about the identity of its product and how it should be treated. Each new dilemma has been confronted as it arose, without the benefit of a larger unifying argument, as a brief review of several recent legislative battles will illustrate.

Removable Chassis.   Throughout the development of the trailer/mobile home specific physical features have been either emphasized or ignored to justify its categorization. One such feature is the chassis. In court cases since the mid-1930s, the question of how a unit was attached to the ground has been used as a basis for classifying it as a dwelling or vehicle. Some courts ruled that anything with a chassis was a vehicle, regardless of whether it was permanently attached to a foundation; others held that the permanency of a dwelling was determined by the user's intent rather than physical characteristics of the abode. The debate continues today, particularly with regard to units built on wood flooring systems that are delivered on removable chassis.

In August 1986, HUD issued a letter instructing its agencies charged with design review to prohibit manufactured homes in which an all-wood floor frame was substituted for the typical metal frame chassis. By rejecting the wood frame, the Department was rejecting the idea of a removable chassis. In fact, the practice of building units with removable chassis had been going on for years, but a HUD sanction had never been requested. Official approval of the removable chassis would have obliterated the technical distinction between manufactured and modular housing.

The issue of the removable chassis is characteristic of the problem of categorizing the mobile home. Writing in the *Federation Focus*, newsletter for the National Manufactured Housing Federation, Dan Gilligan observed:

> The use of the term "chassis" in the official definition of a manufactured home . . . has long caused zoning problems, in that some officials have been prone to consider a structure built on a chassis as a "vehicle" rather than as a "home." However, the chassis represents a different kind of problem when the home is installed on a permanent foundation or over an excavated basement, for in these circumstances it is often expedient for the installer/builder to remove it. It is often overlooked that the official definition of the term "chassis" does not mention, nor does it necessarily connote, that it be made of steel. The term simply refers to the entire transportation system, including the "frame." The definition of "frame" merely uses the words "prefabricated rigid structure."[26]

Several industry lobbying groups proceeded to sue HUD for relief against its August letter, and by March 1987 HUD seemed to be reversing itself. The Department stated that it "had permitted as meeting the statutory definition of 'permanent chassis' designs which integrate the frame function into the mobile home structure," but it went on to assert that it had "never required that manufactured homes must have steel I-beams; integrated frames may be constructed of wood."[27] HUD seemed to be drawing a distinction between the materials that a chassis could be made of, and whether the chassis had to be permanently attached to the unit. The performance specification basis of the HUD code allows for innovations, such as replacing a steel chassis with one of wood, but the code specifies that a unit must be built on a "permanent chassis" regardless of whether it is set on a permanent foundation. In July 1987, the Federal District Court in Washington, D.C., ruled on a suit brought by the Association for Regulatory Reform, an industry lobbyist. It decided that HUD had acted properly, that its interpretation of the mobile home "chassis" did not constitute a new rule, which would have required it to follow a time-consuming rule-making procedure, and that its actions were definitional only. The ruling of the Washington court had not settled the matter. Another suit, filed by the Indiana Manufactured Housing Association in the Federal District Court in South Bend, asked that HUD be enjoined against restricting the production of units with removable chassis. On November 28, 1989 the U.S. District Court in South Bend granted HUD's request for a summary judgment and removed the injunction, which had permitted the industry to continue to build units with removable frames.

New Energy Standards. Home builders, through the NAHB, not only encouraged HUD to require permanently affixed metal chassis on manufactured homes, but supported higher insulation standards. An April version of the 1987 Housing Bill (H.R.4) proposed that manufactured housing meet the same requirements as other Title II single-family housing. These standards are higher than those required by the HUD code and would have the effect of increasing the cost of manufactured housing. A joint Senate/House conference committee on H.R.4 removed the energy provision in October 1987, stating that any increases in energy standards be developed within the authority of the HUD code.

At the same time that Congress was debating the new energy standard for manufactured homes, and ultimately confirming that such standards belonged within the HUD code, HUD itself was proposing a rule change that would have totally deregulated the energy standard. Passage of H.R.4. thwarted the deregulation attempt, but it was far from dead. Earlier that year, FHA commissioner Thomas Demry announced that he supported repealing the entire HUD code. Before that suggestion could make its way into proposed legislation, HUD began divesting itself of some of the responsibility for administering the code, appointing the Council of American Building Officials (CABO) to administer code revisions. CABO was regarded by the manufactured housing industry as antagonistic to its product. Moreover, HUD's authority to delegate responsibility for code revision to a private organization was challenged by members of Congress. In an angry letter to HUD Secretary Samuel Pierce, Jr., representatives Henry Gonzalez and Marge Roukema, of the

House Subcommittee on Housing and Community Development, made the following observations:

> We have watched with dismay the steps taken by your Department to avoid the responsibilities delegated to you by Congress in the National Manufactured Housing Construction and Safety Standards Act. First was the proposal to totally eliminate all energy conserving requirements, leaving manufacturers to struggle with the conflicting requirements of multiple State laws and consumers to struggle with higher utility bills. . . . Second was the selection of the Council of American Building Officials (CABO) to develop revisions to the standards themselves. . . .
>
> In establishing a federal preemptive standard and inspection system, Congress restricted the authority of the States and delegated the responsibility to you, as the Secretary of HUD, for updating and improving the federal construction standards and enforcement system. . . . We urge you to terminate the arrangement with CABO, [and] to use your staff of engineers and architects to develop standard changes where appropriate and to use the National Manufactured Home Advisory Council, as Congress intended, to give you advice on the advisability of necessary changes.[28]

It is likely that attempts to erode or eliminate the HUD code will continue, at least as long as an attitude favoring deregulation prevails over concern for housing affordability and availability.

Legitimacy vs. Availability and Affordability

For over thirty years the mobile home has been an affordable, widely available housing alternative that allowed millions of Americans to own homes. Ironically, its official recognition and regulation at the federal, state, and local level has increased its cost and effectively reduced available land on which to place it. The industry's own quest for legitimacy has lead it to support regulations which also have reduced industry flexibility during recessions while simultaneously moving the product out of the lower end of the housing market. These changes have occurred at the same time that Americans face a new crisis in housing—the affordability gap and the concomitant problem of homelessness.

By current standards, affordable housing requires no more than 25 to 30 percent of a household's gross monthly income. An "affordability gap" opened in the late 1970s, as real housing costs (adjusted for inflation) grew more rapidly than real income. A family already paying 25 percent of its income for housing either had to spend more or find cheaper housing. In the

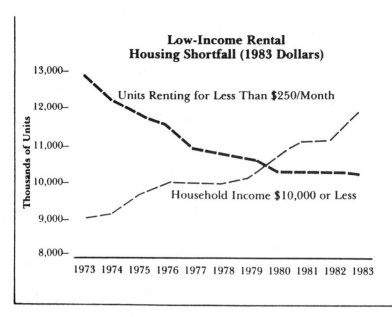

**Low-Income Rental
Housing Shortfall (1983 Dollars)**

One aspect of the gap in affordable housing is in rental units available for
less than $250 a month. This graph, in constant 1983 dollars, shows the de-
cline of affordable rental units in a period in which the number of households
earning $10,000 or less was increasing.

very low end of the rental market, housing costs rose by 34
percent from 1974 to 1985 in constant (adjusted for inflation)
dollars, while real income declined.[29] Households were forced
to devote far more of their income to housing, some as much as
70 percent. Many were simply pushed out of the market and
either had to double up with relatives or join the ranks of the
homeless.[30] Escalating rents, fueled, in part, by a dwindling
supply of rental units, were also affected by rising prices in the
home ownership market.

A Harvard study, *State of the Nation's Housing*, concluded
that in 1985 only 40 percent of households not currently owning
their own home could afford to buy one. Even though mortgage
interest rates began to fall by the mid-1980s, they remained high
when adjusted for inflation. The rising cost of homes also has
meant a larger down payment, an increasingly high hurdle for
the first-time buyer. From 1980 to 1988, the home ownership
rate for those in the 25 to 34 age group dropped from 52.3 percent
to 45 percent.[31] Young, middle-income households found themselves unable to purchase a home and remained in the rental
market, further driving up prices there.

As the affordability gap widens, the more conventional looking manufactured home has found a middle-class market, espe-

Wheel Estate

cially in retirement housing, where it had previously been avoided or ignored.[32] Yet it has simultaneously been retreating from the lower end of the housing market, where, for over three decades, it offered one of the few affordable alternatives.

By the late 1970s the affordability and availability of manufactured housing were being hurt by the increasing difficulty of developing mobile home land. Regulatory and zoning restrictions limited available land, resulting in upward pressure on the price of units and space in existing parks. High development fees made the new developed spaces more expensive. The effects of park space shortages were not felt immediately in all regions, because of heavy overbuilding during the first part of this decade, but by the early 1980s many metropolitan areas had less than 1 percent vacancy. As the tight market encouraged rent increases, the combined lot rent and unit payment became less competitive with rental apartments. At the same time, placing a home on a private lot became more expensive. While many states had made it legally possible to site mobile homes on private lots, finding cities which complied and also had affordable lots available was exceedingly difficult. Minimum lot and unit size requirements raised the cost of such siting, effectively shutting out lower-income households.[33]

As a consequence of moving out of the low end of the affordable housing market, sales of mobile homes have declined. From 1967 to 1976, the total number of mobile homes shipped was 3,799,730. In the following decade, when the HUD code was fully in effect, the total number of homes shipped was down over 30 percent to 2,640,084 units. In addition, the percentage of new single-family dwellings which were mobile homes dropped from 27.7 percent to 14 percent. Mobile homes continued to dominate the low end of the housing market, but they were being chosen by a smaller segment of the home-buying public. In the 1960s, the industry boasted of the number of units under $15,000 that it supplied; by the mid 1980s it was units under $50,000 that defined the low end of the market. In 1977, 62 percent of all new homes that sold for under $50,000 were site-built houses. By 1983, such sales accounted for only 18 percent of the total, while manufactured housing made up the remaining 82 percent. The average new home in 1983 cost $71,840, exclusive of land, while the average mobile home cost $21,000, exclusive of land. From 1976 to 1986, the cost per square foot of a mobile/manufactured home rose from $12.73 to $18.83, while the average cost per square foot for a site-built house rose from $22.59 to $49.05. Even after adding 15 percent to the cost of manufactured housing, for transportation and set-up fees, it was still far more affordable.

The critical economic advantage of owning manufactured housing is being able to site a unit so that monthly land payments or rental costs are still reasonable. In 1986, the average home lot cost $30,800, and the average price of a multisection mobile home was also $30,800. Adding the costs of set-up, transportation, and site preparation, would bring the total to $76,220. A site-built home of comparable size costs $99,225, or 30 percent more. To maintain this cost advantage, however, the buyer must be able to secure comparable financing. Even assuming that the manufactured home buyer finances at a rate three percentage points above the site-built home buyer's, a significant difference in cost will remain. For every percentage difference, however, thousands of potential buyers will be shaved off of the lower end of the market. These buyers still have the option of owning a manufactured home and placing it in a rental park.

A number of factors have been affecting the affordability of buying a unit and renting a park space. The price of new manufactured housing is increasing, though more slowly than the cost of site-built housing. Although a used unit is significantly less expensive, many parks, particularly newer ones, try to restrict placements to new homes. Buying a used unit that is already in a park usually means paying a premium. In parks with a low vacancy rate, the prospective buyer may have little choice

Cost and Size Comparisons of New Manufactured Homes and Site-built Homes Sold, 1984–1988

	1984	1985	1986	1987	1988
Manufactured Homes					
Average sales price (All lengths and widths)	$21,500	$21,800	$22,400	$23,700	$25,100
Cost per square foot	$20.48	$20.57	$20.18	$20.79	$21.36
Average square footage	1,060 sq. ft.	1,060 sq. ft.	1,110 sq. ft.	1,140 sq. ft.	1,175 sq. ft.
Single section					
Average sales price	$17,700	$17,800	$17,800	$18,400	$18,600
Cost per square foot	$19.03	$18.84	$18.84	$19.07	$19.18
Average square footage	930 sq. ft.	945 sq. ft.	945 sq. ft.	965 sq. ft.	970 sq. ft.
Multisection					
Average sales price	$30,450	$30,100	$30,800	$32,400	$33,600
Cost per square foot	$22.30	$21.97	$22.08	$22.82	$23.41
Average square footage	1,364 sq. ft.	1,370 sq. ft.	1,395 sq. ft.	1,420 sq. ft.	1,435 sq. ft.
Site-Built Homes					
Average sales price	$97,600	$100,800	$111,900	$127,000	$138,200
Land price	$19,520	$ 20,160	$ 22,380	$ 25,440	$ 37,314
Price of Structure	$78,080	$ 80,640	$ 89,520	$101,760	$100,886
Cost per square foot	$43.87	$45.18	$49.05	$53.42	$50.57
Average square footage (Living space)	1,780 sq. ft.	1,785 sq. ft.	1,825 sq. ft.	1,905 sq. ft.	1,995 sq. ft.

Source: Quick Facts, Manufactured Housing Institute, 1989.

but to buy a unit already in the park or from the park owner's sales lot.

The low vacancy rate in parks also has escalated rental rates, which have risen more rapidly than the cost of living, at the same time that the price of a unit has been increasing. The lowest end of the park rental market thus is no longer able to afford the mobile home/manufactured housing alternative. Households with a unit already in a park must either absorb rent increases, try to move elsewhere and pay the cost of a move, or sell and run the risk of having to remove the unit from the park, losing much of its built-up equity and appreciation. While the low end of the market is most sensitive to the rental increases, all segments in tight rental markets feel the effects. To what extent this has made consumers choose to rent apartments rather than own a manufactured home in a rental park is not clear, but it is hard to imagine that these conditions have not contributed to the declining market for manufactured housing.

The growing number of foreclosed units in the economically depressed energy development regions of the Southwest has also affected the market for new manufactured housing, though not its affordability. Texas, once the largest producer of manufactured homes, is now the largest source of foreclosed units. Thousands of abandoned units have been left in parks, often stripped of their appliances. Park owners don't want them occupying space, and banks have had a difficult time figuring out what to do with their repos. Refurbishing a unit costs thousands of dollars, and then it often must be transported. To create a better market, banks have been willing to ship units to other regions, consequently spreading the impact on new sales.

The Affordable Housing Demonstration Program

With a widening affordability gap affecting the middle as well as low-income voter, it might have been expected that the Reagan administration, like the Nixon Administration, would have turned to the manufactured housing industry for an unsubsidized solution. Instead, the administration was indifferent at best, and downright antagonistic at worst, toward manufactured housing. Regulation had resulted in greater visibility for the industry at a time when it was beginning to encroach on the lower end of the site-built housing market. Interest groups from the conventional building industry soon were attacking the industry. Fueled by this antagonism, and by their own philosophical support of deregulation, several federal departments and agencies provided a congenial forum for attacks upon manufactured housing. The Reagan Administration's main attempt to address the affordability crisis was the Affordable Housing Demonstration Program.

In 1981, President Reagan appointed a Commission on Housing, headed by William F. McKenna. The McKenna Commission's final report identified housing regulation as a chief culprit behind rising costs:

> For 20 years and more, the public has been fed proposals for new regulation which stress the nobility of the results that are to be achieved by government action and minimize the costs that will be imposed on business and consumers. The time has come to reverse this process, to emphasize the enormity of the costs now imposed upon activities that may not produce a clear public good, often implemented for selfish or obscure purposes.[34]

The Commission estimated that the cost of regulation at all levels added as much as 25 perent to the price of housing.[35] Although the Kaiser and Douglas Commissions of the late 1960s had also cited excessive regulation as an impediment to development, their main concern was with the dampening effect regulation had on the adoption and spread of innovations. They coupled regulatory reform with technological development, and looked toward technological innovation as an important means of reducing housing costs. By contrast, encouraging new technology was not a principal concern of the McKenna Commission. It concluded that existing technology, in the form of industrialized housing, was adequate to meet demand and that it only required the removal of local regulatory roadblocks to achieve greater market diffusion.

Whereas the Kaiser and Douglas Commissions had laid the foundation for Operation Breakthrough, and its commitment of over $70 million to stimulate technological development, the McKenna Commission's recommendations resulted in the Affordable Housing Demonstration Program, a public-private partnership supported by virtually no federal funding. The purpose of the program, in the words of HUD Secretary Samuel Pierce, Jr., was to show that through reform of "outdated and unnecessary building and land use regulation, significant costs savings could be achieved."[36]

One of the program's first demonstrations of affordable housing was developed in 1982 in Elkhart, Indiana, historical center of the mobile home industry.[37] The houses in this demonstration were primarily mobile and modular units produced in local factories, and a couple of site-built houses. Units ranged from an 890-square-foot, two-bedroom modular home, priced at $37,500, to a 2000-square-foot site-built home for $59,900. The average price of the demonstration homes was $48,500, about 16 percent less than the average price of a new house in Elkhart

Exterior and interior of a home in an "Affordable Housing Demonstration" project in Elkhart, Indiana, which consists primarily of manufactured and modular homes. The home shown, built by Schult Homes, was shipped to the site where its chassis was removed and the home set up on a permanent foundation. Additions, like the garage, were built on the site.

County at the time. But the principal savings were realized by reducing lot sizes by about a third of what zoning regulations required and reducing the average floor area of units by about a quarter.[38] Not only were the lower costs achieved by providing less house, but on a cost-per-square-foot basis the demonstration houses were actually more expensive than the average house of the region. These conclusions, however, were not made explicit in the case study of the project published by HUD.

Other demonstration projects in the Affordable Housing program achieved 15 to 20 percent reductions in costs but, again, by providing smaller units on smaller lots, and with narrower roads. The program's tacit message appears to have been: If you want less expensive housing, accept less of a house; and if regulations prevent such houses from being offered on the market, change the regulations. The focus of the Affordable Housing Demonstration and other efforts by the administration to achieve savings through deregulation implicitly denied that significant savings could be achieved through technological innovation. Yet the figures quoted earlier suggest that manufactured housing alone should be able to achieve savings of 30 percent or better, assuming a supportive regulatory environment.

Filling the Gap

If it is a genuine objective of governments at all levels to provide affordable housing, then more concerted attempts to use manufactured housing would appear to be in order. In the area of home and lot ownership, several steps could be taken. Federally guaranteed mortgages, with their lower interest rates and longer terms, could be made more readily available and prospective buyers more aggressively informed of this option. State and local governments could do more to remove barriers to single siting and to allow the siting of less expensive single-wide units that meet reasonable standards for appearance. Along with the single siting of units, greater use could be made of a zoning mechanism, such as the Planned Unit Development (PUD), that allows homes to be clustered on smaller lots. If single siting were allowed on lots that were one fifth smaller, in areas where the cost of land is high, the saving realized could be 15 to 20 percent.

Additional measures are available for the park rental market, including more proactive attempts by local governments to encourage the development of parks, particularly cooperatives. For fixed, low, and moderate-income populations, parks developed with local assistance appear to be a more cost-effective solution to the problem of providing affordable housing than new, subsidized construction. At the state and federal levels, housing voucher assistance programs could be restructured to accommodate manufactured housing as an option.

The challenge in more fully utilizing manufactured housing to close the affordability gap is not a lack of policy alternatives but of political commitment. The stigma of the "trailer camp slum" lingers on, despite the radical transformation of the object. The fear of mobility, regardless of actual immobility, the threat to a geographically fixed community and to neighborhoods composed of narrow economic classes all persist as barriers. It remains for the countervailing pressure of necessity to widen the categorization of housing and the definition of acceptability to allow more Americans to achieve the undisputed cultural ideal of home ownership. Even more pressing is the need to relieve pressures in the rental market which are forcing rates up and exacerbating the crisis of homelessness.

At the Crossroad Again

Procrustes' Bed and Mr. Potato Head

Ancient Greek legend tells of the exploits of Procrustes, a highwayman who would force his victims to lie upon a bed. If they were shorter than the bed, Procrustes would stretch them, and if they were too tall, he would lop off their legs to fit. The term Procrustean is used today to describe a theory or practice that distorts reality to fit a preconceived system. Modern society seems to believe that it is free of such narrowly constraining, myth-laden systems; categorization remains important, but it is supposed to be based on objective analysis, such as the scientific classification of plants and animals.

Land use zoning is a product of the modern tradition of categorization, claiming to base itself on objective criteria related especially to health and safety. Accordingly, a building's height is determined by the requirement that direct sunlight fall on every inch of sidewalk for a minimum amount of time per day, and the placement of adjacent land uses is based on the amount of noise and dirt they produce, or offensive activities they harbor. But the order which zoning and other mechanisms of modern city planning create is far from being myth- or value-free. Constance Perin, who has studied the system of regulation from an anthropological perspective, concludes,

> Land-use planning, zoning, and development practices are a shorthand for unstated rules governing what are widely regarded as

correct social categories and relationships—, that is, not only how land uses should be arranged, but how land users, as a social category, are to be related to one another.

Land-use system [is] . . . a moral system that both reflects and assures social order.[1]

In a very real sense, the mechanisms designed to produce order in the built environment are a Procrustean bed upon which innovations are forced to lie and be measured. Aspects of the innovation which do not fit may be amputated or disguised, and those which fall short may be stretched or otherwise altered to cover minimum requirements. In the end, much of an innovation's utility may be lost. At many points in the development of the mobile home, but especially in the present era, it has been placed on Procrustes' bed and made to fit. The requirements for scatter-siting homes in residential districts, for example, are a template against which a guest who would stay for the night must be measured.

Procrustes' methods are not wholly without merit. The uniformity they enforce makes it possible to coordinate the actions of numerous agencies and to predict their behavior. The Procrustean bed formed by the complex system of housing and land use regulation protects consumers' investment in housing, their single largest purchase. Moreover, it protects the jobs of architects, building contractors, and developers who might lose status, income, and control if a particular innovation were to take hold.

But the predictability and order of category-based regulation has its price. It eliminates potential solutions to needs that would otherwise be met, and it often dampens some of the more creative impulses of society. The hybrid character of the mobile home stands to lose much of its originality and effectiveness in satisfying housing needs as it is made to conform to increasingly narrow standards. This is not to dismiss legitimate health and safety concerns, but rather to suggest that they are at issue in far fewer aspects of design and construction than they may be used to justify. What is really being preserved are the cultural ideals of home and community embodied in traditional forms and practices. Even when those forms symbolize conflicting ideals and behaviors, such as mobility and stability, or individuality and community, their embodiment in conventional form nevertheless assures us that the order of the world remains whole.

A Procrustean approach to categorization is not the only trend evident in the evolution of the form and use of mobile homes. There is a countervailing process that can be described by a less classical reference—Mr. Potato Head. The toy called Mr. Potato Head invites children to see similarities between a potato and human physiognomy. It offers a standard set of facial features—along with accessories such as hats and pipes. The present version of the toy is plastic, but in simpler times a genuine tuber was used. It too invites a child to make analogies. Odd bumps, elongated form, or the deep creases of a potato retrieved from the pantry might suggest an old man, a young woman, a baby, or perhaps the babysitter. Every Mr. (or Mrs.) Potato Head is a hybrid of the random features of a found object and the standard features provided by the toy maker. The toy is nonjudgmental. There is no way to get it wrong, even if an ear is left out or an extra one added.

The Mr. Potato Head approach is clearly evident in the kinds of alterations people make to their mobile homes. The richness of such alterations rests in the play between the standardized object and site-built additions, as well as in the references made to conventional house forms. Evidence of the process of assemblage is left undisguised, adding a richness of its own. While there may be occasional elements of whimsy in many solutions, what is more compelling is evidence of the search for an economical solution to some need while acknowledging and confirming community standards.

All of these qualities of the mobile home are characteristic of vernacular design in America. John Kouwenhoven, whose writing greatly influenced the study of vernacular design, concluded that what distinguishes it is an aesthetic of process:

> It is the ideas, emotions, and attitudes generated by this conscious or unconscious awareness of process which account, I think, for a basic difference between the aesthetic effects of vernacular forms and those of cultivated Western tradition. Inevitably, the forms appropriate to our contemporary world lack the balance, symmetry, the stability, and the elaborate formality to which we are accustomed in the architecture and design of the past. They tend, instead, to be *resilient, adaptable, simple, and unceremonious.* Serenity gives way to tension. Instead of an arrangement of mass we have an aethetic of the tranformation of energy. Only in some such terms as these, it seems to me, can we describe the so-called "American" quality which we detect in our architecture and design. (Italics added)[2]

This aesthetic of process manifests itself in the design of houses which are intended to be temporary and essentially disposable. Kouwenhoven suggests that in the United States there has long been a debate between advocates of so-called permanent homes, made of stone, and those who felt that wooden houses were more appropriate. In 1840, for example, the Report of the Agricultural Survey of Massachussetts recommended the construction of stone houses throughout the Com-

The mobile home as an expression of the aesthetic of process: adaptable and unceremonious.

monwealth. A contemporary farmer derided that recommendation, commenting that stone houses

> are not so cheap . . . not so dry, and not so fit for us. Our roads are always changing direction, and after a man has built at great cost a stone house, a new road is opened and he finds himself a mile or two from the highway. Then our people are not so stationary, like those of old countries, but always alert to better themselves, and will remove from town as a new market opens or a better farm is to be had, and do not wish to spend too much on their buildings.[3]

The stone house and, more generally, the house symbolizing permanence, is favored by the institutional guardians of the built environment, but it is the house of wood, made to be temporary, that better fits the lifestyle of many Americans. J. B. Jackson, who has traced this line of development back to medieval building traditions and into the future, concludes that the mobile home is its obvious progeny. "I am convinced," he writes, "that the trailer or an improved version of it is, for better or worse, the low cost dwelling of the future—lacking in solidity, lacking in permanence, lacking in charm, but inexpensive, convenient, and mobile."[4]

In the mobile home, the aesthetic of process is evident at

several levels. First, in the way that it is made. The thinness which characterizes it is the result of vehicular restrictions, the manufacturing process, and materials. It is a wood structure designed to be light, portable, and efficient. Second, this aesthetic is evident in the collaging of house-like and vehicular features. It is design-by-appliqué, a way of loosely associating meaning, form, and use so that innovations can be rapidly introduced and easily recycled. Finally, this aesthetic of process—of Mr. Potato Head—is evident in the way mobile homes are used, especially their mobility, transformability, and disposability.

The objective of Procrustes' methods is to limit variation and preserve a narrowly defined community standard. As a process it promotes conventionalization of the house's form, relation to the lot, and place within the community. The methods of Mr. Potato Head, by contrast, favor syncretism and a wide variation in form with multiply associations. Pluralism and individual inventiveness in meeting different housing-related needs are openly expressed and celebrated.

The development of the mobile home has moved in fits and starts. At times there has been a high degree of consensus as to what it is and how it should be used, but at other times a combination of necessity and entrepreneurship have challenged the consensus, offering new uses, forms, and meaning. Although there is increased acceptance of the mobile home—in the form of manufactured housing—its current categorization and regulation are preventing it from satisfying housing needs which it met effectively in the past. The industry seems to be stalled in its development, with the Procrustean forces of conservation dominating. The problem for mobile home advocates and those concerned with affordable housing is how to redress the balance and encourage a new round of invention.

One approach is to try to reform the system of categorization. If categorization has been too rigid, narrow, and exclusionary, perhaps a different set of categories could be devised that would recognize the range of mobile homes and their communities. By adapting the system of categorization rather than trying to overthrow it, this approach hopes to avoid resistance from the institutional guardians of the categorization system.

Another approach to moving the industry out of its current malaise is to encourage a new round of innovation. The industry has grown complacent with the compromises it has struck with regulatory authorities: it doesn't want to lose the legitimacy it has gained and is consequently willing to live with a diminishing market. What type of innovation should be promoted is not clear but, the hope is to revitalize the spirit of invention which won the industry its earlier successes.

In the sections that follow an example of each of these approaches is summarized. Frederick Bair, Jr., in a publication for the American Planning Association, *Regulating Mobile Homes*,[5] proposed modifying the current system of categorization to correct its limitations. Arthur Bernhardt, in the concluding section of his study *Building Tomorrow*, advocated new innovation on the part of the industry. Both publications date from the early 1980s, a period when mobile homes sales were already on the decline. Since then, sales have remained stagnant while the affordable housing gap has widened.

Elaborating the System of Categories

The Reagan Administration's approach to manufactured housing was to try to remove categorical distinctions protecting the industry, while encouraging the reduction of local regulation to make all housing cheaper to build and easier to site. Mobile/manufactured housing was to be merged into a single category together with other forms of factory-built dwellings. For its part, the manufactured housing industry lobbied at the federal level to maintain its unique status—and preemption from local building regulation—but at the state and local level it argued against categorical restrictions, specifically those that prohibited placing mobile homes in residential areas. Even here the industry was not consistent, finding it useful at times to preserve protection over certain kinds of land use, especially parks. The combined lobbying efforts of the industry had, in short, moved in contradictory directions, arguing at times for the retention of categorical protections, and at other times for their removal.

One approach to reducing the roadblocks that impede greater use of mobile homes, particularly at the level of local land use regulation, is to create a more elaborate system of categories. Whereas in many communities all types of mobile/manufactured housing are lumped together, so that a thirty-year-old house trailer falls into the same category as a new, multisection manufactured home, a more elaborate categorization system would recognize unit differences and regulate them accordingly.

In 1980, the American Planning Association approached Frederick Bair, Jr., a Florida-based planner long associated with the development of regulations for mobile homes, to write a new set of model guidelines for regulating mobile home land use. A 1960 guideline, written by Bair with Ernest Bartley under the auspices of the University of Florida treated the mobile home as transient and recommended that it be considered a transitional land use at the fringes of expanding cities.[6] His new guidelines recognized a wholly different type of housing and land use, one in which transience was obsolete.

Bair's new classification system addressed construction standards and appearance standards. The construction standard recognized three levels of quality: new HUD code homes, used HUD code (or other earlier state code) homes, and homes built under no code, but still in fair condition. Bair's classification of appearance is a bit more complex. He suggests that a community decide what features a manufactured/mobile home should have to be considered acceptable for zones designated for single-family housing. Such standards might include minimum width/length ratios, exterior materials, roof pitch and style, window size and style, and foundations. The exercise of establishing standards required a community to make its housing values, vis-à-vis visual characteristics, explicit. If it felt that a proper house had to have a saddle roof, it would have to state that. Since every community would develop its own standards, they could be expected to vary from place to place and across regions. Homes which failed to meet acceptable appearance standards could still be placed in the community, but essentially in parks.

Bair's classification system describes six different classes of mobile homes. The community would determine where each class could be placed: as a permitted use (use by right), a conditional use requiring review, or a temporary use. The objective of the entire approach was to remove ambiguity from standards and avoid conflicts over the siting application process. By following the requirements of the code, owners would be assured they could site their Class A home, for instance, in a residential district without seeking a variance or other review.

On its surface, the proposal seems eminently reasonable. It maintains the regulation of building and land use through a system of categorization, while extending it to include a new type of housing. Furthermore, it would work through established regulatory institutions rather than usurping their authority. But the proposal also perpetuates the inherent constraints of the process. By defining acceptable characteristics, it precludes a wider range of designs and favors those with a stereotypic appearance. Thus, a single-wide manufactured home, even though it was house-like in appearance, might be excluded from R-1 zones. At the same time, the proposal does not call for appearance standards for other types of housing.

Bair's classification system may be most valuable in states

CLASS A mobile home with site-built garage attached. This is a 24′ x 36′ double wide, set on a permanent foundation, with a 3:12 roof pitch.

CLASS B or C single wide mobile home with expando section. Built to HUD code or prior code. Site built porches help provide acceptable orientation on the site.

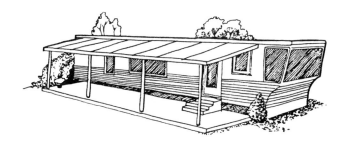

CLASS D or E single wide. Older unit built under prior code or no code. In good to fair condition.

Examples of Class A, B, C, D, and E homes according to Bair's system.

where there has been antidiscrimination legislation or court rulings. In most states where legislation has been passed, both construction and minimum appearance standards are specified for the individual siting of manufactured housing. Communities in such states could nevertheless benefit from Bair's full system, which recognizes a range of mobile homes.

What all systems of categorical regulation, including Bair's, lack, however, is a clear statement of housing needs and goals, which could then be used to promote development of the range of housing required. What such systems also lack are incentives for innovation, particularly innovation which achieves attractive, satisfactory affordable housing.

Promoting Innovation

In the last chapter of his HUD-sponsored study, *Building Tomorrow*, Arthur Bernhardt tried to project a scenario of the future of the industry:

> The mobile home industry thus has two routes for architectural innovation if it wants to participate fully in meeting future market demands. The first is to improve the design quality of the "single" detached mobile home structure. The immediate need is a design of the present product that more clearly communicates the feeling of a "home" and that more strongly fosters the associations of stability, permanence, and integration with a larger residential setting. . . . The industry must perceive the mobile home even more rigorously as a permanent structure, not as a trailer. The ability to grow out of its constricted boxlike shape and respond flexibly to diverse residential as well as nonresidential needs over time, as can conventional buildings, is imperative for greater product acceptance and continued future marketing success. . . .
>
> The second route is to push the industry's systems approach— its well developed, innovative, and highly efficient approach to shelter delivery—into a wider range of residential as well as nonresidential applications. With the use of moveable three-dimensional factory-finished building "components" in higher density applications, demand from diverse market groups can be met.[7]

Bernhardt's first path of mobile home development is readily evident today. The design of units has become increasingly more conventional and house-like, as more and more mobile homes are being sited on private lots and financed as land/home packages. Taking this tack, however, the industry has lost much of its identity and competitiveness with modular manufacturers and merchant builders who also offer industrialized housing. Combined, all three account for some 80 percent of current

Model of a high-rise system using manufactured housing components.

housing construction. Bernhardt observes that the rising incidence of industrialized housing, in general, "is clearly occurring at the expense of the mobile home industry."[8] The merger of several large mobile home manufacturers with modular and merchant builders has created an identity crisis for the industry. If this trend continues, Bernhardt suggests, by the year 2000 a distinct mobile home industry will cease to exist. In addition, as the industry moves increasingly into the production of conventionalized, house-like models and subdivision-type communities, it is abandoning its traditional low-income housing market. Bernhardt recommends that to break out of its crisis of lost identity and diminished sales the industry must be innovative.

Bernhardt's approach to innovation would have the industry concentrate on producing units to be used as single-family housing, which could also be stacked in medium- and high-rise structures. The major market for these units would be site-builders and developers, who would benefit from being able to offer housing at a lower price, thereby expanding their markets. Bernhardt estimates cost savings in the range of 20 percent.

Bernhardt's proposal for stacking modules in low, medium, and high-rise structures is very much like architect Paul Rudolph's 1966 idea of mobile homes as "Twentieth Century Bricks." Rudolph explored the idea in a project built by the Urban Development Corporation of New York State.[9] Stackable low-rise systems were also proposed by some mobile home manufacturers as Operation Breakthrough projects. Bernhardt's basic contribution to this line of thinking is the use of new materials. Steel, aluminum, and even lightweight concrete would replace wood. Units would be finished on the inside, but delivered with unfinished exteriors. Again, the appeal of this proposal is the cost savings that would be realized through factory production and rapid on-site assembly.

Manufactured housing used in an infill project in the South Bronx, New York.

It is not clear, though, why the mobile/manufactured housing industry under this scenario would suffer any less loss of identity than under the first. Nor is it clear how the mobile home used in this way would somehow manage to overcome the institutional barriers that have confronted other forms of industrialized housing. Bernhardt encourages the industry to use its past ingenuity, but does not speculate how that ingenuity might apply here. In the past, innovation in the industry has come from the mix of small, medium, and large manufacturers who were able to enter and exit the business at a relatively low cost. It was also based on a dealership network and a land development system that were similarly flexible. To realize his vision, the investment and the coordination between subsystems of the industry would have to be increased significantly. The inflexibility which hampered Lustron and subsequent efforts at mass producing housing would then pose a danger.

The problem posed by Bernhardt's proposal is not just one of technology or coordination, but of the aspirations of the housing market. What would be lost is precisely what made the mobile home most attractive: that it is an affordable alternative to a conventional single-family house. The mobile home was an alternative within the tradition of industrial vernacular design in America, providing housing that was cheap, flexible, and easy to dispose of when it was no longer needed. Affordability alone does not assure a future for the industry; drawing on its vernacular roots and the unique structure of its organization, it must chart a path to the future consistent with its past and responsive to emerging needs.

Other Roads to the Future

As long-time advocates for this form of housing, with a genuine appreciation of the role it has played, both Bair and Bernhardt offer useful suggestions for removing roadblocks and stimulating the wider use of mobile/manufactured housing. Neither approach, however, fully grasps the vernacular dimensions of the mobile home: the influences that helped form it and that could maintain its vitality. Discerning the wellsprings of that vitality is not easy, but the history sketched in the proceeding chapters offers some suggestions of where to look. It suggests, on the one hand, considering the values underlying the system of categorization regulating land use. Is it possible to bring regulation closer to the communities affected by it, and is it possible to institutionalize more open dialogue so that latent values and conflicts between values can be exposed and dealt with openly? On the other hand, it suggests reviewing the innovative characteristics of mobile homes more closely, particularly the ways they have been modified and used by their different submarkets. Flexibility, which Kouwenhoven identified as a primary characteristic of vernacular design, was responsible for the mobile home's past successes. Can some of the flexibility, lost in its quest for legitimacy, be revived? An alternative approach to reviving the industry would be, first, to think about categorization from the perspective of satisfying needs rather than maintaining order, and second, to consider how the demonstrated flexibility of the design of units and communities could be applied to new submarkets appropriate to the mobile home.

Making Needs Manifest in the System of Categorization

The limitation of any regulatory system based on categorization, whether the distinctions are crude or finely detailed, as Bair proposed, is that it typically fails to address housing goals and community objectives. A system that recognizes more alternatives does not ensure that more affordable housing will be produced. More often, it tends to perpetuate established patterns of development. In many cases, communities have permissive regulations, but engage in "constructive exclusion," a practice in which the only land where certain types of mobile home developments can be built (usually parks) is land already so occupied. Permissive regulations also do not help when land prices and building permits and fees are prohibitive. If the need for affordable housing is to be met, then communities must set production goals tied to incentives.

Although Bair takes great pains to suggest how communities might determine acceptable appearance standards, he fails to suggest how they might determine their housing goals. To be sure, comprehensive plans, which are part of the process of regulating land use by zoning, always include a discussion of broad community goals, but such goals tend to be translated indirectly in terms of allocating land use. A more effective approach is allocating permission to build, and awarding such permission to developers on the basis of their satisfying stated goals.

Lawyer and planner Kirk Wickersham, Jr., suggests an incentive-based system of regulation in *The Permit System: A Guide to Reforming Your Community's Development Regulation.*[10] He proposes that communities establish a series of goals. When developers approach the city for permits, their proposals are evaluated and assigned points based on response to community goals. Developers with the highest point totals are awarded permits. For this system to operate, the community must control its growth, so the number of permits issued is effectively tied to a population target. Implicitly, the effectiveness of the system depends on a competitive development market. If there is strong demand and a lot of people want to build, then developers will have an incentive to respond to communities' goals. When the market is soft, however, builders will not feel compelled to address them.

It is important to recall that the original system of zoning developed in the 1920s was designed to be run by an elite group of community leaders whose sense of civic responsibility was supposed to shield the process from corruption. In practice, however, as the system evolved it became dominated by powerful interests and less responsive to the needs of the people of the community.[11] Moreover, the power to zone is derived from the state, and local interests have often exploited that power to keep segments of the state's population out of particular communities. The objective of the permit system is to bring regulation back to the community and to demystify it, to give adequate recognition to clear and pressing needs, and to reduce the power of special interest groups. None of this assures the poor and those of moderate income that they will receive better housing, but it at least removes some of the barriers.

If the production of a specific number of affordable housing units is made a community goal, the permit system can create effective incentives to realize it, especially when housing prices are rising rapidly. Although it has not been used specifically in this way, such a system could also be conducive to the use of mobile/manufactured housing. It should provide a forum for the full discussion of housing needs and values, in which the merits of mobile/manufactured housing as affordable housing are fully considered along with other alternatives.

Yet such a forum will be of little use to the mobile/manufactured housing industry if it continues to pursue legitimacy by abandoning its traditional role of meeting the housing needs of low and moderate-income households. Instead, the industry might recognize that its product has several submarkets, and that making modestly sized and priced single-wide mobile homes does not preclude it from making more house-like, luxurious sectional models. It might return to actively promoting quality community developments. Its efforts to do so ceased in the early 1970s, when park development was at a high point, but conditions have changed markedly since then. Finally, the industry should seek to form a coalition with affordable housing advocacy groups, promoting the use of its product for that goal.

All this suggests that the industry may be facing a bifurcation not unlike what it experienced in the mid-1950s, when mobile home and recreational vehicle manufacturers went their separate ways. At present, the larger manufacturers in the industry seem to be pursuing the image and idea associated with manufactured housing, in lieu of mobile homes. This, together with the enactment of the HUD code, has encouraged smaller manufacturers to leave the industry and turn to producing modular homes. An alternative might be for the industry to differentiate mobile and manufactured housing and promote regulations distinct to each. It could then market manufactured homes at the higher end of its market, emphasizing their placement in subdivisions, while promoting the use of mobile homes in rental or cooperative parks for the affordable housing market.

Letting the Market Speak

One of the interesting product developments since the enactment of the HUD code is the park model. In the original code, a mobile home was defined as a transportable dwelling, at least 8' x 32'. Smaller models were considered recreation vehicles, which fell under the regulatory review of the Department of Transportation and the Federal Trade Commission. In 1980, the HUD code was amended to increase the minimum dimensions to 8' x 40', with an area of 320 square feet. HUD, however, has essentially been uninterested in regulating units between 320 and 400 square feet. Neither has the recreation vehicle industry wanted to take responsibility for units in this size range. As a result of this regulatory gap, park models currently enjoy some of the invisibility which long protected the mobile home.

What is interesting about the park model's emergence as a special class of dwelling is that it demonstrates the persistence of a market that was in danger of being abandoned as most manufacturers moved on to bigger models. The park model is designed specifically for park locations, especially for smaller lots in older parks, and for ease of maintenance, which is particularly attractive to older, seasonal occupants. Park models, however, have been relatively expensive, partly because they are designed to appeal to the more affluent second-home market.

Similar to the park model in design, and parallel in their development, are small modular units used as "grannie flats." Designed for the backyards of private homes, they provide housing for elderly people who, though living with relatives, wish to preserve an independent place of their own. Marketed in California under the name ECHO houses, a zoning variance is

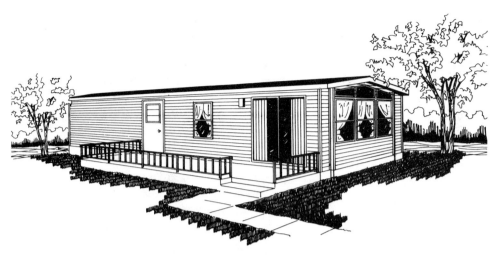

Park models such as the Shore Park by Skyline, are typically one-bedroom twelve-foot wide units with a total floor area of approximately 400 square feet.

usually required to place them in a residential area. ECHO housing is being promoted around the country by senior citizen lobbying groups. Despite the clear need for this type of housing, and the large market it could potentially serve, mobile home manufacturers have ignored it even as they continue to build park models.

The ease with which the mobile home can be expanded, also invites further innovation and market development. Relatively few manufacturers have responded to users' apparent demand for a componentized mobile home, designed for expansion. The appeal here is not only the affordability for a new household that can begin with the purchase of a minimal core unit, but the opportunity to vary the appearance of homes as they are expanded over time to meet changing family needs. Park models, ECHO housing, and componentized mobile homes are emerging market niches unmet or ignored by conventional developers of housing. They represent some of the areas in which mobile home sales might expand.

Along with innovations in unit design, developments in parks seem to be taking place, which perhaps will help revitalize the industry. The cooperative parks discussed in Chapter 5 are one such development. At a time when new parks are becoming larger to absorb development and management costs, forming coops is a way to develop smaller parks which blend in more easily with existing neighborhoods. Although expertise in developing such parks is scarce, the manufactured housing industry might try to market its product to nonprofit Community Development Corporations, which are devoted to the production of affordable housing, and promote the creation of new housing-oriented parks.

The development of new parks need not depend exclusively on the nonprofit sector. A largely undeveloped market seems to exist for parks which rent not only lots, but units. Gary McDaniels, President of ROC propoerties in Denver, suggests that a new type of all-rental park could offer cheaper housing than rental apartments, while providing more privacy. McDaniels believes that such parks could be maintained by rotating units out of service after about ten years.

The line of industry development expressed in the term manufactured housing also offers opportunities for further expansion, as is evident in the increased emphasis on developing subdivisions rather than parks, in the mix of both modular and manufactured homes in some communities, and in ordinaces that require manufactured homes for individual lot siting. These developments all aim to push the product further into the middle-class, middle-aged housing market. It might be reason-

The Ada-Room manufactured by United in the 1950s was an early response to the demand for an expandable mobile home.

able to promote extending the HUD code to include all types of factory-built housing, thus enabling them to enjoy the benefits of preemptive regulation. But to include the single-wide mobile home in this new expanded category of housing risks sacrificing affordability for, at best, questionable improvements in safety, durability, and appearance.

The current, tacit, bifurcation of the industry into mobile homes and manufactured housing could result in a wider range of housing possibilities. Such a development, however, is far from inevitable, despite the presence of specific submarkets for each type of product. On one hand, increased institutional recognition has reduced the industry's flexibility and it could have trouble successfully negotiating the transition. On the other hand, the industry has failed to clarify its objectives. Over the past sixty years, it has not been particularly good at understanding itself and the dynamics of its market, but this was not a serious liability in the past. With the visibility and status that manufactured housing has achieved in the last ten to fifteen years, the situation has fundamentally changed. If the industry narrowly courts respectability by promoting more conventional looking and expensive units, then it may lose not only a good share of its market, but aspects of the mobile home as an innovation which have made it such a valuable housing alternative.

The industry associations have confronted individual crises —the FEMA flood regulation, the chassis ruling, and revised energy standards—as they emerged. Now a larger, guiding vision of the role of the industry is needed, if for no other reason than to avoid contradictory pleadings. At the very least, the industry could make a clear commitment to producing affordable, low, and moderate income housing. Perhaps accepting a bifurcation of markets and products would help clarify its efforts. For their part, government agencies and housing institutions have beat the drum loudly, signifying commitment to the cause of affordable housing, but their good intentions have failed to narrow the gap. In their efforts to institutionalize the mobile home, they seem to have lost sight of a larger responsibility to alleviate the crisis in low and moderate-income housing, and the role that the mobile / manufacturing industry might play.

An innovation's ultimate contribution is not simply that it meets some need more effectively, but that it alters a socially constructed sense of reality and broadens it to accept new forms of action and thought. As an innovation, the mobile home's contribution in reshaping the American understanding of housing is unfinished. It would be ironic if the recognition of mobile/manufactured housing's legitimacy were to result in a new kind of invisibility; one in which it lost its identity as a unique innovation and saw it collapsed into anonymity among other forms of industrialized building. If legitimacy resulted in a loss of affordability along with the last vestiges of mobility, what would remain of the mobile home as an innovative contribution to housing?

Notes

Preface

1. An excellent account of the ideal of industrialized housing is Gilbert Herbert's *The Dream of the Factory-Made House* (Cambridge, MA: MIT Press, 1984), which ends by suggesting that the mobile home is the true progeny of the ideal of the factory-made house.

2. Margaret Drury's *Mobile Homes: The Unrecognized Revolution in American Housing* (New York: Praeger, 1972) is essentially a literature review, but it also offers several provocative insights about the role of mobile homes in American housing.

3. Center for Automotive Safety, *The Low Cost Housing Hoax* (New York: Grossman, 1975).

4. Arthur Bernhardt, *Building Tomorrow: The Mobile/Manufactured Housing Industry* (Cambridge, MA: MIT Press, 1980).

5. Thomas E. Nutt-Powell, *Manufactured Homes: Making Sense of a Housing Opportunity* (Boston: Auburn House, 1982).

Chapter 1

1. The Byrd's home was built before the Mobile Home Construction and Safety Standards were implemented on June 15, 1976. The sequence of construction today would be essentially the same, though certain practices, such as mounting exterior walls on top of carpeting, have changed.

2. The descriptions in this section are based on the author's observations in Muncie, Indiana. Muncie is the site of Robert and

Helen Lynd's classic studies of American community life, *Middletown* (New York: Harcourt, Brace, and Co., 1929) and *Middletown in Transition* (Harcourt, Brace, and Co., 1937), hence the use of the name here.

3. *Quick Facts About the Manufactured Housing Industry* (Chantilly, VA: Manufactured Housing Institute, 1989).

4. Ibid.

5. Survey conducted by the Foremost Insurance Company, of 24,000 manufactured home households reported in *Quick Facts* (1989).

6. For a discussion of the problems of affordability see William Apgar, Jr., and Denise DiPasquale, *State of the Nation's Housing* (Cambridge, MA: Joint Center for Housing, Harvard University, 1989).

7. These estimates are based on a study conducted by the City of Sunnyvale, California in 1986 in preparation for a mobile home park conversion ordinance. Costs of moving in other areas of the country may be lower.

8. The idea that housing has symbolic value, including status, has been considered by many authors, especially Franklin Becker, in *Housing Messages* (Stroudsburg, PA: Dowden, Hutchinson & Ross, 1977).

9. Kenneth Tremblay and Don Dillman, *Beyond the American Housing Dream: Accommodation to the 1980s* (New York: University Press of America, 1983).

10. Ibid., 114.

11. Frederick Bair, Jr., is a professional planner with a longstanding interest in reforming zoning practices to accommodate the use of mobile homes. His statement is quoted by Drury in *Mobile Homes.*

12. On the neighborliness of park living, see, for example, Sheila Johnson, *Idle Haven* (Berkeley: University of California Press, 1971), and John Deck, *Rancho Paradiso* (New York: Harcourt Brace Jovanovich, 1972).

13. 1984 Foremost survey reported in *Quick Facts.*

14. For a description of "tramping," see Kay Peterson, *Home Is Where You Park It: A Guide to RV Living as a Lifestyle* (Chicago: Follett, 1977).

15. So. Burlington Cty. N.A.A.C.P. v. Mount Laurel Tp. 92 N.J. 158 (1983).

16. See Bernhardt, *Building Tomorrow.*

17. Drury, *Mobile Homes*, 82.

18. The term *boundary* has been widely used in the social sciences, particularly by writers influenced by systems theory. The use of the word here follows from the work of Kai T. Erikson in the sociology of deviance: "A human community can be said to maintain boundaries . . . in the sense that its members tend to confine themselves to a particular radius of activities and to regard any conduct that drifts outside of that radius as somehow inappropriate or immoral" (*Wayward Puritans* [New York: John Wiley, 1966], 12). In a similar way, an innovative alternative is deviant, in that it

falls outside the radius of prescribed activities and, consequently, threatens society.

19. *Comeau v. Brookside Village* 633 SW2d 790 (1982).

20. Edward H. Levi, *An Introduction to Legal Reasoning* (Chicago: University of Chicago Press, 1948), 1.

21. Ibid., 3.

22. *Robinson Township v. Knoll* 410 Mich. 293, 302 N.W. 2d 146 (1981).

Chapter 2

1. Quoted in Warren Belasco, *Americans on the Road* (Cambridge, MA: MIT Press, 1979), 31.

2. *Automobile and Trailer Travel*, 1:1 (Jan.–Feb. 1936), 26.

3. Quoted in Kenneth Jackson, *Crabgrass Frontier* (New York: Oxford University Press, 1985), 160.

4. Belasco, *Americans on the Road*, 74.

5. J. J. Flink, *America Adopts the Automobile: 1895–1910* (Cambridge, MA: MIT Press, 1970).

6. Belasco, *Americans on the Road*, 52.

7. Ibid., 35.

8. Company brochure, Auto-Kamp Trailer Co., Saginaw, MI, n.d.

9. In C. E. Nash, *Trailer Ahoy* (Lancaster, PA: Intelligencer Printing Co., 1937), 88.

10. Nerissa Wilson, *Gypsies and Gentlemen* (London: Columbus Books, 1986).

11. See Carlton M. Edwards, *Homes for Travel and Living* (East Lansing, MI: Carl Edwards & Associates, 1977), especially chapter 8, "The Growth of Industry Suppliers."

12. Edwards, *Homes*, 184.

13. Ibid., 272.

14. Quoted in Roderick Nash, *Wilderness and the American Mind* (New Haven: Yale University Press, 1982), 146.

15. "200,000 Trailers," *Fortune* (March 1937), 105.

16. Ibid., 108.

17. Robert Silbar, "The Unmentionable Debt to the Yacht," *Trailer Travel* (July 1939), 14.

18. Taylor Meloan, *Mobile Homes: The Growth and Business Practices of the Industry* (Homewood, Illinois: Homewood Press, 1954), 5.

19. Company brochure, Wolfe Bodies, Inc., Detroit, MI, n.d.

20. *Automobile and Trailer Travel*, 1:2 (February 1936), 20.

21. Blackburn Sims, *The Trailer Home: With Practical Advice on Trailer Life and Travel* (New York: Longmans, Green and Co., 1937).

22. For a description of the split coach, see *Motor Vehicle Monthly*, 66:1 (1950), 29.

23. Edwards, *Homes*, 7.

24. *Automobile and Trailer Travel*, 1:1 (Jan.–Feb. 1936), 10.

25. Ibid., 11.

26. Ibid., 26.

27. Corwin Willson, "Diagnosing Trailer Fever." *Automobile and Trailer Travel*, 1:4 (July 1936), 17.

28. Ibid., 19.

29. Corwin Willson, "The Mobile House," *Architectural Record* (July 1936), 64–65.

30. William Stout, "The Highway Home of Tomorrow," *Trailer Caravan* (October 1936), 8.

31. Le Corbusier, *Toward a New Architecture*, trans. Frederick Etchells (New York: Praeger, 1927), 268.

32. Stout, "The Highway Home," 8.

33. R. C. Pebworth, "Trailers Grow Up Into Houses Without Wheels," *Automobile and Trailer Travel*, 3:6 (June 1938), 14.

34. Estimates by the manufacturer suggested that transportation costs would range from twenty to thirty cents a mile. Presumably the costs would be twice that for the double unit. The manufacturer felt that the economic distance for transport was within five hundred miles of the factory.

35. The Federal Housing Authority (FHA) was established by the National Housing Act of 1934. FHA approval of industrialized housing would be essential in making that form of construction competitive. In 1939, an FHA-backed development in Wilmington, Delaware, could offer a furnished six-room house for $5,150; but with the FHA mortgage only $550 was required as a down payment and the monthly payment was $29.61 (figures from Jackson, *Crabgrass*, 205). If a trailer home could only be secured through a vehicle rate loan, with its shorter period of maturation, monthly costs would be higher. In addition, it should be recognized that a major impetus behind the establishment of the FHA was to re-employ construction workers idled by the Depression. Labor-saving methods of construction were not necessarily desirable in view of this objective.

36. Karl M. Tomfohrde, *Special Report on Trailers and Trailer Camps*, WPA project number 15245. (Boston, MA: State Planning Board, June 1939), 4.

37. Ibid., 26.

38. On this point see, Brian Horrigan, "The Home of Tomorrow, 1927–1945" in *Imaging Tomorrow*, ed. Joseph J. Corn (Cambridge, MA: MIT Press, 1987), 137–163.

39. "200,000 Trailers," *Fortune* (March 1937), 108.

40. Tomfohrde, *Special Report on Trailers*, 23.

41. This estimate is based on two contemporary surveys: one done at Yellowstone National Park in the summer of 1936, and another done by the Palace Corporation (cited in Meloan, *Mobile Homes*). Wilcox and Clark, also estimated that ten percent of trailerites were year-round users. They suggest that the majority were migratory retirees (now called "snowbirds"). C. Clark and C. E. Wilcox, "The House Trailer Movement," *Journal of Applied Sociology*, 22 (1939), 503–16.

42. Attributed to James L. Brown, President of the Trailer Coach Manufacturer's Association.

43. Ernestine Evans, "Resettlement by Trailer," *The Nation*, 143:7 (August 1936), 181.

44. Whereas in 1928 only 68,000 homes were foreclosed, in 1930 there were 150,000 foreclosures, and nearly 200,000 in 1931. By Spring 1933, almost half of all the homes in the United States were technically in default.

45. Katherine Lynch, "When Is a Trailer Not a Trailer," *Trailer Caravan*, 1:5 (January 1937), 13, 34.

46. "Toledo, Ohio, Ordinance Cited by T.C.M.A. as Model," *Trailer Travel*, 3:6 (June 1938), 15–16.

47. While the industry at the time endorsed the idea of limiting the period that a trailer could remain in a community, in endorsing the ninety-day period cited in the Toledo ordinance it was trying to counter far more restrictive time limits, such as that of two days imposed by Rochester, New York.

48. *Municipal Law Journal*, 4 (1936).

49. P. H. Elwood, "Trailer Test," *Time* (November 23, 1936), 66.

50. Barnet Hodes and Gale Roberson, *The Law of Mobile Homes*, 3d ed. (Washington, D.C.: The Bureau of National Affairs, 1974), 105.

51. By 1937, all but four states had size limitations on travel trailers. The maximum allowable height varied from 11' in Connecticut to 14'6" in Utah, with the average being 12'6". The maximum length of the trailer ranged from 26'6" in Kentucky, to 60' in Nevada; with the average being 35'. The maximum width in all states was 96", except in Rhode Island where a width of 102" was permitted. (*House Trailers: A Survey of Laws Governing Ownership and Use*, National Highway Users Conference, Washington, D.C., 1937).

52. 175 Misc. 249, 22 N.Y.S.2d 501 (1940), cited in Hodes and Roberson, *The Law of Mobile Homes*, 98.

53. 214 Ind. 75, 14 N.E. 2d 579, 115 A.L.R. 1395 (1938).

54. The use of sanitary codes remains a means of restricting the use of mobile homes. See, for example, the decision of the High Court in Texas cited in chapter 1.

55. Cited in Hodes and Roberson, *The Law of Mobile Homes*, 97.

56. *The House Trailer, Its Effect on State and Local Government*, prepared by the American Municipal Association in cooperation with the American Public Welfare Association, the American Society of Planning Officials, and the National Association of Housing Officials: Report No. 114, February 1937.

57. Clark and Wilcox, 513.

58. The term *feature* is used here to describe an aspect of an artifact which can be discriminated from the whole. In linguistics the test of commutation is used to identify a feature: a feature is a discrete aspect of a word which, when changed, alters the meaning of the artifact. See Juan Pablo Bonta, *Architecture and Its Interpretation* (New York: Rizzoli, 1979).

59. Quoted in Edwards, *Homes*, 222.

60. James L. Brown, "TCMA Goes on Record in Favor of Regulation" *Trailer Travel* (April 1939), 12.

61. Edwards, *Homes*, 238.

Chapter 3

1. A description and analysis of life in Ypsilanti during the war is provided by Lowell Carr and James E. Steiner in *Willow Run: A Study of Industrialization and Cultural Inadequacy* (New York: Harper Bros., 1952).

2. Carr and Steiner had asked two women to keep diaries of their experiences in the trailer parks. This excerpt is from one of the diaries (110).

3. Carr and Steiner, *Willow Run*, 96.

4. Ibid., 119–120.

5. Scrapping wartime trailers was important to the industry as well as the government, since a flood of used trailers could depress postwar markets.

6. A summary of the industry's arguments appeared in "Mobile Homes for Defense," *Trailer Travel* (February 1942), 9.

7. In 1937, trailer sales had reached a high of $17,000,000. By 1939, they had dropped to $10,000,000. In that year, 77,886 trailers were manufactured, still up from the total for 1938 of 4,571 (Meloan, *Mobile Homes*, 20; Edwards, *Homes*, 106).

8. "Building for Defense," *Architectural Forum* (March 1941), 171.

9. Edwards, *Homes*, 111.

10. The members of the trailer committee were Norman Wolfe, Fred Burt, and Walter Wells (Ibid.). Note that while Edwards refers to the "committee trailer" as being on display for the first time in April of 1943, such a unit was already described in the NHA bulletin issued in January of that year. I have assumed here that Edward's date is off by one year.

11. "What Is 'Sub-Standard' Housing," *Trailer Travel* (September 1943), 6.

12. "No More Trailers," *Business Week* (July 17, 1943), 19.

13. "What Is 'Sub-Standard' Housing," *Trailer Travel* (September 1943), 7.

14. In 1942, the government took control of the private sale of trailers. Companies doing over 50 percent of their business with the government could provide their employees with a certificate enabling them to purchase a trailer.

15. Cecil L. Dunn, "The Trailer Industry and the Trailer Coach Residents of Southern California" (Los Angeles: Cecil L. Dunn & Co., 1948).

16. As late as 1975, some of these trailers were still in use on the campus of the University of Indiana in Bloomington.

17. Quoted in Richard Bender, *Crack in the Rear View Mirror* (New York: Van Nostrand, 1973), 6.

18. This essay by Le Corbusier first appeared in *L'Esprit Nouveau* and was later incorporated in *Toward a New Architecture*, 210.

19. National Committee on Public Policy, *Technological Forecast* (Washington, D.C.: U.S. Government Printing Office, 1937).

20. "FSA Prefabricates $930 Homes for Sharecroppers in Missouri," *Architectural Forum* (November 1938), 393–94.

21. Burnham Kelly, *The Prefabrication of Houses* (Cambridge, MA: MIT Press, 1953), 33.

22. Estimate by the Twentieth Century Fund Housing Committee.

23. They did, however, discuss trailers as recreation vehicles; see, for example, "The Trailer Industry," *Architectural Record* (August 1936), 161–64.

24. Alfred Bruce and Harold Sandbank's, *A History of Prefabrication* was originally published in 1943 by the John B. Pierce Foundation, a group dedicated to the development of prefabricated housing. It was later republished by Arno Press (New York, 1972).

25. Kelly, *Prefabrication*, 47–48.

26. Ibid., 176.

27. In 1942, the first association of prefabricated house manufacturers was formed as the Prefabricated Home Manufacturers Association (later the Prefabricated Home Manufacturers Institute). Its purpose was to disseminate information, establish industry standards, study distribution problems, improve manufacturing techniques, make cost and accounting studies, and exchange ideas.

28. Kelly, *Prefabrication*, 37.

29. In the early 1950s, the Army erected several thousand of these houses in Oak Ridge, Tennessee for its A-bomb facility.

30. Kelly, *Prefabrication*, 38.

31. These estimates are based on Kelly, *Prefabrication*, and Meloan, *Mobile Homes*.

32. In Europe this method was called "serialized production."

33. For a brief summary of the Wyatt Program see Kelly, *Prefabrication*, 68–70.

34. In 1948 there was a bill in the House (HR 6122) which would have amended the Servicemen's Readjustment Act to provide federal guarantees for one half of the cost of a house trailer. It was hoped that this would reduce financing costs, but the bill was not enacted (Meloan, *Mobile Homes*, 89).

35. Much of my account is based on Kelly, *Prefabrication*, and Tom Wolfe and Leonard Garfield, "A New Standard of Living: The Lustron House, 1946–1950," in *Perspectives in Vernacular Architecture, III* (Columbia, MO: University of Missouri Press, 1989), 51–61.

36. For a detailed account of the business practices of merchant builders, see Ned Eichler, *The Merchant Builders* (Cambridge, MA: MIT Press, 1982).

37. A brief but excellent summary of Levitt's work is found in Jackson, *Crabgrass*, 234–38.

38. For the effects of postwar programs in favoring the develop-

ment of large-scale developers see Barry Checkoway, "Large Builders, Federal Housing, and Postwar Suburbanization," in *Critical Perspectives on Housing,* ed. R. Rachel Bratt, et al. (Philadelphia: Temple University Press, 1986), 119–38.

39. Another postwar builder, Jim Walters, took the unfinished house idea further. Working in a low-income Southern market, he offered customers a housing shell on a serviced site and left the finishing to the new owner. See T. Schlesinger and M. Erlich, "Housing: The Industry Capitalism Didn't Forget," in *Critical Perspectives on Housing,* 139–64.

40. See Arthur A. Levitt, "A Community Builder Looks at Community Planning," *Journal of the American Institute of Planners* (Spring 1951), 80–88. Also see Edward P. Eichler and Marshall Kaplan, *Community Builders* (Los Angeles: University of California Press, 1967).

41. "Spartan Builds a Silver City," *Trailer Dealer* (October 1951), 133.

42. In fact, after the war the trailer industry suffered under an excise tax that was not lifted until 1953.

43. "The Trailerite Is a Typical American," *Trailer Travel* (July 1945), 5.

44. John Steinbeck, *Travels With Charley* (New York: Viking Press, 1962), 91–92.

45. Ibid., 93–94.

46. Survey reported in "The West's Third Largest City," from a Trailer Coach Association catalog of 1956 trailer show models, unpaged.

47. One later variation in the assembly line system was the development of the sideways assembly line, introduced in the early 1950s by Rex Anderson of the ABC factory in Bay City, Michigan. In this process the units are moved along sideways on dollies (Edwards, *Homes,* 108). Today both end to end and sideways assembly lines are used by different factories.

48. Edwards, *Homes,* 107.

49. In 1970, the number of firms was up again to about 360 manufacturers with 600 plants; but by 1980 there were only 180 firms with 420 factories.

50. See Bernhardt, *Building Tomorrow.*

51. The ease with which design could be changed has been hampered by the HUD procedures that require approval of all designs and modifications.

52. Meloan, *Mobile Homes,* 63.

53. Mike Moose, et al., *Immobile Home Syndrome* (Fayetteville: University of Arkansas, 1973), 17.

54. Booz, Allen and Hamilton, "Sales and Distribution Survey" (April 19, 1951), cited by Meloan, *Mobile Homes,* 54.

55. This practice, known as "closed parks," is illegal today. A related practice was to charge tenants an "exit fee" to remove their unit from the park.

56. Based on a survey conducted by Bernhardt in 1977 (Bernhardt, *Building Tomorrow*, 163).

57. In 1952, the Mobile Home Manufacturers Association began sponsoring a survey of nationwide sales data; since manufacturers and dealers seemed to have difficulty understanding and making use of such information, MHMA conducted a workshop (Meloan, *Mobile Homes*, 71).

58. Bernhardt, *Building Tomorrow*, 13.

59. The idea of a loose-fitting system is analogous to that of "cloud-like" systems discussed by Bender in *Crack in the Rear View Mirror*. He suggests that the traditional conception of industrialized building as "clock-like" leads to the pursuit of precisely coordinated activities that may be too rigid to accommodate the character of the housing market. He suggests that cloud-like organization would be more appropriate (see 118–26).

60. Theodore Morrison, "House of the Future," *House Beautiful* 66 (September 1929), 292. Quoted in Horrigan, "Home of Tomorrow," 139.

61. "The Industry Capitalism Forgot," *Fortune* (August 1947), 61–67.

62. "What Became of the Fuller House," *Fortune* (May 1948), 168.

Chapter 4

1. Survey conducted by Marketing Information Associates for the Mobile Home Manufacturers Association. Results published in "Meet Your Best Customers," MHMA, 1953.

2. The Palace Corporation continued to produce the folding trailer till it went out of business in 1960, after a fire. Folding trailers were still being manufacturered in the 1960s by the Magnolia Company, under the name Leisurama.

3. The term "Tenwide" refers specifically to the Marshfield home, while the term "ten-wide" refers generically to all 10-foot-wide models.

4. Frey's brother-in-law, John Bertschie, had built a 21-foot trailer for himself and his wife during the Depression, so that he could travel around the country as an itinerant carpenter. Bertchie later became a partner with Frey and three of their brothers and started the Rollohome company after the war.

5. Quoted from a letter from Elmer Frey, August 5, 1987.

6. Frey, August 5, 1987.

7. Letter from R. E. McMackin to Elmer Frey, March 2, 1956.

8. California survey by C. L. Dunn, 1948. The sample for the second survey, conducted by Carlton M. Edwards of Michigan State University, was 1629 readers of the *Mobile Home Journal*. (Results reported in Drury, *Mobile Homes*, 1972, 18–21.)

9. Robert M. French and Jeffery K. Hadden, "An Analysis of the Distribution and Characteristics of Mobile Homes in America," *Land Economics* (May 1965), 138.

10. The first twelve-wide was introduced by the Har-Mac Corporation of Stratford in the spring of 1959. That August, a 12-foot-wide model was introduced by Marshfield Homes.

11. *Trailer Dealer Magazine,* 1953.

12. "A Symposium on Prefabrication," *House and Garden* 68:12 (December 1935), 65–72.

13. This position was most clearly expressed by the early advocates of industrialized building, working before the First World War. Of their approach, Gilbert Herbert observed, in *The Dream of the Factory-Made House*: "The meaning of 'dwelling' is the point at issue here, and it remains a critical point for prefabrication to the present day. The most conservative forces are in operation, when we build a home—and the term 'conservative' is used here deliberately, with no prejudicial connotations. The function of the home is to conserve, to protect privacy, family life, cultural and social values, and traditions. It is a reflection of very deep needs, for security, continuity, conformity, in an area of emotional intensity, dealing as it does with one's personal immediate environment, rich in symbolic meaning. The early prefabricated house [before the First World War] challenged and denied most of these attributes: this was understood by the manufacturers, who thus never even presented it to their fellow citizens as an option to be rejected. In this they perhaps lacked courage, but they certainly showed sensitivity to the temper of the times (19)."

14. Kelly, *Prefabrication,* 90.

15. The relationship between regulatory authorities and the public with respect to attitudes toward the appearance of housing also profoundly concerned prefabricated builders. Kelly observed, in the *Prefabrication of Houses*: "Though the design [of a prefabricated house] is superior to current practice, from the point of view both of design and production 'people like what they know' and do not like this design because it is new; the banks consider the house too great a financial risk because of the public reaction; without loans few houses can be built; and the design remains unknown and unaccepted (87)."

16. In the late 1940s, some units did offer the option of a tub under the bed (the mattress hinging up into the wall revealing a tub beneath). Such an arrangement probably compounded problems with condensation and also violated the normative expectation that sleeping and bathing areas should be separate (a convention which had been established only recently with the popular use of fixed plumbing).

17. Meloan, *Mobile Homes,* 46.

18. The model designed by the Wright Foundation was also featured in a study sponsored by the Wisconsin Department of Natural Resources, *Production/Dwelling: An Opportunity for Excellence* (Spring Green, WI.: Frank Lloyd Wright Foundation, 1970).

19. In Homer Barnett's *Innovation: The Basis for Cultural Change* (New York: McGraw-Hill, 1953), his use of the term syncretism and the companion term, conventionalization derives from the work

of the British gestalt psychologist Frederick Barlett, specifically, from his experimental studies described in *Remembering* (New York: Cambridge University Press, 1932).

20. Portions of this section appeared originally in "The Mobile Home: Lessons in Industrial Vernacular Design," *Open House International*, 9:3 (1984).

21. In some states, like Georgia, to remove the tires was made illegal as a fire precaution, the assumption being that a burning unit or those adjacent to it could be pulled out to prevent the spread of a fire.

22. Jane Liebetrau, "Mobilehome Design-Outside," *Trailer Topics* (March 1958), 18.

23. "The Grounded Trailer," *Trailer Travel*, 5:12 (1940), 7.

24. Lillian and Griffith Borgeson, *Mobile Homes and Travel Trailers* (New York: Fawcett Publications, 1959), 28.

25. H. B. Ellis, "Our Immobile Mobile Home," *Trailer Topics* (January 1961), 36.

26. Dick Poplin, "The House With a Trailer Inside," *Trailer Topics* (January 1962), 39–40.

27. See Sam Davis, "Mobile Home," in *The Form of Housing*, ed. Sam Davis (New York: VanNostrand, 1977), 187.

28. See, for example, John Habracken's *Supports* (New York: Praeger, 1972), and Lars Lerup's *Building the Unfinished* (Beverly Hills, CA: Sage Publications, 1977).

29. I am using the term *dwelling* here in the phenomenological sense as developed by Heidegger in "Building Dwelling Thinking," *Martin Heidegger: Basic Writings* (New York: Harper & Row, 1977), 323–39, and by Norberg-Schulz in *The Concept of Dwelling* (New York: Electa/Rizzoli, 1985).

30. For an analysis of the psychological and cultural significance of the quality of complexity, see Amos Rapoport and Robert E. Kantor, "Complexity & Ambiguity in Environmental Design," *AIP Journal*, 33:4 (July 1967), 210–21; and Amos Rapoport, *Human Aspects of Urban Form* (New York: Pergamon, 1977), cf. 207–220.

31. On the analysis of social and personal images of housing, see Franklin Becker, *Housing Messages*.

32. A discussion of some of the intended and unintended functions and meanings of attic and cellar are found in Perla Korosec-Serfaty, "The Home, from Attic to Cellar," *Journal of Environmental Psychology*, 4:4 (1984), 172–79.

33. Perla Korosec-Serfaty, "Experience and Use of the Dwelling," in *Home Environments*, ed. I. Altman and C. M. Werner (New York: Plenum Pless, 1985), 65–86.

34. John B. Jackson, "The Movable Dwelling and How It Came to America," *Discovering the Vernacular Landscape* (New Haven, CN.: Yale University Press, 1984), 98.

35. Robert Venturi, Denise Scott Brown, and Steven Izenour, *Learning From Las Vegas* (Cambridge, MA: MIT Press, 1977), 85.

36. Andrew Jackson Downing, *The Architecture of Country Houses* (New York: Dover, 1969).

37. On the idea of association as a basis for aesthetic experience, see Peter Collins, *Changing Ideals in Modern Architecture* (Montreal: McGill University Press, 1972).

38. George L. Hersey, *High Victorian Gothic* (Baltimore: Johns Hopkins Press, 1972).

39. Quoted from an interview by Henry Allen with Steven Izenour, "That's No Trailer, That's My Home," *Washington Post Magazine* (September 24, 1978), 30.

Chapter 5

1. Author's interview with Sid Adler, April 23, 1987.

2. One of the few mobile home manufacturers that has engaged in vertical integration—in which one firm manufactures, deals and develops land—is Fleetwood Homes.

3. A survey conducted by *Trailer Dealer* in 1965 found that a fifth of all dealers were park owners. By 1977 over a third of all park owners also operated or planned to open a dealership. Of those involved in both businesses, over 46 percent had started out in parks, while about 26 percent had begun in dealerships (reported in Bernhardt, *Building Tomorrow*, 223–24).

4. Al Sweeney, "Trailer Park Growth Now on a Huge Scale," *Trailer Travel* (June 1937), 15.

5. Alexander Wellington, "Trailer Camp Slums," *Survey*, 77:10 (October 1951), 418, 421.

6. David R. Nulsen and Robert H. Nulsen, *Mobile Home and Recreation Vehicle Park Management* (Beverly Hills, CA: Trail-R-Club of America, 1971).

7. Author's interview with Phyllis Yohey, February 4, 1976.

8. Quoted in Welford Sanders, *Regulating Manufactured Housing*, American Planning Association, Planning Advisory Report 398, December 1986, 4.

9. The practice of constructive exclusion is cited in Bernhardt, *Building Tomorrow* (1981), 337.

10. Independence, as a strategy in the adaptation to innovation is described by Barnett in *Innovation*, 346–52.

11. Ernest R. Bartley and Frederick H. Bair, *Mobile Home Parks and Comprehensive Community Planning*, Public Administration Clearing Service, Studies in Public Administration, no. 19 (Gainesville, FL: University of Florida, 1960), 12–13.

12. The results of this survey of local zoning practices is reported in Bernhardt, *Building Tomorrow*, 338–45.

13. Charles Geisler and Hisayoshi Mitsuda conclude, "the simple fact is that many mobile home residents have moved beyond urban jurisdictions to escape exclusionary zoning or threats of displacement as land beneath them appreciates. Once in the countryside, however, mobile home owners and renters re-encounter their urban/suburban antagonists in the form of local elites or well-to-do second home owners. Thus discrimination in the hinterlands continues, perpetuated by class-specific differences in mobile home

acceptance—differences capable of making the 'lower class' attributes of mobile homes self-fulfilling." ["Mobile Home Growth, Regulation and Discrimination in Upstate New York," *Rural Sociology* 52:4 (1987), 532–43.] The fact that more mobile homes are concentrated in rural areas does not reflect a lack of prejudice as much as lower land costs and fewer zoning restrictions in general.

14. *Mobile Home Park Planning Kit* (Chicago: Mobile Home Manufacturers Association), issued periodically.

15. Author's interview with Herbert Behrends, March 3, 1987.

16. The concept of the neighborhood unit plan was first formalized by Clarence A. Perry in his monograph *The Neighborhood Unit*, published as part of the 1929 plan for New York City (New York: Russell Sage Foundation). By the early 1950s it had become the standard for planning new housing developments.

17. Suzanne Keller, *The Neighborhood Unit* (New York: Random House, 1968).

18. David Hager, "Trailer Towns and Community Conflict in Lower Bucks County," *Social Problems*, 1:1 (1954), 34.

19. L. Skelter, "Exploding Trailer Fallacies," *Trailer Life* (July 1951), 47.

20. Two studies which consider, in part, social interaction in parks are: *Energy Consumption and Social Interaction in Mobile Home Parks, Champaign County, Illinois*, ed. Steven Parshall (Urbana-Champaign, IL: Department of Architecture, University of Illinois, 1974); and Allan Wallis, *Mobile Homes: A Psychological Case Study of Innovation in Housing* (Ph.D. Dissertation, City University of New York, 1981). Compare these with the physical patterns recommended for promoting social interaction in multifamily housing in, Clare Cooper Marcus, *Housing as if People Mattered* (Berkeley, CA: University of California Press, 1986).

21. Elaine Kendall, *The Happy Mediocrity* (New York: G. P. Putnam, 1971).

22. James Gillies, *Factors Influencing Social Patterns in Mobile Home Parks* (Los Angeles: Trailer Coach Association, 1965).

23. John Deck, in *Rancho Paradiso* (New York: Harcourt Brace Jovanovich, 1972), and Sheila Johnson, in Idle Haven (Berkeley: University of California Press, 1971) describe housing-oriented parks with elderly residents.

24. Peterson, *Home Is Where You Park It*, 64–65.

25. For other reviews of mobile home landlord–tenant law during this period, see Lyle F. Nyberg, "The Community and the Park Owner Versus the Mobile Home Park Resident: Reforming the Landlord–Tenant Relationship," *Boston University Law Review*, 52:3 (1972), 810–30; and Robert S. Hightower, "Mobile Home Park Practices: The Legal Relationship Between Mobile Home Park Owners and Tenants Who Own Mobile Homes," *Florida State Law Review*, 3 (1975), 104–26.

26. Hodes and Roberson, *Law of Mobile Homes*, 320.

27. Survey reported in Bernhardt, *Building Tomorrow*, 260.

28. Ibid., 260.

29. Edwards, *Homes*, 190.

30. Le Corbusier, *The Marseille Block* (London: Harvill Press, 1953), 44.

31. Allison and Peter Smithson, *Ordinariness and Light* (Cambridge, MA: MIT Press, 1970), 117.

32. Ibid., 121.

33. David Greene, "Gardener's Notebook," *Archigram*, ed. Peter Cook (New York: Praeger, 1973), 110.

34. E. K. Thompson,"Paul Rudolph's '20th Century Brick' Used in Cluster Apartments," *Architectural Record* (May 1970), 42–45.

35. Ordinance 2210-87, passed April 1986.

36. On the problem of expiring use, see Phillip Clay and James Wallace, "Preservation of Existing Housing Stock," in *MIT Housing Policy Project,* ed. Langley Keyes and Denise DiPasquale (Cambridge, MA: MIT Center for Real Estate Development, 1988).

37. Letter from Bill Turney, President of the Florida Manufactured Housing Association, to Holt Blomgren, President of the National Manufactured Housing Federation, dated September 19, 1986.

38. These estimates are from a petition submitted to FEMA, "In the matter of: National Flood Insurance Program (44 CFR 59,60)," dated February 27, 1987. A subsequent estimate by FEMA found 166,000 flood-prone sites, but only 40,000 of them were subject to more than shallow flooding (3 feet or less).

Chapter 6

1. "Message from the President of the United States Transmitting the Second Annual Report on National Housing Goals," Committee on Banking and Currency, Washington, D.C.: U.S. Government Printing Office, April 1, 1971.

2. Center for Automotive Safety, 1975, 10.

3. National Commission on Urban Problems, *Building the American City: Report of the National Commission on Urban Housing* (Washington, D.C.: U.S. Government Printing Office, 1968); *A Decent Home: Report of the President's Committee on Urban Problems* (Washington, D.C.: U.S. Government Printing Office, 1968).

4. For a summary report on the activities and results of Operation Breakthrough, see *Operation Breakthrough—Lessons Learned About Demonstrating New Technology*. U.S. General Accounting Office (Washington, D.C.: U.S. Government Printing Office, 1976).

5. Bender, *Crack in the Rear View Mirror*, 11.

6. National Commission on Urban Problems, *Building the American City*, 260.

7. Quoted in Bender, *Crack in the Rear View Mirror*, 11.

8. In fact this was not the first time that the industry had engaged an independent lab to develop voluntary construction standards (see Edwards, *Homes*).

9. The only states which had not adopted the code were Hawaii, Massachusetts, Rhode Island, Vermont, and Wyoming.

10. Louisiana, Montana, West Virginia, Michigan, Oklahoma, Missouri, New Hampshire and Nebraska.

11. Center for Automotive Safety, 1975, 90.

12. A brief account of the development of the legislation authorizing the HUD code is given in Bernhardt, *Building Tomorrow*, 378.

13. Title IV of the Housing and Community Development Act of 1974.

14. U.S. Department of Housing and Urban Development, *Policy and Program Recommendations to Encourage Land Ownership in Mobile Home Communities*, 1981.

15. Despite the longstanding participation of the FHA and VA in manufactured housing finance, the Farmers Home Administration, which is an important source of mortgages in rural areas, did not begin making manufactured housing loans (under its 502 and 515 programs) until Fall 1986.

16. The secondary purchase of manufactured housing loans applies only to units on owner-occupied sites, where such units are permanently set on agency-approved foundations, and where the home has a conventional site-built appearance.

17. U.S. Department of Housing and Urban Development, *Policy and Program Recommendations*, 1981.

18. Manufactured Housing Institute, *Quick Facts*, 1989.

19. In the first nine months of 1987, for example, the delinquency rate on mobile home loans was 3.29 percent versus 5.33 percent for conventional homes.

20. Welford Sanders, *Regulating Manufactured Housing*.

21. *Geiger v. Zoning Hearing Board of North Whitehall*, 507 A2d 361 (1986).

22. *The Report of the President's Commission on Housing* (1982), 85.

23. *Technology, Trade, and the U.S. Residential Construction Industry. Special Report, OTA-TET-315* (Washington, D.C.: U.S. Government Printing Office, September 1986), 76.

24. In 1980, HUD estimated that to implement its code would add $380 to the cost of the average mobile home. This estimate probably did not include administrative costs, but only material costs. See Bernhardt, *Building Tomorrow*, 381.

25. See "Table 4. The Nation's Top Producers of Mobile Homes," in *Technology, Trade, and the U.S. Residential Construction Industry. Special Report, OTA-TET-315*, Office of Technology Assessment. (Washington, D.C.: U.S. Government Printing Office, September 1986).

26. *Federation Focus* 10:15 (August 25, 1986), 1.

27. Motion for summary judgment filed by the U.S. Department of Housing and Urban Renewal in the United States District Court for the District of Columbia, March 27, 1987.

28. Letter dated August 24, 1987, from Representative Henry B. Gonzalez and Marge Roukema to Samuel R. Pierce, Jr.

29. William Apgar, Jr., and Denise DiPasquale, *State of the Na-*

tion's Housing (Cambridge, MA: Joint Center for Housing Studies, Harvard University, 1989).

30. While there are many causes of homelessness, the most signifi-cant cause is economic: the inability to meet housing payments. See, for example, Langley Keyes, *Homelessness*, MIT Working Papers, Center for Real Estate Development, August 1988.

31. Apgar and DiPasquale, *State of the Nation's Housing*, 1989.

32. A report issued by the MIT-Harvard Joint Housing Center concluded that "when home ownership costs increase, the trade-up market diminishes and remaining buyers tend to look for smaller, simpler homes and less expensive options, such as condominiums and mobile homes. . . . [As a result] condominiums almost tripled their share of newly built homes between the mid-1970s and the early 1980s, while mobile homes increased their share by about 25-30%." Kermit Baker and H. James Brown, "Home Ownership and Housing Affordability in the United States: 1968–1984," (Cambridge, MA: MIT-Harvard Joint Center for Housing Studies, 1985), 32–33.

33. A review of mobile home land use controls which stops short of an analysis of costs is found in M. Furlong & T. Nutt-Powell, *Development Controls for Mobile Home-Component Housing—A Ten Year Review of the Law* (Cambridge, MA: Joint Center for Urban Studies, Harvard University, 1980).

34. *The Report of the President's Commission on Housing*. William F. McKenna, Chair. (Washington, D.C.: U.S. Government Print-ing Office, April 1982), xxxiv.

35. For earlier and in many respects more comprehensive reviews of the cost of government regulation of housing, see Stephen R. Seidel *Housing Costs and Government Regulation* (New Brunswick, NJ: The Center for Urban Policy Research, Rutgers University, 1978), and B. Frieden (Cambridge, MA: MIT Press, 1979).

36. Letter from Samuel R. Pierce, Jr., n.d., in *The Affordable Housing Demonstration: A Case Study—Elkhart, Indiana* (Washing-ton, D.C.: The Department of Housing and Urban Development, January, 1984), iv.

37. Information on the demonstration project is drawn from the report *The Affordable Housing Demonstration*, 1984.

38. The 25 percent figure is an estimate based on the given sizes of the demonstration units and the average size of a new home in the region. No size was given for average new homes in the country.

Chapter 7

1. Constance Perin, *Everything in Its Place: Social Order and Land Use in America* (Princeton, N.J.: Princeton University Press, 1977), 4. On the idea of land use regulation as a means of expressing and maintaining a moral social order also see Judith de Neufville, "Symbol and Myth in Public Choice: The Case of Land Policy in the United States," Working Paper 359, Institute of Urban and Regional Development, University of California, Berkeley, July 1981.

2. John A. Kouwenhoven, "What Is 'American' in Architecture?" *The Beer Can by the Highway* (Garden City, N.Y.: Doubleday, 1961), 156.

3. Quoted by Kouwenhoven in "The Two Traditions in Conflict," in *Made in America: The Arts in Modern Civilization* (Garden City, N.Y.: Doubleday, 1962), 49.

4. J. B. Jackson, "The Movable Dwelling," *Discovering the Vernacular Landscape*, 100.

5. Frederick H. Bair, Jr., *Regulating Mobile Homes*, American Planning Association Publication 360, Planning Advisory Service, Chicago, April 1981.

6. Bartley and Bair, *Mobile Home Parks*.

7. Bernhardt, *Building Tomorrow*, 405.

8. Ibid., 492.

9. Rudolph's project suffered severe maintenance problems and has since been torn down.

10. Kirk Wickersham, Jr., *The Permit System: A Guide to Reforming Your Community's Development Regulation* (Boulder, CO: Indian Peaks Publishing, 1981).

11. There are a number of books on the problems of zoning, but one of the most readable remains Richard F. Babcock's *The Zoning Game* (Madison, WI: University of Wisconsin Press, 1966).

Illustration Credits

Chapter 1

p. 4 Photo by author
p. 6 Bernhardt, *Building Tomorrow*, 114
p. 6 Photo by author
p. 8 Manufactured Housing Institute
p.11 Photo by author
p.18 Photo by author
p.23 Photo by author
p.26 Photo by author

Chapter 2

p.33 Cecil R. Roseberry, *Glenn Curtiss: Pioneer of Flight* (Garden City, N.Y.: Doubleday, 1972). Original courtesy of Glenn Curtiss, Jr.
p.34 Courtesy National Auto History Collection, Detroit Public Library
p.37 *Trailer Travel*, 1:5 (1936), 17
p.38 A. Frederick Collins, *How To Build a Motor Car Trailer* (Philadelphia: J. B. Lippincott, 1936)
p.40 *Trailer Travel*, 4:2 (1939), 35
p.41 Donald O. Cowgill, *Mobile Homes*, Washington, D.C.: *A Study of Trailer Life*, American Council on Public Affairs, 1941
p.42 *Trailer Travel*, 2:6 (1937), 17

p.43 *Trailer Travel*, 2:8 (1937), 69

p.44 *Trailer Travel*, 1:1 (1936), 15

p.46 *Trailer Travel*, 1:1 (1936), 26

p.48 *Trailer Travel*, 1:1 (1936), cover

p.49 *Trailer Travel*, 3:17 (1938), 12

p.53 Schult Homes, Middlebury, IN

p.53 Schult Homes, Middlebury, IN

p.54 *Trailer Travel*, 4:3 (1940), 16

p.56 *Trailer Topics*, 2:5 (1938), 9

p.57 *Trailer Topics*, 2:8 (1938), 13

p.60 Reprinted from *Architectural Record* (July 1936), 65. © McGraw-Hill, Inc. All rights reserved. Reproduced with permission of publisher.

p.63 *Trailer Caravan*, 1:3 (1937), 7

p.63 *Trailer Travel*, 3:6 (1939), 15

p.65 *Trailer Caravan*, 1:7 (1937), 29. Reprinted from Chicago *Tribune*.

p.65 *Trailer Travel*, 2:9 (1939), 13

p.69 *Trailer Travel*, 2:5 (1937), 77

p.72 *Trailer Caravan*, 1:5 (1936), 13

p.75 Dye Hawley

p.75 *Trailer Caravan*, 1:7 (1937), 6

Chapter 3

p.84 *Trailer Travel*, 8:1 (1943), 5

p.86 *Trailer Travel*, 7:11 (1942), inside cover

p.88 *Trailer Travel*, 7:2 (1942), 8

p.89 *Trailer Travel*, 7:2 (1942), 8

p.90 *Trailer Travel*, 7:2 (1942), 8

p.94 *Trailer Travel*, 10:10 (1945), cover

p.95 *Trailer Life*, 10:3 (1945), 11

p.10 Schult Homes, Middlebury, IN

p.106 Burnham Kelly, *The Prefabrication of Houses* (Cambridge, MA: MIT Press, 1953), ills. 13 and 49

p.110 *Trailer Topics*, 11:3 (1947), 33

p.113 *Trailer Life*, 6:12 (1941), cover

p.115 *Trailer Topics*, 3:4 (1937), 9

Chapter 4

p.127 *Trailer Topics*, 19:1 (1958), 51

p.128 *Trailer Travel*, 11:5 (1947), 65

p.129 *Trailer Topics*, 8:8 (1947), 75

p.132 Elmer Frey, Marshfield Homes, Marshfield, WI

p.137 *Trailer Life*, 4:1 (1954), 38

p.137 *Mobile Life,* MHMA Yearbook (1957), 80

p.139 *Mobile Home Trailer Dealer* (1955)

p.140 *Trailer Life,* 4:1 (1954), 46

p.141 *Trailer Topics,* 11:10 (1950), 17

p.142 *Mobile Life,* 7:2 (1957), 17

p.144 Company brochure

p.146 Marlette Homes brochure

p.147 Taliesin Associated Architects, *Production/Dwelling: An Opportunity for Excellence* (Spring Green, WI: Frank Lloyd Wright Foundation, 1970), 42, 43

p.148 *Trailer Topics,* 16:3 (1955), 21

p.150 *Trailer Travel,* 8:8 (1943), inside front cover

p.153 Photo by author

p.155 Photo by Donna Morganstern

p.156 Photo by Paul Heath

p.158 Nashua Homes brochure

p.159 *Mechanics Illustrated* (October 1983), 47

p.161 U.S. Forest Service, *Wood Dwelling Construction* (Washington, D.C.: U.S. Government Printing Office, 1964)

p.162 Robert Venturi, Denise Scott Brown, and Steven Izenour, *Learning from Las Vegas* (Cambridge, MA: MIT Press, 1977), 158

p.164 Drawings from John Downing's *Encyclopedia,* in George L. Hersey, *High Victorian Gothic* (Baltimore: Johns Hopkins University Press, 1972)

p.165 Photo by author

Chapter 5

p.168 Photo by author

p.172 *Trailer Travel,* 3:1 (1938), 5

p.176 Drawing by author

p.177 Photo by author

p.181 Mobile Home Manufacturers Association

p.182 Clarence A. Perry, "Neighborhood and Community Planning," *Regional Plan of New York and Its Environs,* vol. VII (New York: Committee on Regional Plan of New York and Its Environs, 1929), 36 [Used by permission of Regional Planning Association]

p.184 *Guidelines for Improving the Mobile Home Living Environment* (Washington, D.C.: U.S. Department of Housing and Urban Development, 1978)

p.186 Kaufman & Board Co.

p.186 Photo by author

p.187 Photo by author

p.189 Photo by author

Index